The Franciscan Journey

Embracing the Franciscan Vision

Secular Franciscan Order

Orientation + Inquiry + Candidacy

Lester Bach OFM Cap

+ **IMPRIMI POTEST** - John Celichowski OFM Cap - Minister Provincial of the Province of St Joseph of the Capuchin Order - February 26, 2009.

ISBN - 0-944996-40-X

+ Published in the United States of America by Smoky Valley Printing - P.O. Box 189 - Lindsborg, KS 67456-0189 - Phone 785-227-2364 - Fax 785-227-3360.

+ United States Conference of Catholic Bishops - USCCB Publishing - 3211 Fourth St NE - Washington D.C. 20017

Catechism of the Catholic Church (CCC)
Compendium - Catechism of the Catholic Church
United States Catholic Catechism for Adults

©1993 Libreria Editrice Vaticana/Publisher: Pauline Books and Media (Encyclicals)-Boston, MA

God is Love (Deus Caritas Est) - Benedict XVI
Saved in Hope (Spe Salvi) - Benedict XVI
Sacrament of Charity (Sacramentum Caritatis) - Benedict XVI
Christianity and Social Progress (Mater et Magister) - John XXIII
Evangelization in the Modern World (Evangelii nuniandi) - Paul VI

+ Costello Publishing Co. Inc - P.O. Box 9 - Northport, NY 11768

Vatican Council II, Constitutions / Decrees / Declarations - Austin Flannery OP - General Editor

+ New City Press - 202 Cardinal Road - Hyde Park, NY 1215318

Clare of Assisi, The Lady - Regis Armstrong OFM Cap
Francis of Assisi - The Saint / The Founder/ The Prophet (3 Volumes)
Regis Armstrong OFM Cap/Wayne Hellman OFM Conv/Wm Short OFM

+ Franciscan Institute - St Bonaventure University (SBU) - St Bonaventure, NY 14778

Build with Living Stones - Franciscan Institute
De Illis Qui Faaciunt Penitentiam - The Rule of the SFO, Origins, Development, Interpretation - Robert Steward OFM
St. Francis and the Third Order - Raffaele Pazelli OFM

+ Orbis Books - Maryknoll, NY 10545

Engaged Spirituality - Joseph Nangle OFM
Poverty and Joy - Wm Short OFM

+ St Anthony Messenger Press - 28 W. Liberty St - Cincinnati, OH 45202

Franciscan Prayer - Ilia Delio OSF

+ Crossroads Publishing Co - 370 Lexington Ave - New York, NY 10017

Francis of Assisi - Arnaldo Fortini (Copyright - Helen Moak - Translator)

+ Paulist Press -- 997 Macarthur Blvd - Mahwah, NJ 07430

Sacramental Guidelines - Kenan Osborne OFM

+ Twenty-Third Publications - 185 Willow St - Box 180 - Mystic, CT 06355

On the Way to Work - Vinal Van Benthem SFO

+ Loyola Press - 3441 N. Ashland Ave - Chicago, IL 60657

Spirituality@work - Gregory F. A. Pierce

CONTENTS

++

INITIAL FORMATION

++

Numbers in parenthesis are articles of the Rule

PREFACE

Assisting newcomers to embrace the Secular Franciscan way of life is the responsibility of the local SFO Council, formation personnel and the membership, all guided by the Holy Spirit. They invite newcomers to become people:

A) with a Franciscan spirit, perspective, and ideals;
B) with the ability to reflect gospel values in their lives and accept conversion as needed;
C) with a willingness to accept the SFO as a primary and permanent commitment;
D) with a desire to build up the Church and the Kingdom of God;
E) with a sense of Franciscan responsibility for social action;
F) with a desire for contemplative prayer.

Called by the Spirit, newcomers learn, integrate, and express the Franciscan spirit in daily life.

The SFO Rule/Constitutions guide us. *Formation* means much more than sharing information. Newcomers are expected to integrate information into the way they live. The Franciscan spirit embraces the values, attitudes and perspectives of the Gospel. It is more than an intellectual accumulation of facts. Information must *transform* our lives to reflect gospel values, attitudes, and perspectives. Many personal changes of attitudes, perspectives, and opinions are expected as you journey through initial formation. If not, something is missing in the formation process.

Formation engages people in ministry. Service to others is part of who and what we are. *Profession* in the SFO, a permanent commitment, calls Franciscans to offer service to all people - in the Church, in the world and in fraternity life. Franciscans are loyal to the People of God (Church). The Church, guided by the Holy Spirit, confirms our Rule and Consitutions as our way to serve God. The Holy Spirit guides us on our Franciscan journey (vocation).

Respect and reverence color the way we deal with people, however difficult that may be. Whatever we say or do, whatever attitudes we bring to issues, whatever judgments we have about others, we choose to avoid anything - words, actions, or attitudes - that would fracture our relationship with one another. Franciscans avoid whatever would separate us from others.

I ask not only on behalf of these, but also on behalf of those who will believe in me through their word, ***that they may all be one****. As you, Father, are in me and I am in you, may they also be in us, so that the world may believe that you have sent me.*

John 17:20-21

The SFO Rule calls people to nurture gospel qualities in their lives. They learn about contemplative prayer. They deal with issues of peace and justice both in the Church, in the world and in their own lives. They go *from Gospel to life and life to Gospel* (SFO Rule #4). They understand that they are stewards of material goods. A realistic sense of poverty leads to a simple lifestyle and trust in God. They use material goods as needed but also find themselves ready to share with others who are in need. They imitate God's generosity and accept the loving generosity of others. Our entire life is lived in the spirit of St. Francis of Assisi.

Franciscans develop a sense of freedom, guided by the Holy Spirit, following the words of Jesus, and loved with an eternal passion by Father, Son and Holy Spirit. As love relationships blossom in our lives, we discard things that hinder our love of God, the Church, the world, all people, and all of creation. God gives us a sense of community-love that brings us joy and moves us to serve others, especially those in greatest need. We learn to graciously accept such love when we are the needy ones. The SFO is our primary commitment. Joining other groups must not interfere with our Franciscan way of life which is a 24/7 commitment.

Welcome to
The Franciscan Journey!
Embracing the Franciscan Vision

Chapter one

Orientation in the SFO

Orientation - the first step in entering a fraternity.
Minimum of three months.

Orientation is the first phase of formation in the Secular Franciscan Order. You become acquainted with Secular Franciscans and they get to know you.

Together, we determine whether you have a vocation to the SFO. The "discovery" period begins in *orientation* and extends into *inquiry*. These phases of formation help discern your vocation through reflection, dialogue, and prayer. There are necessary requirements as you begin the journey.

Together, we discover your situation in the Church, your knowledge of the Creed* as well as your personal attitudes and perspectives. This aids your discernment to see if you are called to the Franciscan way of life. If it becomes clear that you have a Franciscan vocation we offer integration time, ministry opportunities, prayer experiences, and information to nurture your vocation. If we discern that you do not have a vocation to the SFO, we encourage you to follow the vocation to which the Spirit calls you. In either case the result is good news.

SOME REQUIREMENTS

1. Rule 23 *Membership in the Order is attained through a time of initiation, a time of formation, and the profession of the Rule.*

---

* **References**: United States Catechism for Adults - USCCB / Catechism of the Catholic Church (CCC).

2. The journey of formation, ***which should develop throughout life,*** *begins with entrance into the fraternity. Mindful that the Holy Spirit is the principal agent of formation and always attentive to collaboration with Him, those responsible for formation are: the candidate, the entire fraternity, the council with the minister, the master* (director) *of formation and the assistant.*

Constitutions - article 37.1, 37.2

1. Rule 23 *The request for admission to the Order is presented by the aspirant to the minister of a local or personal fraternity by a formal act, in writing if possible.*

2. Conditions for admission are: to profess the Catholic faith, to live in communion with the Church, to be of good moral standing, and to show clear signs of a vocation.

3. The council of the fraternity decides collegially on the request, gives a formal answer to the aspirant, and communicates this to the fraternity.

Constitutions - article 39.1, 39.2, 39.3

2. The candidates are guided to read and meditate on Sacred Scripture, to come and know the person and writings of Francis and of Franciscan spirituality, and to study the Rule and Constitutions. They are trained in a love for the Church and acceptance of her teaching. The laity practice living their secular commitment in the world in an evangelical way.

3. Participation in the meetings (gatherings) *of the local fraternity is an indispensible presupposition for initiation into community prayer and into fraternity life.*

Constitutions - article 40.2, 40.3

Initial formation (Inquiry/Candidacy) prepares you for permanent profession as a Secular Franciscan. Our *way of life* **must take priority** in your life. When choices must be made between SFO requirements and that of other groups, SFO takes priority. However, we realize that family and other serious situations may occasionally take priority.

Secular Franciscans (including newcomers) are required to be present at the regular gatherings of the fraternity. Newcomers also need to attend formation sessions. There may be times when attendance is difficult for various serious reasons. **Courtesy** requires members to inform the Council (or formation director) when an absence is necessary.

Periods of formation

1. Orientation:

a. Orientation is a time for determining a person's interest, eligibility and disposition to enter into the initial formation process (cf. Guidelines for Initial Formation in the SFO in the USA - Page 25).

b. The period of orientation shall consist of not less than three (3) *months.*

National Statutes - article 19.1a, 1b

2. Initial formation

a. ***Inquiry*** *- The period of inquiry, which begins with the ceremony of Introduction and Welcoming* (cf. Ritual of the SFO - Page 9), *shall consist of not less than six* (6) *months.*

b. ***Candidacy*** *- The period of Candidacy, which begins with the rite of Admission* (cf. Ritual of the SFO - Page 11) *shall consist of not less than eighteen* (18) *months and not more than thirty-six* (36) *months.*

c. All persons in initial formation, in addition to attending their formation sessions, must participate in the meetings of the local fraternity as this is an indispensible presupposition for initiation into community prayer and into fraternity life (Cf. Constitutions - Article 40.3).

d. To be admitted to the SFO in the United States, a person must be a fully initiated member of the Catholic Church (i.e. having received the sacraments of Baptism, Chrismation/ Confirmation, and Holy Eucharist) in addition to being an actively practicing Catholic.

National Statutes - article 19.2a, 2b, .2c, .2d

2. The conditions for profession or promise of evangelical life are:

+ *attainment of the age established by the national statutes;* (21 years - National Statutes - Article 19.3a)
+ *active participation in the time of formation ....;*
+ *the consent of the council of the local fraternity.*

Constitutions - article 41.2

1. Profession is the solemn ecclesial act by which the candidate, remembering the call received from Christ, renews the baptismal promises and publicly affirms his or her personal commitment to live the Gospel in the world according to the example of Francis, and following the Rule of the SFO.

 # Note that our relationship to the Church is special for Franciscans. We examine our ecclesial relationship during the process of *initial formation,* especially in Candidacy.

2. Rule 23 *Profession incorporates the candidate into the Order and is by its nature a perpetual commitment. Perpetual profession, because of objective and pedagogical reasons, may be preceded by temporary profession, renewable annually. The total time of temporary profession may not be longer than three years.*

Constitutions - article 42.1, 42.2

+++

We do not take formation lightly. Nor do we expect sudden decisions about embarking on our Franciscan way of life. *Orientation* and *Inquiry* initiate your understanding of the SFO way of life. Generally the discernment of a vocation is achieved by the end of *inquiry.* The 3 months of *orientation* and 6 months of *inquiry* provide time and information to make a good decision. We will share guidelines with you to help with your discernment.

Orientation explores issues that assist in discerning your vocation. Initially this may seem overwhelming. But we move gently. We are sensitive to your ability to understand and embrace our Franciscan way of life or to discover that the Spirit is calling you to another way of life. In the formation process we walk with you prayerfully and respectfully. We are generous in sharing our Franciscan way of life. We expect you to be **fully engaged** in the formation process. That includes doing the *Readings* at the end of each chapter of this book.

He (Francis) used to tell them: "As you announce peace with your mouth, make sure that greater peace is in your hearts. Let no one be provoked to anger or scandal through you, but may everyone be drawn to peace, kindness, and harmony through your gentleness. For we have been called to this: to heal the wounded, bind up the broken, and recall the erring. In fact, many who seem to us to be members of the devil, will yet be disciples of Christ."

Legend of the Three Companions - Francis of Assisi - The Founder Vol II - Page 102

I wish to know in this way if you love the Lord and me, His servant and yours; that there is not any brother in the world who has sinned - however much he could have sinned - who, after he has looked into your eyes, would ever depart without your mercy, if he is looking for mercy. And if he is not looking for mercy, you would ask him if he wants mercy. And if he would sin a thousand times before your eyes, love him more than me so that you may draw him to the Lord; and always be merciful with brothers such as these.

A Letter to a Minister - Francis of Assisi - The Saint - Vol 1 - Page 97

Let us refer all good to the Lord, God Almighty and Most High, acknowledge that every good is His, and thank Him "from whom all good comes for everything." May He, the Almighty and Most High, the only true God, have, be given, and receive all honor and respect, all praise and blessing, all thanks and glory, to Whom all good belongs, He Who alone is good.

Fragments - Francis of Assisi - The Saint - Vol 1 - Page 90

If you abide in me, and my words abide in you, ask for whatever you wish, and it will be done for you. My Father is glorified by this, that you bear much fruit and become my disciples. As the Father has loved me so I love you; abide in my love.

John 15:7-9

NB: Franciscans need knowledge of the Catholic faith. In the course of these sessions we will incorporate basic teachings of the Catholic Church. We will use both the *United States Catholic Catechism for Adults* and the *Catechism of the Catholic Church.* Information on the creed will be part of various chapters. Our understanding of and relationship to the Church (ecclesiology) will be incorporated in like manner.

Readings/Questions for dialogue

First paragraph - Page 109
Franciscan Prayer - Ilia Delio OSF

Earlier exhortation - Chapter 1
Francis of Assisi - The Saint - Vol 1 - Page 41-42

God is Love *(Deus Caritas Est)* - Benedict XVI
Paragraph 19

1. What brought you to this fraternity of the Secular Franciscan Order? What is the role of the Holy Spirit in your decision to come to us?

2. Name and describe some of the requirements for joining the SFO? How would you evaluate your openness to fresh ideas? How ready are you to change personal opinions as you embrace Franciscan perspectives that differ from your own? Are you willing to engage in dialogue to clarify your own and other person's opinions?

3. List the sacraments you have received in the Catholic Church and share documents for baptism and confirmation.

4. Does anything in your life keep you from receiving the Eucharist? If so, how will you deal with these issues?

5. Share ideas about our Franciscan way of life that you gleaned from the quotes of St. Francis (cf. Page 5).

6. Scripture reflection: Mark 2:15-17 - How does this text call for embracing important Franciscan values?

+++

The deepest identity
of a Secular Franciscan
is based on their relationship
with Jesus Christ,
God's gift to the People of God.
We believe that the Church
has the mission to bring the spirit
of generosity, forgiveness, reconciliation,
and celebration to all people.
Franciscans are dedicated
to do whatever is needed not only
to proclaim the gospel message by words,
but also to make it evident in their lives.

Whether they speak the word
or live the word,
they bring the message
to the Church and the world.
They go from the *Gospel to life
and life to the Gospel.*
It is never just talk.
It becomes a life of love
as Jesus' life was one of love,
even to death on the cross.
Secular Franciscans, through life itself,
share love with all people
and all of creation.
They gently call people to love
through the example
of their personal lives
as well as
their community life
in fraternity.

Chapter two

Three Orders Structures Discernment

The Franciscan family is composed of three distinct Orders.

The **First Order** is a community of men who make solemn vows to follow the Rule given by St Francis (1223). They live in community and serve in a variety of ministries - especially among poor and marginalized people.

In time, the First Order divided into three separate branches - the Order of Friars Minor (OFM) / the Order of Friars Minor, Conventual (OFM Conv) / and the Order of Friars Minor, Capuchin (OFM Cap).* Each branch follows the Rule written by St. Francis. Each branch of the First Order has Constitutions which indicate their differing interpretation of the Rule. These branches of the First Order are juridically independent. However, collaboration is common among them, especially in ministries and sharing spirituality. The Franciscan spirit shows itself in each of these branches. Each branch has a special relationship to the SFO.

The **Second Order** of St. Francis is called the Poor Clares. These women joined the Order founded by St. Francis and St. Clare of Assisi. Contemplation is an important part of their charism. They also find ways to serve the poor and care for others as part of their charism. Like their Franciscan brothers of the First Order, they were renewed and reformed in the course of time. The Poor Clare reforms include the

---

* For a concise history of the First Order - Cf. *Francis & His Brothers* - Dominic Monti OFM - St Anthony Messenger Press

Poor Clares, Colletines, Capuchin Poor Clares and other groups who follow Clare's Rule of life.

The **Third Order of St. Francis** was initially a group of laity who chose to follow the spirit of St. Francis in their secular state - the Third Order *Secular*. As time went on, some of these people chose to take vows and live in community. They are called the Third Order Regular.

This development within the Third Order of St Francis brought about a variety of Franciscan groups.

1. Men within the Third Order came together and took vows to live a Franciscan life in community. As they grew, the Church gave them the status of a religious order known as the **Third Order *Regular*** (TOR) of St. Francis. The Church gave them a special relationship to the SFO.

2. A revised **Third Order Regular** rule has been adopted by large numbers of Franciscan religious, both men and women. Numerous Franciscan groups follow the revised Rule of the Third Order Regular.

3. The laity who chose to live their lives in the secular world in the spirit of St. Francis became known simply as the **Third Order *Secular*** of St. Francis. They brought the spirit of St. Francis into their world.

Seculars are committed both to the Church and the world. They follow Francis' lead in concern for and service of the "little ones" of society. In the middle ages their refusal to bear arms diminished some of the warlike spirit that flooded that era. They sought to find better ways to settle conflicts.

From 1209, and thoughout the centuries, the Third Order Secular embraced the spirit of St. Francis. Though it was dedicated to Francis' way, there were times when it became more devotional than service-oriented. The SFO shows different faces throughout its history.

The Holy Spirit has blessed the Church and the world with over 800 years of Franciscan life. The First and Second Order, the TOR and the Secular Franciscans of today bring the spirit of Francis to the 21st century and beyond.

After Francis' initial rule, there were three different Papal rules for the Third Order Secular, approved at three different times (1289/1883/1978). The 1978 Rule was approved by Pope Paul VI on June 24, 1978. The Third Order of St Francis is now known as *The Secular Franciscan Order* (SFO / Latin - Ordo Franciscanus Secularis - OFS).

+++

SFO formation requires you to read, understand, and implement the SFO Rule in daily life. The formation program prepares you for permanent *profession* as a Secular Franciscan. During *initial formation* you learn to live the life of a Secular Franciscan. *Ongoing formation* continues the formative process after profession. Franciscan theology and spirituality offer fresh ways of perceiving and responding to reality in the Church and the world.

The rule and life of the Secular Franciscan is this: to observe the gospel of our Lord Jesus Christ by following the example of St. Francis of Assisi, who made Christ the inspiration and the center of his life with God and people.

Christ, the gift of the Father's love, is the way to him, the truth into which the Holy Spirit leads us, and the life which he has come to give abundantly.

Secular Franciscans should devote themselves especially to careful reading of the gospel, going from gospel to life and life to the gospel.

SFO Rule - #4

Dialogue will be a normal process both during initial and ongoing formation. When you discern that you have a vocation to the Franciscan way of life, we will continue to share your journey of formation and help you implement the Rule in your life as a secular Franciscan.

Organizational structure

The SFO developed structures that serve the spirit/vision of St. Francis. Structures are meant to develop unity within the Franciscan family and maintain the vision. Structures serve the vision. When a structure no longer serves the *Franciscan vision* we change the structure.

The SFO organizational structure is similar at the various levels. An elected council exists at each level of the SFO. It includes a Minister/President - vice-minister - secretary - treasurer - formation director - and spiritual assistant. Depending on needs, other councilors can be added. This council of servant-leaders look for ways and means to serve the fraternity members and promote the common good.

1. **International level.** (Elected offices - six year term)

The International Fraternity is constituted by the organic union of all the Catholic Secular Franciscan Fraternities in the world. (Cf. Constitutions - article 69.1) *The International fraternity is guided and animated by the International Council of the SFO* (CIOFS - i.e. Concilium Internationale Ordo Franciscanus Secularis), *with its seat* (location) *in Rome* (Italy), *by its presidency and by the general minister or international president* (Cf. Constitution - article 69.2). *The "presidency" of the International Council of the SFO is constituted within the international council of which it forms an integral part* (Cf. Constitutions - article 70.2)

The *International fraternity* is the union of all Catholic SFO fraternities throughout the world. It is guided by the *International Council* and the *International Presidency.* The *International Presidency* is composed of: Minister General, Vice-minister General, seven Presidency councilors (who serve in various capacities), a YOUFRA (Young people's) repesentative and the four General Spiritual Assistants. The *Presidency* is similar to an executive council at the other levels of the SFO. The meetings of *seculars and councils,* at all levels, are called "chapters." (The regular meeting of a local fraternity is called a "Gathering.")

Spiritual assistants (SA's), from the First Order and the TOR, are part of the international presidency. They are called the *Conference of General Spiritual Assistants (4 Friars)*. They "assist" the *Presidency* and the *International council.*

2. **National level.** (Elected offices - three year term)

On the national level the regional ministers (and national executive council) form the *National Fraternity* (NAFRA). They represent the regions throughout a country (The USA has 30 regions). The *National Fraternity* (NAFRA) meets annually. Every three years they elect a *National Executive Council* (NEC) to conduct the business of the SFO in the USA (Cf. Constitutions - article 66.2). The NAFRA "chapter" has legislative authority for the whole country. Major issues dealt with by the National Executive Council (NEC) need approval by NAFRA for major decisions to become binding (e.g. budgets - statutes - policies).

One friar from each of the three branches of the First Order and the TOR form the *Conference of National Spiritual Assistants* (CNSA - 4 friars) in the USA. The president of CNSA (2 year term) serves the National executive council (NEC). All *four* friars attend the annual "chapter" of the National Fraternity (NAFRA). They "assist" the national level of the SFO and spiritual assistants throughout the USA.

3. **Regional level.** (Elected offices - three year term)

A *region* is a contiguous geographic area in the USA. Each region assumes a name, e.g. *La Verna Region, Tau Region* etc. There are 30 SFO regions in the USA (2010).

The *Regional Fraternity Council* is composed of the local *fraternity ministers* in a particular region and the members of the *Regional Executive Council* (including the regional SA). The *Regional Fraternity Council* meets annually (at their "chapter"). Every three years it elects a *Regional Executive Council* (REC) to conduct the business of the region. These "chapters" approve major decisions of the REC (e.g. budgets - guidelines etc).

1st Order and TOR friars (Total of four), whose province has fraternities in the region, are part of the *regional* council. Because of a lack of friars, regions often have less than four regional spiritual assistants. This has also opened the door for non-friars to be appointed as regional SA's

Friars and others who are appointed as regional SA's are expected to take the training program provided by CNSA. The regional SA's implement the *altius moderamen* and provide the *vital reciprocity* between the SFO and the First Order/TOR at the regional level. A major superior (provincial) of the First Order/TOR makes the appointment or delegates a provincial spiritual assistant to do so.

4. **Local level** (Elected offices - three year term)

The local fraternity is the foundational structure of the SFO. The perpetually professed members of the local fraternity constitute their "chapter." The local council is elected (every three years) by the active, perpetually professed members of the fraternity (Cf. Constititons - article 77.1) who are not excused from attendance (National Statutes -article 18.6). The local council (including the SA) serves the fraternity at the local level.

After he had washed their feet, ... he said to them," ... You call me Teacher, and Lord - and you are right for that is what I am. So if I, your Lord and Teacher, have washed your feet, you also ought to wash one another's feet. For I have set you an example, that you should also do as I have done to you."

John 13:12-15

The local SA is appointed by the major superior (or his delegate - PSA) of the 1st Order/TOR Province to which a fraternity is bonded. Bonding occurs when a province's major superior (or delegate) establishes a fraternity or accepts its transfer from another province. A lack of friars allows for the appointment of Sisters, Clergy or SFO members as local SA's after completing the training course for spiritual assistants (Cf. Constitutions - article 89.4). **Please read article #21 of the SFO Rule.**

Discernment

The call to enter the SFO is given by the Holy Spirit. It is a call (vocation) to live life in the spirit of St. Francis and according to the Rule/Constitutions of the SFO. Because it is a special calling, it is important to determine if you have a vocation to the SFO or to some other way of life. We call this process *discernment.*

Responding to the call of the Holy Spirit is important. If you have a vocation to the SFO you give your best effort to our formation program. It will bring you to *profession* in the SFO after at least 27 (or more) months of formation. On the other hand, if we mutually discover this is not your vocation, you are free to discern where the Holy Spirit is leading you. Both cases are good decisions and good news.

In the next few pages we will offer criteria to assist you in making a decision about your vocation

Applicants to the SFO must be knowledgeable Catholics in good standing, active in the Church and living the Catholic faith in everyday life.* They must have a good moral character indicated by their lifestyle. We expect applicants to have received Baptism, Confirmation, Eucharist and the sacrament of Reconciliation. It helps if applicants have documentation for baptism and confirmation. Local formation personnel will help you in this process.

We need to be clear about your willingness and ability to attend both the formation sessions and the regular fraternity gatherings. It is a serious concern if you are not able to regularly be present at fraternity and formation gatherings. It may mean that a vocation is absent or that now is not the time to pursue it. If the situation changes and you become able to attend the regular gatherings, you would be welcome to re-enter the formation program.

---

* Please read Pages 122-123 in the *United States Catholic Catechism for Adults* - doctrinal statements on the "Church."

It is important to ascertain your marital situation. A healthy marriage is no problem. If you are divorced that would not, of itself, be an obstacle to entering the SFO. If you are a baptized, practicing Catholic, married, divorced, or single, you are welcome. However, if, after a divorce, a second marriage is attempted without the benefit of an annulment, it would hinder your entrance to the SFO. Dialogue with the formation personnel of the local fraternity will help to settle these issues.

The local *Fraternity Council* decides on your acceptance. It is guided by the recommendation of the formation director and/or formation team. You engage in dialogue with the formation personnel who make the recommendation. The local council may also choose to do a personal interview with applicants. The local council represents the fraternity in these decisions.

Other helps for discernment

The following guidelines are meant to help you and the formation people determine your vocation. Use them wisely and prayerfully with respect for one another. If there is doubt about your vocation, **the fraternity gets the benefit of the doubt.** We do not expect ready-made saints. We recognize the need for reflection in discerning your vocation. This is done prayerfully and with respect. The criteria that follow are tools to assist discernment. Though certainly not infallible, they offer a sense of direction. Use them with that spirit.

Signs that may indicate
***the presence of a vocation to the SFO*.**

1. People with a sense of concern and compassion for others and have a spirit of dialogue in conversations/discussions.

2. People whose ambition is service-oriented (not dominating). People with a good motivation for entering the SFO.

3. People who choose to learn from others and realize their need for learning throughout their lives.

4. People with good listening skills who willingly share their ideas and opinions. People who listen well and share as is appropriate. People willing to grow in these qualities.

5. People who are practicing Catholics.

6. People with a personal faith-relationship with Jesus, not simply an intellectual knowledge about Jesus. People who desire to follow Jesus and his Gospel, the heart of Franciscan life.

7. People ready and able to deal with life-issues, both personal and communal, no matter how difficult.

8. People who are willing to recognize themselves as imperfect and sinners in need of conversion. People who do not judge others but find ways to help them.

9. People with a desire to show reverence for all of creation and a sense of courtesy and respect for all people.

10. People with communication skills and a willingness to dialogue with others. People with a good sense of humor.

11. People willing to enbrace a counter-cultural stance that is frequently part of SFO life. Secular Franciscans share creative ideas and life stories with one another.

12. Married people with a sacramental marriage who are continuing to grow in their spousal relationship. Divorce is not an obstacle for joining the SFO. (However, attempting a second marriage without an annulment would hinder your entrance into the SFO).

13. Single people who are practicing Catholics and are willing to learn about our Franciscan way of life.

Signs that may indicate that *__a vocation to the SFO is not present.__*

Some of these signs can be diminished by a willingness to change. Such an attitude can make a difference in the discernment.

1. People who are individualistic and lack a sense of community or who are extremely competitive and must "win" in every situation.

2. People who are self-absorbed, always trying to "get ahead" of others. People who are over-extended and exhausted by too much involvement in all kinds of projects and issues.

3. People who are self-righteous and need to be "right" in every situation.

4. People who seek to control and manipulate others. People who expect service but never serve anyone else.

5. People with serious difficulties in inter-personal relationships.

6. People who talk-talk-talk and rarely listen. - or - People who are too quiet and never reveal their real ideas or opinions. People who are overly serious or overly flippant.

7. People who already belong to a religious Order or another Third Order. An individual may not belong to more than one *public association of the faithful.*

8. A person who is a non-Catholic.

9. A person with serious inter-personal problems, has serious problems with relationships, or someone who simply wants to escape family or work problems by joining the SFO. *__We are NOT a therapy group!__*

10. A person with extreme personal devotions who tries to

force them on others. Dominating personalities will disrupt fraternity life.

11. A gossipy person or someone with unbending opinions, who is prejudiced, arrogant or irresponsible in family or work life is NOT a good candidate for the SFO.

12. A person who is rigid, domineering, a know-it-all, or uses violence, power or prestige to get his/her way will find our sense of dialogue and concern impossible to follow.

13. A person who is simply a "professional" joiner of every kind of group is not a good candidate for the SFO.

14. People who are extremely selfish or self-centered will find community life difficult if not impossible.

15. Catholics who are divorced and re-marry without the benefit of a church annulment.

Be prayerful while discerning a vocation. Ask the Holy Spirit for guidance. Discern with reverence and prayerfulness. A vocation to the SFO will mean many life-changing decisions. This will continue throughout life. If a vocation to the SFO is not present, you will be free to discover where the Spirit is calling you.

Blessed is the servant who does not consider himself any better when he is praised and exalted by people than when he is considered worthless, simple, and looked down upon, for what a person is before God, that he is and no more.
Admonition XIX - Francis of Assisi -The Saint - Vol I - Page 135

Readings/Questions for dialogue

Praises of St. Francis - Bernard of Besse
St Francis of Assisi - The Prophet - Vol 3
Page 63-65

19

Legend of the Three Companions
St. Francis of Assisi - The Founder - Vol 2
Chapter III - Page 71-74

God is Love *(Deus Caritas Est)* - Benedict XVI
Paragraphs 36-37

1. Give a general overview of the three Orders of St Francis. What is the difference between the three Orders?

2. What is the relationship of the First Order/TOR to the SFO? How do they assist one another? (Also - Cf. chapter 33 - Page 353ff in this book)

3. Describe the structure of the SFO? How do the various levels affect one another?

4. What is a "chapter" in the SFO? What role does it serve?

5. Who has legislative authority at the various levels of the SFO organization? What is the role of the executive council (or the international Presidency) at the various levels?

6. As you reflect on various criteria for discerning a vocation, what conclusion do you have (at this point) about your own vocation to the SFO? Give reasons for your answer.

7. Why is prayerfulness important in discerning a vocation to the SFO or the absence of a vocation to the SFO?

8. Having a dialogue with a formation person to discuss your vocation is helpful. When will you do it?

9. Why is your attendance at the regular gatherings of the fraternity (as well as the formation sessions) important?

10. Scripture reflection: Acts 15:3-23. How does this text offer a model for settling disputes?

The first principle is human dignity.
This principle reflects the biblical
teaching that we humans are made
in the image of God.

Human dignity is a
key ethical foundation
for sustainable community.
Because of God's image within us,
every person has the right to all
that is needed to guarantee human dignity.

Also all persons have the duty
to defend human dignity
for themselves and for others,
and to bring to fulfillment
by their own gifts and efforts
all that the image of God implies.

The deepest meaning
of the image of God within us
is that we are co-creators with God,
that we share in God's own creativity.
Yet the consumer society rejects this teaching.
It tries to convince us:

* *that we are what we buy and consume,*
* *that our joy is not from our creative power,*
* *that we need what others say we need.*

This Land is Home to Me (1975)
**At Home in the Web of Life* (1995)
<u>Appalachian Pastoral Letters</u>
(By over 30 Bishops)
Page 73

Chapter three

Francis
Clare
Catholic Doctrine

St. Francis (1182-1226) and St. Clare (1194-1253) lived in Assisi, Italy. They belonged to different classes in the social structure of Assisi. Clare's family was of the nobility/aristocracy of Assisi. Francis' family belonged to the rising social class of merchants. Power was mainly in the hands of the nobles. Francis' father, Pietro Bernadone, longed to move up the power/social ladder of Assisi.

Society was changing. Wealth was becoming a source of power. Pietro's wealth came from his cloth business. He was frequently absent on buying trips to France and other countries. But wealth alone was not enough to enter the power structure. It was imperative to become part of the nobility if he wished to move up the social scale.

Francis knew that becoming a knight was one way to move up the social ladder in Assisi. His father, Pietro Bernadone, obviously approved Francis' desire to become a knight. As a knight he could marry into the aristocracy and move up the social ladder.

War and violence were a normal part of life in Italy during Francis' lifetime. In 1199-1200 the people rebelled against the emperor's power structure in Assisi. The "Rocca," which towered over Assisi, was stormed and captured by the ordinary citizens of Assisi. Clare's family (and Clare) fled to Perugia to escape the violence. The spirit of the times often used violence to achieve goals. Early in life Francis experienced the use of violence to achieve social goals.

When Assisi battled with Perugia (1202), Francis was part

of Assisi's army. It was an opportunity to make a name for himself and move toward knighthood. Sad to say, Perugia prevailed at Collestrada, and many men of Assisi were taken prisoner, including Francis. Prisons were not noted for their gentle treatment of prisoners. Francis survived but became quite ill. He was ransomed by his father (in 1203) after about a year in prison.

Returning home he needed time to recuperate. His mother, Pica, took loving care of her son. Little by little he regained his strength. But as he joined his friends in parties and fun-times, he found them to be less exciting than before his captivity. His time in prison had made him more reflective. Things didn't seem the same for Francis. But he didn't know where to go or what to do. So he continued to do what he had done before his imprisonment - to party!

Another opportunity for knighthood (1205) came when Gautier de Brienne, a famous warrior, gathered an army to fight on the side of the Papacy against the German emperor. Again, Francis' father furnished him with fine armor. Once more Francis went forth on the journey to become a knight.

What happened next really confused him. While resting in Spoleto, on the way to Apulia, he had a dream.

It was night when he arrived in Spoleto and, anxious about his trip, he retired for the night. Half asleep, he heard a voice asking him where he intended to go. He outlined to him his whole plan. The voice then asked him: "Who can do more for you? The lord or the servant?" "The lord," he answered. "Then why are you abandoning the lord for the servant, the patron for the client?" To which Francis responded: "Lord, what do you want me to do?" "Go back," it said, "to your own land to do what the Lord will tell you."

It seemed to him that divine grace had suddenly made him a different man. But when it was morning, he returned home as he had been told.

And when, on the way back, he reached Foligno, he sold the horse he was riding as well as the wardrobe with which he had equipped himself for the expedition to Apulia, and put on cheaper clothing.

The Anonymous of Perugia - Francis of Assisi - The Founder Vol II - Page 36

In this year of 1205 the Holy Spirit moved this young man in a new direction. He would be a knight, but a knight of the Lord. A new beginning is taking shape. But first there is the matter of dealing with his father.

The following months were not peaceful for Francis. Pietro thought his son had lost his senses. He cajoled him. He held him in captivity in his home's basement. He was embarrassed by Francis' actions and felt stunned by his strange behavior. When Francis came to the shop and took some rolls of fabric and sold it in another town, Pietro was furious. This contest of wills came to a public conclusion when Pietro brought Francis before the Bishop. Pietro demanded that Francis return everything he had received from him.

On that winter day, far from being shamed, Francis saw this as an important moment. In public, before the bishop, he undressed himself, took all his clothes and laid them before his father. With his father and the townspeople standing around, using words that had deep meaning for Francis, he spoke clearly of his new call - from this day forward his Father would be: *Our Father in heaven ...*

The whole story of Francis' conversion fills many more pages in the writings on his life. Much is left out in this short telling. This is only the beginning. Francis' life and works fill books, articles and other resources that are available for further study.

During these early days, Francis came to understand that having "things" and "stuff" is not necessarily a source of happiness and peace. To ignore people who are poor or leprous or marginalized seemed to him to be sinful. He sought to relate to all of them. They were all brothers and sisters. In fact, his contact with lepers brought him to a new point in understanding the ways of Jesus. He attributes his contact with lepers as the source of his vocation.

The Lord gave me, Brother Francis, thus to begin doing penance in this way: for when I was in sin, it seemed too bitter for me to see lepers. And the Lord Himself led me among them and I showed mercy to them. And when I left them, what had seemed bitter to me was turned into sweetness of soul and body. And afterwards I delayed a little and left the world.

The Testament (1226) - Francis of Assisi - The Saint - Vol 1 - Page 124

Francis' love of Lady Poverty went further than discarding "things." He needed some "things" to live. But he realized that things we call necessary can also make us their slaves.

We lose freedom of movement and sharing because we must take care of "things." Even today we recognize how much of our time is spent in being able to buy "things" and maintain "things" and repair and re-paint "things," and replace "things," and get new "things" to be up-to-date or "in style." Worry about "things" saps our energy. Lack of "things" can make us depressed or sad or angry.

Francis' nakedness before the bishop and townspeople is a symbol of what it means to "trust" our *Father in heaven.* Francis stands us on our heads. Standing upright, things seem secure and permanent. When we stand on our heads we see things in a new light. Things are dependent on God's gracious hands to keep them from falling into space. The bigger they are, the more they are in danger.*

Francis was captured by his love of Lady Poverty. She was a symbol of his love for Jesus, his words and ways. He repeated the gesture of divesting when he came to die and

---

*Cf. Francis of Assisi - G.K. Chesterton - Image Books - Page 74

asked his brothers to lay him naked on the ground. In this way he repeated his trust in *Our Father in heaven* as he prepared to greet Sister Death. He asked the brothers to lay him naked on the ground when they saw that Sister Death was near.* He knew that as he brought nothing material into the world, he would leave without possessing anything but his life, given over and consecrated to God.

Clare grew up in Assisi. Clare's father, Favrone di Offreduccio, was one of Assisi's nobles. The men (Uncles) in her family were knights and military men. They supported the Emperor, Frederick II. The ordinary people of Assisi wanted to get out from under the power of the Emperor and showed little love for the Offreduccio family. When civil war broke out in Assisi (between 1199 and 1200), Clare's family was forced to flee to Perugia. Clare was about six or seven years old at the time. The family returned several years later when things settled down.

Her mother, Ortolana, was a woman of devotion and pilgrimages. Clare at times joined in her mother's pilgrimages. These were tough pilgrimages, with difficult travel and penitential practices both on the way and at the goal of the pilgrimage.

Clare was dedicated to relationships and had a special concern for the poor. The townspeople recognized her generosity to and concern for the poor and needy. She and her sisters, Catherine (Agnes), and Beatrice, showed a generous concern for the poor of Assisi.

With all the military men in the house, even in Perugia, the house echoed with swords and clanging armor and talk of wars and battle. She heard the lamentations over lost battles and friends who died in war. After several years the family was able to return to Assisi from their exile in Perugia.

---

* Cf. Francis of Assisi - Fortini - Page 612

The young girls of the family were becoming beautiful young women. Clare's teen years were filled with tales of violence and loss and - concern for the poor.

Clare was still in her teens when Francis renounced his goods before the bishop of Assisi. When she turned seventeen the family began to speak of marriage for her. Clare was expected to get married and bring new life to the family. At least, that's what members of the family thought. But Clare did not wish to marry. She felt a different call. Though Francis was still the object of jokes and teasing around Assisi, Clare wanted to speak with him. Her friend, Bona, arranged the meetings.

Little by little Francis' dream became Clare's dream. For over a year they met, apparently without Clare's family being aware of the meetings. The Spirit of God touched them and the dream that they shared. It confirmed Clare's desire to follow the way of life Francis shared with her.

On March 27, 1211, Palm Sunday, Clare went to San Rufino, the Cathedral of Assisi. She was dressed as beautiful as a bride. The Palm Sunday celebration was beautiful and the prayers touched her heart. Carried away in reverie, she stayed in her place while everyone moved forward to receive palm branches from the bishop. When Bishop Guido noticed her, he came to her place and gave her a palm branch as though it were part of the rite.

As night descended on Assisi, Clare prepared to join Francis and his brothers. She left the house late that night and headed to the little church of the Portiuncula. The brothers welcomed her. She took off her jewels and fine clothes. Then she received from Francis the rough habit of the friars. She knelt and loosened her hair. Francis cut it. Now she is a servant of the great King. The friars accompany her to the Benedictine convent of San Paolo Delle Ancelle di Dio. In a short time Clare, and those who joined her, would come to their first home, San Damiano, outside the walls of Assisi,

The development of the Poor Clares has begun. A Franciscan lifetime of contemplation and service begins. Clare remained faithful to the call of the Holy Spirit throughout her life. In a way, her dedication became a source of support for Francis. Later, writing to Agnes of Prague (whom she never met personally), Clare penned these words in a letter to Agnes:

But because one thing is necessary, I bear witness to that one thing and encourage you, for love of Him to Whom you have offered yourself as a holy and pleasing sacrifice, that you always be mindful of your commitment like another Rachel always seeing your beginning.

What you hold, may you hold,
What you do, may you do and not stop.
But with swift pace, light step, unswerving feet,
so that even your steps stir up no dust,
may you go forward
securely, joyfully, and swiftly,
on the path of prudent happiness,
believing nothing,
agreeing with nothing
that would dissuade you from this commitment or
would place a stumbling block for you on the way,
so that nothing prevents you
from offering your vows
to the Most High in the perfection
to which the Spirit of the Lord has called you.

Second Letter to Agnes of Prague (1235)
Clare of Assisi - The Lady
Regis Armstrong OFM Cap - Pages 47-48

Francis' and Clare's friendship was never exclusive. Relationship with others was always part of their lives. Francis and Clare offer us a mirror in which to discover the gospel spirit they both embraced. Their love reached out to everyone and to all of creation.

28

Catholic Doctrine

People called to the Secular Franciscan way of life are expected to understand their Catholic faith. We will not write another Catholic Catechism, but there are some beliefs that are very important to our Franciscan spirit.

Beloved, let us ***love one another,*** *because love is from God; everyone who loves is born of God and knows God. Whoever does not love does not know God, for God is love. ... Beloved, since God loved us so much, we also ought to love one another.*

1 John 4:7-8, 11

It is our belief as Franciscans that God's love is what prompted God to send Jesus to earth to be with us. Sin is not what influenced God to send Jesus. Rather, whether we had sinned or not, Jesus would have come among us because God's love seeks to be with us. That love is made visible in the humanity of Jesus, the Christ. Only secondarily did this love rescue us from our sin and unfaithfulness. Hence, one theological truth of faith for Franciscans is - **God's love finds expression in the Incarnation.** God chooses to come among us because God loves us.

Jesus shows us what love looks like in everyday life. The words and actions of Jesus offer a model of how to deal with the issues of life and faith. Jesus is at the heart of all we are. Without Jesus and the Holy Spirit we would be lost. Jesus is the love of God made flesh (Incarnation).

With all wisdom and insight he has made known to us the mystery of his will, according to his good pleasure that he set forth in Christ, as a plan for the fullness of time, to gather up all things in him, things in heaven and things on earth. ... In him you also, when you heard the word of truth, the gospel of your salvation, and had believed in him, were marked with the seal of the promised Holy Spirit ...

Ephesians 1:8-10, 13

Personal faith in Jesus Christ is fundamental. This requires a personal faith-relationship with Jesus, not just an intellectual knowledge of facts *about* Jesus. As Jesus put it: *Those who **abide** in me and I in them bear much fruit, because apart from me you can do nothing!* (John 15:5). Revelation reached its zenith in Jesus Christ. Jesus is God's final Word to us. No new public revelation will be given by God before the final manifestation of Jesus.*

+ *Jesus Christ, the fullness of Revelation, entrusted his mission to the Apostles. They transmitted Christ's Gospel through their witness, preaching, and writing - under the guidance of the Holy Spirit - meant for all peoples until Christ comes in glory. ...*

+ *"The Church, in her doctrine, life and worship perpetuates and transmits to every generation all that she herself is, all that she believes"* (*Dogmatic Constitution on Divine Revelation* - Vatican II - no 8, Paragraph 1). *This is what is meant by the term* Tradition.

United States Catholic Catechism for Adults - USCCB - Page 31-32

Jesus established a believing community (Church) to transmit God's revelation to people. This happens through scripture, tradition, and the magisterium. Through the written words of scripture God reveals the way to walk and how to live as children of God. Jesus is the teacher who is known as *the way, the truth and the life*!

Tradition shares the truth through living transmission of the message of Jesus. Sound tradition is in accord with Scripture and the words of Jesus. If people believe a tradition that wanders from Scripture or is in conflict with approved Church teaching, they follow a false tradition.**

"The whole body of the faithful ... cannot err in matters of belief. This characteristic is shown in the supernatural appreciation of faith (sensus fidei) *on the part of the whole*

---

* Cf. United States Catholic Catechism for Adults - USCCB - Page 18.
** Cf. United States Catholic Catechism for Adults - USCCB - Page 24-26.

people, when, 'from the bishops to the last of the faithful,' they manifest a universal consent in matters of faith and morals." (LG 12 cf. St. Augustine, De praed. sanct. 14: PL 44, 980)

Catechism of the Catholic Church - No. 92

Sacred Scripture is inspired by God and is the Word of God. *Therefore, God is the author of Sacred Scripture, which means he inspired human authors, acting in and through them. Thus, God ensured that the authors taught, without error, those truths necessary for our salvation.* Inspiration *is the word used for the divine assistance given to the human authors of the books of Sacred Scripture. This means that guided by the Holy Spirit, the human authors made full use of their talents and abilities while, at the same time, writing what God intended.*

United States Catholic Catechism for Adults - USCCB - Page 26-27

The focal point of revelation is the transmission of God's message to all people. Sharing the love and vision of the Father, Son and Holy Spirit is a primary responsibility of the Church.

*The teaching office of the college of bishops is called the "**Magisterium.**" When all the bishops throughout the world, together with the Pope, in the fulfillment of their teaching office, proclaim a doctrine that has been divinely revealed, it must be accepted with the obedience of faith by the whole People of God. "The Church, through its magisterium, has been entrusted with the task of authoritively interpreting what is contained in revelation, so that 'all that is proposed for belief, as being divinely revealed, is drawn from the one deposit of faith'* (*Dei Verbum*, no. 10). *In some cases these doctrines have been explicitly defined; in others, they are universally considered to be an essential and irreformable element of the one Catholic faith."* (USCCB, *The Teaching Ministry of the Diocesan Bishop* [1992]).

United States Catholic Catechism for Adults - Page 133

The Church is an assembly of people gathered by God into one community. Through this community God's message is transmitted. The Holy Spirit empowers the Church to proclaim the Gospel. Building the kingdom of God is the mission of the Church.*

The Church has structures to transmit the vision the Trinity seeks to share with us. Like Jesus, who has both a divine and a human nature so, too, the Church. The Church is a complex reality that has human and divine elements. **

Another element of faith is our belief in the **real presence of Jesus in the Eucharist.** Jesus instituted the Eucharist at the Last Supper. The Eucharist is the memorial of Christ's saving life, death and resurrection, made present to us. Jesus gives himself totally to us in the Eucharist.

Under the consecrated species of bread and wine, Christ himself, living and glorious, is present in a true, real and substantial manner: His Body and Blood, with his soul and divinity. (CCC. no. 1413 - Council of Trent: Denzinger/Schonmetzer 1640, 1651)

United States Catholic Catechism for Adults - USCCB - Page 226

I cannot possess Christ just for myself; I can belong to him only in union with all those who have become, or who will become, his own. Communion draws me out of myself toward him, and thus also toward unity with all Christians. We become "one body," completely joined in a single existence. ... A Eucharist which does not pass over into the concrete practice of love is intrinsically fragmented ...

God is Love *(Deus Caritas Est)* - Benedict XVI - Paragraph 14

Eucharistic spirituality is not just participation in Mass and devotion to the Blessed Sacrament. It embraces the whole of life. ... Hence the Eucharist, as the source and summit of the Church's life and mission, must be translated into spirituality, into a life lived "according to the Spirit" (Romans 8:4; cf. Galatians 5:16, 25).

Sacrament of Charity *(Sacramentum Caritatis)*
Benedict XVI - Paragraph 17

---

* Cf. United States Catholic Catechism for Adults - USCCB - Page 113-121.

** Cf. United States Catholic Catechism for Adults - USCCB - Page 122.

In a later chapter we will speak of **the resurrection**, a fundamental belief of our Catholic faith.

+++

Readings/Questions for dialogue

God is Love *(Deus Caritas Est)* - Benedict XVI
Paragraphs 12, 14, 19, 29

1 Celano - Chapter VIII
St. Francis of Assisi - The Saint - Vol 1
Page 196-199

Let everyone be struck with fear etc
St Francis of Assisi - The Saint - Vol I
Letter to the Entire Order - Page 118

1. Share your impressions of Francis and Clare and their response to the call of the Holy Spirit. How were their lives changed? What role did prayer play in their conversion?

2. Do any of Francis' or Clare's experiences reflect your own life-experiences? Explain.

3. How would you describe the relationship between Francis and Clare? What brought them together?

4. How did the situation of society affect the life of Francis? What brought him to a new way of assessing the ways of society?

5. Having answered #4, how did his new conversion-insights affect Francis' choice of a way of life? What kind of impact did it have among those who knew him?

6. How did Clare come to accept Francis' perceptions about the Gospel and Jesus? Explain.

7. What is your reaction to the requirement of the SFO that

you understand your faith-beliefs? Why is it required?

8. *God is love.* God's people are expected to reflect God's love in everyday life. What are some love-conversions that are needed in your personal life?

9. Which truths of the faith do you find you need to learn more about? Why?

10. Scripture reflection: Matthew 5: 1-16. How do Jesus' words about the beatitudes touch you? What beatitude seems to elude your grasp in daily life? How would you suppose Francis and Clare responded to the Beatitudes? Explain.

+++

Charity goes beyond justice,
because to love is to give,
to offer what is "mine" to the other;
but it never lacks justice,
which prompts us to give the other
what is "his," what is due to him
by reason of his being or his acting.
I cannot "give" what is mine to the other,
without first giving him what pertains
to him in justice. If we love others
with charity, then first of all
we are just towards them.
Not only is justice not extraneous
to charity, not only is it not an alternative
or parallel path to charity;
justice is inseparable from charity,
and intrinsic to it.

Charity in Truth (Caritas in Veritate)
Benedict XVI - Paragraph 6

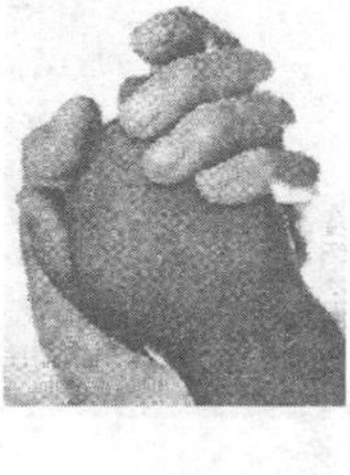

At the beginnning of **inquiry**
we introduce newcomers
to the fraternity
and welcome them.

A ritual for this simple ceremony
is found on page 9 and 10 of the
Ritual of the Secular Franciscan Order

The rite serves as a model.
Fraternity formation people
can add or subtract elements
to make it more meaningful
for everyone concerned.

The rite is simple.
Involve both newcomers and
the members of the fraternity.
Hospitality is the key word.
A welcoming spirit will make
the newcomers feel at home.

Chapter four

Inquiry in the SFO

Inquiry - the first phase *of initial formation*
(A minimum of six months)

You perceived a bit of the rhythm of formation sessions during *Orientation*. The second step in the formation process is your *initial formation* in the SFO. It is a two-step program. The first step is called *Inquiry*. It lasts for at least six months. The second step is *Candidacy,* which lasts from 18 to 36 months. The specific length of candidacy is determined by the local council or by regional guidelines.

Inquiry is a time of continuing discernment of your vocation and learning more about our way of life. We will examine a number of topics:

a. Continuing discernment of your vocation during these next six months.
b. A look at lay/secular spirituality.
c. Continued exploration of the spirit of Francis and Clare and getting acquainted with some of their writings.
d. A brief history of the SFO and the development of the SFO *Rule* of 1978.
e. An introduction to Scripture study.
f. Reflections concerning the Church and the spirit of Vatican II.

INQUIRY

a. **Inquiry** - *The period of inquiry, which begins with the ceremony of introduction and welcoming, shall consist of not less than six (6) months.*

c. All persons in initial formation, in addition to attending their formation sessions, must participate in the meetings (gatherings) *of the local fraternity as this is an indispensible presupposition for initiation into community prayer and into fraternity life.* (Cf. Constitutions - article 40.3).
National Statutes - article 19.2a, 19.2c

The call to the SFO is a vocation. The Holy Spirit invites someone to follow the Franciscan spirit as their way of living and serving the People of God. The SFO is not an isolated group doing its "own thing." It exists within the Catholic Church and finds its home there. The Church approves our way of life, approves our Rule and Constitutions and frequently invites us to greater dedication in living our way of life.

The call of the Spirit can begin in many ways. It may be because St. Francis is an attractive figure and people want to find out more about him. It can happen because someone you know is a secular Franciscan and their example attracts you. It may happen when you are praying and sense a need to learn more about Francis. It may occur because of some fraternity action that fits your desire to serve. It may occur because of your personal research, or information in your parish bulletin, or brochures in your church. It may be your friendship with a live Franciscan. Or it may be something entirely different that draws you.

The Holy Spirit is creative. The call may come in many forms. Your presence with us speaks of a readiness to discover your vocation. We assist you. *Orientation* began the process with guidelines to help you. The formation personnel are present to help. Your quiet prayer time will be part of the process. You might re-read some of the ideas found on pages 15 to 18 in this book. By the end of *inquiry* you can come to a decision about your vocation to the SFO

The Franciscan family, as one among many spiritual families raised up by the Holy Spirit in the Church, unites all members of the people of God - laity, religious, and priests - ***who recognize that they are called*** *to follow Christ in the footsteps of Saint Francis of Assisi.*

In various ways and forms but in life-giving union with each other, they intend to make present the charism of their common Seraphic Father (Francis) ***in the life and mission of the Church****.*

SFO Rule - #1

The Secular Franciscan Order holds a special place in this family circle. ... the brothers and sisters, led by the Spirit, strive for perfect charity in their own secular state. By their profession they pledge themselves to live the gospel in the manner of Saint Francis by means of this rule approved by the Church.

SFO Rule - #2

St. Francis wrote the following words that focus on Jesus Christ.

Let every creature
in heaven, on earth, in the sea and in the depths,
give praise, glory, honor and blessing
To Him Who suffered so much,
Who has given and will give in the future every good,
for He is our power and strength,
Who alone is good, Who alone is almighty,
Who alone is omnipotent, wonderful, glorious
and Who alone is holy, worthy of praise and blessing
through endless ages.
Amen

Later Admonitions & Exhortation
Francis of Assisi - The Saint - Vol 1 - Page 49-50

In a letter to his converts in Colossae, Paul calls us to an awareness of the primacy of Jesus Christ.

He (God) *has rescued us from the power of darkness and transferred us into the kingdom of his beloved Son, in whom we have redemption, the forgiveness of sins.*

He (Jesus) *is the image of the invisible God, the*

firstborn of all creation, for in him all things in heaven and on earth were created, things visible and invisible, whether thrones or dominions or rulers or powers - all things have been created through him and for him. He himself is before all things, and in him all things hold together. He is the head of the body, the church; he is the beginning, the firstborn from the dead, so that he might come to have first place in everything. For in him all the fullness of God was pleased to dwell, and through him God was pleased to reconcile to himself all things, whether on earth or in heaven, making peace through the blood of his cross.

Colossians 1:13-20

The Constitutions support St. Paul's words - Re: Christ:

Rule 10 *"Christ, poor and crucified," victor over death and risen, the greatest manifestation of the love of God for humanity, is the book in which the brothers and sisters, in imitation of Francis, learn the purpose and the way of living, loving, and suffering. They discover in Him the value of contradictions for the sake of justice and the meaning of the difficulties and the crosses of daily life. With Him, they can accept the will of the Father even under the most difficult circumstances and live the Franciscan spirit of peace, rejecting every doctrine contrary to human dignity.*

Constitutions - article 10

Our growth in Franciscan spirituality consistently enriches our relationship with Jesus. Spirituality, in this sense, means our way of perceiving things and people. We are not naive nor out-of-touch-with-reality. Quite the contrary. We grow in our ability to see reality with the eyes of the Trinity.

Maintaining relationships is no easy task. Being consistent in finding ways to bring about unity is part of our spirituality. Learning how to deal with tough issues and people requires creative skills. Conflicts will arise in our lives. *HOW* we deal with conflictual situations and people is what matters rather than *whether* they occur.

To respond in reverent ways to difficult situations and people calls for openness to the guidance of the Holy Spirit. We respond with a sense of respect and reverence, avoiding attitudes/actions that would separate us from one another. This is no easy task. But we bring this spirit to the Church and the world. Everyone in the Church or the world may not follow our way, but we will be faithful to it.

One does not make the world more human by refusing to act humanely here and now. We contribute to a better world only by personally doing good now, with full commitment and wherever we have the opportunity, independently of partisan strategies and programs. The Christian's program - the program of the Good Samaritan, the program of Jesus - is "a heart which sees." This heart sees where love is needed and acts accordingly

God is Love *(Deus Caritas Est)* - Benedict XVI - Paragraph 31.b

When the Holy Spirit calls us to follow Francis, and we accept the call, we have made our choice. We are committed to achieve whatever the SFO Rule requires of us. SFO members, like other people, will have to deal with conflicting opinions and ideas. We may use limited human responses when conflicts arise. We can dominate or "turn off" others; become angry and separate from them; give others the "silent treatment;" show our "know-it-all" attitude; refuse to deal with the issue; label others as "devils/nazis;" or use a variety of negative ways to deal with one another in conflictual situations.

In these and other human situations Franciscans avoid whatever would diminish or destroy relationships. We are called to bring about unity. It may require the ability to listen; or to forgive; or to reconcile; or to apologize; or to discontinue a dominating attitude; or to allow that others may have good ideas etc.

United by their vocation as "brothers and sisters of penance," and motivated by the dynamic power of the gospel, let them conform their thoughts and deeds to those

of Christ by means of that radical interior change which the gospel itself calls "conversion." Human frailty makes it necessary that this conversion be carried out daily. ...

SFO Rule - #7

In this spirit of conversion, they should live out their love for the renewal of the Church, which should be accompanied by personal and communal renewal. The fruits of conversion, which is a response to the love of God, are the works of charity in the interactions with the brothers and sisters.

Constitutions - article 13.2

Which leads to another important dimension of Franciscan life. If we are going to bring the Franciscan spirit to the Church and the world we need one another.

Community is not an additive to our way of life. Creating a supportive community, creating a model of reverence and respect, learning the ways of forgiveness and acceptance is no easy thing. One lifetime may not be enough. But we faithfully work together to achieve it. Community life calls for faithful collaboration. We check out the implications of these Franciscan ideas and quotations. It is not enough to nod and say "Amen." That is easy. Accepting the personal consequences of the call to conversion may not be so easy.

Most of us have developed firm ideas about how to deal with life, do it "my way" - without much reflection. Change is not always easy nor attractive nor understood nor practiced in our personal lives. The SFO Rule requires us to actually "deal" with it in our personal lives.

In the Franciscan "conversion process" we examine our personal lifestyle, ideas, and opinions to discover their source. The Franciscan spirit may reveal a contrast between how we live and how we accept personal changes. To convert to the Franciscan spirit may not be easy. We open our lives to the Holy Spirit. The Holy Spirit enables us to follow our Franciscan vocation and embrace conversion.

The Spirit, in fact, is that interior power which harmonizes their hearts with Christ's heart and moves them to love their brethren as Christ loved them, when he bent down to wash the feet of the disciples (Cf. John 13:1-13) *and above all when he gave his life for us.*

The Spirit is also the energy which transforms the heart of the ecclesial community, so that it becomes a witness before the world to the love of the Father, who wishes to make humanity a single family in his Son.
God is Love (*Deus Caritas Est)* - Benedict XVI - Paragraph 19

Conversion is never a one-time affair. We don't suddenly "get religion." Conversion requires consistent comparison of our personal lives with the gospel requirements for following Jesus. We will discover many things in our lives that call for change.

E.g. How do we perceive marginalized people? How do we maintain relationships with people who engage in criminal activity or are pro-choice? How do we assess the value of someone who is handicapped? How do we deal with people who insult or denigrate us, especially if done publicly? How do we care for creation? How do we assess the qualities of individuals running for political office or holding a political office? How do we deal with failures of people in authority in the Church, civil society, families or groups? How do we create an atmosphere of acceptance for friends, children, spouse, immigrants? How do we support servant-leaders in the SFO?

The Franciscan spirit touches the whole of life. The SFO **is not a devotional society** that lets you do what you want as long as you pray. Rather, it expects that your grasp of the Franciscan spirit will find expression in the actions of your daily life.

The more ardent the love for the Eucharist in the hearts of the Christian people, the more clearly will they recognize the goal of all mission: "to bring Christ to others." Not just a theory or a way of life inspired by Christ, but the gift of his very person. Anyone who has not shared the truth of love with his brothers and sisters has not yet given enough.

Sacrament of Charity *(Sacramentum Caritatis)*
Benedict XVI - Paragraph 86

Our Franciscan way of showing love is spelled out in the SFO Rule and reflected in the SFO Constitutions. We do not embrace an esoteric community. The SFO Rule and Constitutions guide us to live realistic and practical Franciscan lives. *Initial formation* helps recognize the Rule and Constitution's call for conversion to gospel values.

Gaining inspiration from the example and the writings of Francis and, above all, filled with the grace of the Holy Spirit, ***each day*** *the brothers and sisters faithfully live the great gift which Christ has given: the revelation of the Father. They should bear witness before all:*

+ *in their family life;*
+ *in their work;*
+ *in their joys and sufferings;*
+ *in their associations with all men and women, brothers and sisters of the same Father;*
+ *in their presence and participation in the life of society;*
+ *in their fraternal relationships with all creatures.*

Constitutions - article 12.1

Nothing and no one we encounter is left untouched by the Franciscan spirit. People should know they have a friend when we are present. Friendship does not ignore people's responsibility for their actions; nor does forgiveness automatically excuse people from changing the things that made forgiveness necessary; nor does reconciliation exclude the changes that are required for restoring friendships.

c) Charity, furthermore, cannot be used as a means of engaging in what is nowadays considered proselytism. Love is free; it is not practiced as a way of achieving other ends. ... Those who practice charity in the Church's name will never seek to impose the Church's faith upon others. They realize that a pure and generous love is the best witness to the God in whom they believe and by whom they are driven to love. A Christian knows when it is time to speak of God and when it is better to say nothing and to let love alone speak.

God is Love *(Deus Caritas Est)* - Benedict XVI - Paragraph 31c

Franciscans bring their whole life into conformity with the Gospel through the spirit of Francis of Assisi. The SFO Rule and Constitutions assist us in recognizing the need for growing and maturing in the vocation given by the Holy Spirit. It spells out the Franciscan way of following the Gospel. Ignorance of the Rule and Constitutions is not a virtue for Franciscans. Intellectual knowledge of the Rule and Constitutions is never enough.

Living the spirit spelled out in the Rule and Constitutions is the criterion that proves the legitimacy of our calling. Our vocation expects us to give flesh, in daily life, to the words of our Franciscan profession. Love of people, conversion, reconciliation, forgiveness, contemplation, love for all of creation, prayerfulness, etc. become normal for us. These words of Francis sound like a passionate challenge:

"Your will be done on earth as in heaven."
That we may love You
with our whole heart by always thinking of You,
with our whole soul by always desiring You,
with our whole mind by always directing
all our intentions to You,
and by seeking Your glory in everything,
with all our strength by exerting
all our energies and affections of body and soul
in the service of Your love and of nothing else;
and we may love our neighbor as ourselves
by drawing them all to Your love
with our whole strength,
by rejoicing in the good of others as in our own,

by suffering with others at their misfortunes,
and by giving offense to no one.

A Prayer inspired by the Our Father
Francis of Assisi - The Saint - Vol 1 - Page 158-159

+++

Readings/Questions for dialogue

SFO Constitutions
Articles 11, 12.2, 13.1

St. Francis of Assisi - The Saint - Vol 1
Prayer inspired by the Our Father - Page 158-160

God is Love *(Deus Caritas Est)* - Benedict XVI
Paragraph 31

1. What ideas struck you most forcefully in this chapter? How did you react to them?

2. Describe the relationship of the SFO to the Catholic Church? What does loyalty to the Church require of us when the Church needs some rebuilding (renewal)?

3. At this point give your thumbnail description of the SFO.

4. Please explain why we need the Holy Spirit to follow the Franciscan gospel way of life?

5. Why is your attendance at regular gatherings considered so important to the SFO? (The same is true of your presence at the formation sessions). If at this time you are unable to be present, (for long periods) how does this influence your discernment?

6. Scripture reflection: Mark 3:1-6. What does this story tell you about doing good? When is silence a poor way to show love? What was wrong with curing the man with the withered hand? What does this story teach us about people who may not like our Franciscan spirit put into action?

The ideal of the monastic orders was complete withdrawal from the world. A new type of religious order, however, arose in the thirteenth century whose aim was to pursue the monastic ideals of renunciation, poverty and self-sacrifice while staying in the world in order to convert it by example and preaching. These were called "friars," from the Latin word, "fratres," meaning "brothers." They were also called mendicant orders because of their practice of begging alms to support themselves. ... They were, in part, an instinctive response to the new social conditions caused by the rise of towns, the revival of commerce, and the growth of the population. The shift of population from the countryside to the towns posed a big problem for the Church, whose venerable structures were geared to the old rural, feudal society. It stood in danger of losing touch with the masses who had moved away from the rural parishes and who now lived in the slums, clustered outside the walls of medieval towns. The mendicant orders proved a godsend in the new urban apostolate.

A Concise History of the Catholic Church
Thomas Bokenkotter - Page 149

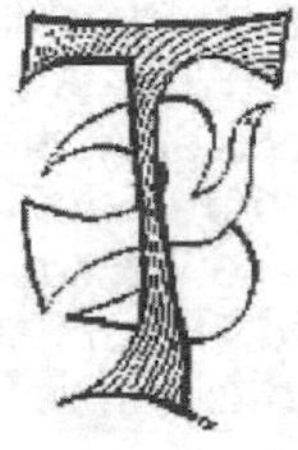

Chapter five

Lay Secular Spirituality

Secular Franciscans need to understand secular Franciscan spirituality. Though all spiritualities ultimately draw people to Jesus and his Gospel, the path to such intimacy shows differences. St. Ignatius of Loyola's spirituality attracts the men who follow him. Benedictine founders established a spirituality that touched their followers and was linked to monastic ideals. The followers of St. Dominic focus on ministries that fit their spirit.

Each group has a spirituality that ultimately leads to Jesus and the God who loves them joined to an outreach to others. We will find common threads in each of the tapestries of their spirit. But they are not exactly the same. Indeed, each group attracts individuals who seem to fit the "spirit" of the group. It is a special calling or vocation for each individual.

Each group brings a different gift to the Church and the world. Religious gather in community and collaborate in ministries that reflect their spirit. They vow to serve the Church by living life in the spirit (charism) of their founder.

Laity who live in the secular world need a structure that helps them live in the spirit of their founder. Lay groups need a spirit that reflects not only the spirit of the founder, but *how* the spirit finds expression in secular life. They need a secular spirituality to be successful in living their calling in the secular world. Their "specific way" of living the spirit of their founder is expressed in their everyday secular life.

If seculars merely imitate Franciscan Religious they will fail in their role of reshaping the world in the blueprint of the Gospel. Their presence in the world gives them a special entre' into the halls of legislation, in the structures of justice, in the fairness of wages and work conditions, in the ways of settling conflicts, in the ability to embrace immigrants or accept the poor and marginalized, in developing a wholesome family life. The spirit shows in celebrations and worship and in love for one's family and one's neighbor.

A secular spirituality embraces family life, spousal relationships and human rights. Secular Franciscans bring a contemplative prayerfulness to their daily lives that keeps them in touch with the Trinity. They serve the Church and its people. They find ways to affirm a gospel stance in the common life of the People of God. They remain in the world but choose to be free from its negative actions and values. Secular Franciscans bring a positive viewpoint and perspective that springs from their vocation to follow the spirit of St. Francis of Assisi.

The SFO is a lay order. The word "order" means participation in the discipline and penitential practices of Franciscan spirituality while retaining the autonomy typical of their lay and secular condition.*

The Rule of 1978 enables the SFO to be autonomous. From 1471 to 1978 we might say that it was in a state of substantial inferiority, subject to the First Order and the TOR. In its fresh situation, it is in a *life-giving union* with the rest of the Franciscan family. The First Order/TOR collaborates with ("assists") the SFO while not dominating it nor diminishing its autonomy.

Insight into being a real order, but a *lay order,* requires our understanding. Collaboration among the Franciscan family members is a work in progress. The relationships within the Franciscan family respond to the requirements of a

*Cf. Address to the SFO General Chapter - John Paul II - June 14, 1988.

secular order composed mainly of lay people. The laity are involved in the world and in the ordinary activities of family, work and society. (Cf. Preparatory Document for the SFO General Chapter of 2008). It is an ongoing task to develop a *life-giving union* within the Franciscan family while recognizing the SFO as an autonomous family member.

The foundation for unity comes from baptism. Profession reinforces the promises of baptism. Our call to the Franciscan way of life points out the path for us to follow. This baptismal source of unity reaches beyond the boundaries of states, languages, cultures, and social classes. We are one in Christ. We are called to spread the Gospel and influence the world and the Church with the Gospel of Jesus flavored by our Franciscan spirit.

Moreover, let the laity band together to remedy those secular institutions and conditions which are an inducement to sin, so that they may be brought into line with the rules of justice, favoring rather than hindering the practice of virtue.

... Because of the very economy of salvation the faithful should learn to distinguish carefully between the rights and duties which they have as members of the Church and those which fall to them as members of human society. They are to do their best to ensure that the two work together harmoniously, remembering that in all temporal matters they are to be guided by a christian conscience, since not even in temporal business may any human activity be withdrawn from God's dominion.

Lumen Gentium - Vatican II - Paragraph 36

Secular Franciscans develop love in full measure so that it becomes their natural reaction to life and people and problems and celebrations. The SFO Rule is clear on this when it states: ... *In these fraternities the brothers and sisters, led by the Spirit,* ***strive for perfect charity*** *in their own secular state* (SFO Rule - #2).

Some important ideas:

1. Baptism *makes us members* of the community of believers, the People of God called "Church." God calls us to intimacy with Jesus and to love one another.

Baptism, the gate to the sacraments, necessary for salvation in fact or at least in intention, by which men and women are freed from their sins, are reborn as children of God and, configured to Christ by an indelible character, are incorporated in the Church, is validly conferred only by washing with true water together with the required form of words.

Code of Canon Law - Canon 849

2. Baptism brings the *responsibility* to listen to and implement the word of God. The gifts of the Spirit enable us to do what we could not do alone. ... *because apart from me you can do nothing.* (John 15:5). ... *the fruit of the Spirit is love, joy, peace, patience, kindness, generosity, faithfulness, gentleness and self-control. There is no law against such things.* (Galatians 5:22-23)

3. Within the baptismal community the Holy Spirit calls people with a variety of gifts to *contribute* to building the Kingdom of God in our world.

Now there are varieties of gifts, but the same Spirit; and there are varieties of services, but the same Lord; and there are varieties of activities, but it is the same God who activates all of them in everyone. To each is given the manifestation of the Spirit ***for the common good.***

1 Corinthians 12:4-7

4. Baptism invests the People of God with participation in *priestly* service. Baptism unites them with Christ and the Church (People of God). They offer themselves and their activities to God as their spiritual sacrifice. Franciscans accomplish this through faithfulness to the SFO Rule and a life-long effort to witness to the Gospel in all they do.

Thus, in the spirit of "the Beatitudes," and as pilgrims and strangers on their way to the home of the Father, they should strive to purify their hearts from every tendency and yearning for possession and power.

SFO Rule - #11

5. Baptism invites the baptised to *prophetic* service, accepting the word of God and being faithful in living the Gospel. They bear witness in the world to God's way of achieving peace, joy, love and justice. Franciscans are faithful to the way of life to which the Spirit calls them. This faithfulness witnesses to the spirit of the Gospel and St. Francis' charism in responding to the Gospel.

Mindful that they are bearers of peace which must be built up unceasingly, they should seek out ways of unity and fraternal harmony through dialogue, trusting in the presence of the divine seed in everyone and in the transforming power of love and pardon.

SFO Rule - #19

6. Baptism gives us *a place* in the Kingdom of God and its mission in history. Christians seek to leave the kingdom of sin and enter the kingdom of love patterned by Jesus. Franciscans seek to establish a society where peace and justice, joy and acceptance, understanding and forgiveness, reconciliation and relationships, become the natural consequence of their call to the Franciscan way of life.

Therefore, even when occupied with temporal affairs, the laity can and must be involved in the precious work of evangelizing the world. ... it is the duty of all lay people to cooperate in spreading and building up the kingdom of Christ. The laity, consequently, have the duty to work hard ***to acquire a deeper knowledge of revealed truth*** *and* ***earnestly to pray*** *to God for the gift of wisdom.*

Lumen Gentium - Vatican II - Paragraph 35

Secular Franciscans, together with all people of good will, are called to build a more fraternal and evangelical world so that the kingdom of God may be brought about more effectively. ... let them exercise their responsibilities ***competently*** *in the Christian spirit of service.*

SFO Rule - #14

Within the family called *People of God,* the manner of service is influenced by the spirit of various founders. In our case that founder is St. Francis of Assisi. Prompted by the Holy Spirit, we bring the Franciscan spirit to all we do. It is our gift to the Church and the world.

To gift the Church with our Franciscan spirit we must know it well and live it faithfully. Both *initial* and *ongoing formation* keep us attentive to our Franciscan charism. We deal with life with a Franciscan spirit because the Spirit calls us to this way of living. It is our way to serve both the Church and the world with the spirit of St. Francis.

Accordingly, all Christians, in the conditions, duties and circumstances of their lives and through all these, will grow constantly in holiness if they receive all things with faith from the hand of the heavenly Father and cooperate with the divine will, making manifest in their ordinary work the love with which God has loved the world.

Lumen Gentium - Vatican II - Paragraph 41

7. The SFO Rule *spells out* the way the Spirit wishes us to do God's will. When we are called to the Secular Franciscan way of life, the SFO Rule spells out the way God desires us to live. Faithfulness to the SFO Rule and Constitutions is the way we build God's kingdom. Among these ways are:

... going from gospel to life and life to gospel (SFO Rule - #4); *... encounter the living and active person of Christ in their brothers and sisters, in Sacred Scripture, in the Church, and in liturgical activity* (SFO Rule - #5); *... let prayer and contemplation be the soul of all they are and do* (SFO Rule - #8); *... place themselves on an equal basis with all people, especially with the lowly, for whom they shall strive to create conditions of life worthy of people redeemed by Christ* (SFO Rule - #13).

There is more. But these texts illustrate how the SFO way of life helps determine how to be faithful to God through our Franciscan vocation. Secular Franciscan holiness is connected to the faithful living of a secular life, touching the whole of life with the Franciscan spirit.

So then, putting away all falsehood, let all of us speak the truth to our neighbors, for we are members of one another. Be angry but do not sin; do not let the sun go down on your anger, and do not make room for the devil. Thieves must give up stealing; rather let them labour and work honestly with their own hands, so as to have something to share with the needy. Let no evil talk come out of your mouths, but only what is useful for building up, as there is need, so that your words may give grace to those who hear. And do not grieve the Holy Spirit of God, with which you were marked with a seal for the day of redemption. Put away from you all bitterness and wrath and anger and wrangling and slander, together with all malice, and be kind to one another, tender-hearted, forgiving one another, as God in Christ has forgiven you. Therefore be imitators of God, as beloved children, and live in love, as Christ loved us and gave himself up for us, a fragrant offering and sacrifice to God.

Ephesians - 4:25 to 5:2

Trinitarian spirituality colors our Franciscan spirit. It is not specifically ours alone nor does it only touch Franciscans. But it influences and colors what we call our "charism."

The Trinity is three persons - Father, Son and Holy Spirit. **The Trinity is not three Gods but one - one nature with three persons. All three are equally God and all together are God**. A relationship of love binds them together. They are a unity of persons in one divine nature. Each is fully God in a way distinct from one another. They relate to each other and live within the atmosphere of that relationship.*

---

*Cf. Catechism of the Catholic Church - #253-255 / United States Catholic Catechism for Adults - USCCB - Page 51-53 - *God is the Trinity*.

We recognize the vital relationship the Father, Son, and Holy Spirit have with one another. It is a relationship that has no jealousy, no turf-wars, no hidden agendas nor anything that would diminish or destroy the relationship.* The Trinity models what love does best - it makes us one!

It is through Jesus that we come to know this Trinity of persons. The humanity of the Son, Jesus, makes present to us this God who is Trinity. The message of God to us is Jesus. It is through Jesus that St. Francis of Assisi came to recognize the role of the Trinity in his life.

Jesus led him among lepers and Francis learned the power of compassion. Jesus led him to Scripture and Francis learned to embrace biblical ideals. Jesus led him to the Church and Francis understood her role in revealing Jesus to the world. Jesus led him to constant conversion and Francis understood the meaning of penance and pain by walking the passion path with Jesus. Jesus brought him to revel in the resurrection as the gift of a loving Father and Francis embraced Sister Death as the pathway to new life.

Jesus led him to relate to all of creation because it is an outpouring of God's love. Jesus brought Francis to the Trinity and taught him to be a seraphic lover. Jesus taught him to forgive and moved him to be faithful to his calling. Jesus taught him how to relate to God in prayer and Francis engaged in prayerful contemplation. Jesus taught him to know that words and example must blend and show a unity that reveals integrity. So Francis prayed:

Almighty, eternal, just and merciful God,
give us miserable ones
the grace to do for You alone
what we know you want us to do
and always to desire what pleases You.
Inwardly cleansed,
interiorly enlightened,

---

* Cf. Catechism of the Catholic Church - #255

and inflamed by the fire of the Holy Spirit,
may we be able to follow
in the footprints of Your beloved Son,
our Lord, Jesus Christ,
and, by your grace alone,
may we make our way to You,
Most High,
Who live and rule
in perfect Trinity and simple Unity
and are glorified
God Almighty,
forever and ever.
Amen

A Letter to the Entire Order
Francis of Assisi - The Saint - Vol 1
Pages 120-121

Relationship (love) is the heart of the Trinity. Our ability to relate to people, to God, and to the whole of creation is at the heart of Franciscan life. Respect and reverence for people must not be sidetracked because people are ornery, stubborn, criminal, indifferent, arrogant or possess other negative qualities. We are called to show a respectful and reverent way of dealing with all people.

Our human feelings are not always loving when we meet hard-to-love people. We may be angry, frustrated, irritated, hateful, fearful, threatened, or have negative feelings in their presence. We need to deal with our feelings and seek to achieve some level of unity with people. Our conversion never ends. *Human frailty makes it necessary that this conversion be carried out daily* (SFO Rule - #7).

No one can elude negative people nor escape situations that make respect, reverence and love so demanding. If we are the ones who show negative qualities, the SFO way of life requires us to the change *which the Gospel itself calls "conversion"* (SFO Rule - #7). Since none of us is perfect, and we are inadequate, conversion becomes part of life. Franciscans make this choice through their *profession*.

St. Francis offers a bit of advice when he writes:

A servant of God cannot know how much patience and humility he has within himself as long as he is content. When the time comes, however, when those who should make him content do the opposite, he has as much patience and humility as he has at that time and no more.
Admonition XIII - Francis of Assisi - The Saint - Vol 1 - Page 133

Personal reflection will give flesh to the many demands that are required to maintain relationships. Family situations are loaded with opportunities to discover better ways of relating. Spousal arguments or conflicts with children will require us to develop better ways of relating. Dealing with neighbors and gangs and cliques requires special work to keep relationships alive and healthy. Dealing with Church matters, parish closings, poor leadership, abuse and misuse within groups, both in the Church and society, do not give much support for maintaining relationships.

Working for a corporation that sees all competitors as the "enemy" requires a special moral sense if relationships are to continue. The desire for riches (greed) and power can have a debilitating effect on relationships. Rumor-mongering and acceptance of half-truths and lies can destroy relationships. The excesses of political campaigns can separate people instead of bringing them together to work for the common good. Bringing love to work, family situations, our church and the world is no easy task for Franciscans.

Franciscans deal with these issues day in and day out. *How* we deal with them requires not only personal wisdom but the collaboration of people of good will. Fraternity members and others are sources for discovering ways to achieve progress in these secular areas. Franciscans are determined to avoid whatever diminishes relationships and to engage in whatever would enhance unity.

In their family they should cultivate the Franciscan spirit of peace, fidelity, and respect for life ... (SFO Rule - #17);

... they should strive to move from the temptation of exploiting creation to the Franciscan concept of universal kinship (SFO Rule - #18)*; ... husbands and wives in particular should bear witness in the world to the love of Christ for his Church* (SFO Rule - #17)*; Messengers of perfect joy in every circumstance, they should strive to bring joy and hope to others* (SFO Rule - #19); *... following the example of Saint Francis of Assisi, who made Christ the inspiration and center of his life with God and people* (SFO Rule - #4); *With Jesus, obedient even to death, they should seek to know and do the will of the Father. They should give thanks to God for the gift of freedom and for the revelation of the law of love. ... They should take on the risk of courageous choices in their life in society with decisiveness and serenity.* (Constitutions - article 12.2).

+++

Readings/Questions for dialogue

Poverty and Joy - Wm Short OFM
Orbis Books - Pages 30 to 36

United States Catholic Catechism for Adults
USCCB - Pages 51 to 53 - *God is the Trinity*

Catechism of the Catholic Church
#261 to #267

1. Describe your understanding of the meaning of "spirituality." What is the focus of Franciscan spirituality?

2. How do spiritualities differ from one another? What is the source of these differences?

3. What demands come with baptism into the community of faith? Describe how we are priests and prophets.

4. How do you feel about the requirements of the SFO Rule that you have learned so far? Why is it important to recognize the call to the SFO way of life as God's way of

inviting you to a certain way of living?

5. Explain, in your own words, how the Trinity's inner life influences Franciscan spirituality.

6. How does the "love" Franciscans speak about differ from society's way of speaking about love?

7. At this point, what personal changes (conversions) are needed in your life to embrace the Franciscan spirit?

8. Scripture reflection - Luke 8:9-15. How would you apply this parable's explanation to areas in your personal life? (You may discover that each explanation means something for your own life)

+++

The SFO General Chapter of 2002
addressed a number of issues:
+
Here is what they said about our
Presence in the world.

The chapter is concerned that many fraternities confine themselves to their own boundaries rather than opening themselves to the larger Franciscan world.

+ *We call on all Secular Franciscans to involve themselves in the areas of justice, peace, and safeguarding creation.*

+ *Fraternities are called to reflect on the "Spirit of Assisi" so that the spirit of Assisi might become incarnated throughout our Franciscan world.*

+ *The SFO is committed to involvement in public life and in the world of labor. This must be rooted in fraternity in whatever way it is possible. We are are expected to be a concrete and authentic leaven in society wherever we go.*

+ *A commitment in favor of the family, its defense, the recognition of its importance in the life of every society, nation and culture. The family has an irreplaceable value. It is the stronghold of every fraternity in the world.*

The "TAU" Cross

The external sign
of the SFO
in the United States
*is the **TAU.***

USA National Statutes
Article 16.4

The holy man (Francis) *venerated this symbol*
with great affection, often spoke of it
with eloquence and signed it
with his own hand in the letters he sent,
as if his whole desire were,
according to the prophetic text,
"to mark with a Tau the foreheads
of those moaning and grieving," (Ezekiel 9:4)
of those truly converted
to Jesus Christ.

Major Legend of St. Francis - St. Bonaventure
Francis of Assisi - the Founder - Vol II - Page 556

Chapter six

Writings & Stories of Francis & Clare

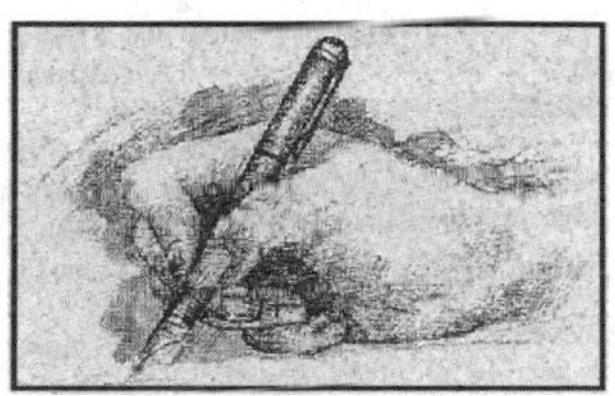

The truth about people is often revealed through stories. Franciscan stories about Francis and Clare reveal particular qualities that blossomed in their lives. In this chapter we will share text sources as well as a few stories and personal writings of Francis and Clare. In each situation we learn something about them and their way of living the Gospel. The writings and stories are found in Franciscan texts.

We will not exhaust Franciscan sources in this chapter. We will simply share some sources (texts) written by Francis and Clare or written about them.

Francis of Assisi

Vol 1 - The Saint / Vol II - The Founder / Vol III - The Prophet
New City Press - 202 Cardinal Rd - Hyde Park, NY. 12538

This is a three volume set of writings of Francis and biographies and writings about Francis.

Volume one - *The Saint*

+ The writings of St. Francis - his own words and ideas

+ Thomas of Celano's *Life of St. Francis* - 3 "books" - 2 official biographies of Francis and an account of the miracles at his canonization.

+ Liturgical texts - Francis' canonization required new liturgical texts - Thomas of Celano and Julian of Speyer met this need.

+ The life of St. Francis - Julian of Speyer - 13 chapters - based on, but shorter than, Thomas of Celano, and better adapted to public reading during meals and gatherings.

+ A Versified Life of St. Francis - Henri d'Avranches - divided into 14 "books" - Poetic interpretation of Thomas of Celano.

+ The Sacred Exchange between St. Francis and Lady Poverty. An allegory to encourage followers to live an authentic vision of poverty. It is a rich text of the early Franciscan movement.

+ Related Documents.

Volume two - *The Founder*

+ Anonymous (John?) of Perugia - Beginnings of the founding of the Order and the deeds of the first followers of Francis.

+ The Legend of the Three Companions - Provides insight into Francis, his youth, struggles with his father, and the emerging consciousness of his call to a gospel life. It illustrates the evolution of the primitive fraternity. It can serve as a companion piece to the *Anonymous of Perugia.*.

+ The Assisi Compilation - Anecdotes about Francis - an uneven, sometimes puzzling, compiling of stories about Francis.

+ The Remembrance of the Desire of a Soul - Two texts by Thomas of Celano about 15 years after his first writings.- a collage of memories stitched together by Thomas in his unique style.

+ The Treatise on the Miracles of St. Francis - Thomas of Celano uses some of his earlier writings and adds other sources concerning the miracles granted through the intercession of Francis.

+ An Umbrian Choir Legend - Adds little to our knowledge of Francis, but offers some later information about the Order around 1260.

+ A Letter on the Passing of Francis - There is much unknown about the author of this text and the text itself. It seems to be a sort of encyclical letter written by someone in authority about the death of Francis and his stigmata.

+ Legends & Sermons about St. Francis - St. Bonaventure of Bagnoregio - At the request of a General Chapter of the Order, St. Bonaventure, the minister general, wrote this mystical and spiritual biography of St. Francis. It is often called the *Legenda Major*. Writing a similar work that could be used liturgically was called *Legenda Minor.* It focuses on Francis' spirituality and could be used in choir prayer. This section of volume two of *Francis of Assisi* also includes some of St. Bonaventure's sermons on Francis.

+ Related documents - More texts on Francis' life.

Volume three - *The Prophet*

This volume contains texts about Francis as well as many of his companions. It also has liturgical texts. Most of these texts were written after 1277 and the latest around 1396. A few texts of this volume are listed below:

+ Collection of sayings of the Companions of Blessed Francis. Some uncertainties occur in these writings as they conflict among themselves and with other sources. Interesting ideas and opinions.

+ The Little Flowers of St. Francis (Fioretti) - cc 1384-1396 - A translation of stories of Francis and companions. It broadens popular devotion to St Francis with stories and incidents from Francis' life! Written more than a century after Francis' death, it is not always accurate but enjoyable.

These fundamental texts are surrounded by a host of biographies, writings on Franciscan spirituality, sermons by followers of St. Francis and Clare and reflections on Franciscan life. Feel free to explore them

Clare of Assisi - The Lady* - *Early Documents

Revised edition - 2006
Regis Armstrong OFM Cap - New City Press
202 Cardinal Road - Hyde Park, NY 12538

This book contains writings of and about St. Clare of Assisi.

Part 1 - *The Writings of Clare of Assisi.*

Her own words to friends and followers.

+ *Letters (four) to Agnes of Prague.* Clare encourages Agnes in her vocation, in prayerfulness, and in the wonder of being called by God to a Franciscan life. We do not have Agnes' letters to Clare at the present time.

+ *Testament of Clare.* Autobiographical writings. It includes glimpses into her struggle in writing the Rule and getting papal approval after years of struggle. It is a sort of "last will" to her sisters.

+ *Clare's blessing for her Poor Clare sisters.* Clare blesses not only those alive in her time, but also those who would come to the Poor Clares in the future. The blessing echoes the style of blessing given by Francis to Brother Leo on La Verna.

Part II - *"Together with my Sisters"* *Toward the Form of Life* *(Rule)*

+ The writings in this section of the book cover a potpouri of letters, from Popes, Cardinals and others. Also Clare's "privilege of poverty."

+ *The Rule for the Poor Clares.* Clare struggled for many years to have her form of the Rule approved by the Church. Popes and advisors thought it could not be lived in the form she had given. She persisted and her form of the Rule was approved shortly before her death. Clare is the first woman to write a religious rule and she began a new epoch for women in the life of the Church.

Part III - *Writings that concern Clare, the Poor Ladies, and Francis and His Brothers.*

+ The writings in this section refer to different testimonies about Clare. Other writings contain references to Clare and the Poor Ladies.

+ Includes Papal documents referring to Clare and the Poor Ladies

+ This section includes the Acts of canonization and the Legend of St Clare. It incorporates other documents relating to Clare and Francis.

Francis and Clare
The Complete Works

Regis Arnstrong OFM Cap - Ignatius Brady OFM
Paulist Press - 545 Island Rd - Ramsey, NJ 07446

+ This book contains the writings of Francis and Clare published in 1982 as part of the *Western Classics Series* of Paulist Press. It contains the same material found in previously cited texts of the writings of Francis and Clare.

Clare of Assisi

A biographical Study - Ingrid Peterson OSF
Available from the Franciscan Institute - St Bonaventure University
St Bonaventure, NY 14778

+ Within this study Ingrid Peterson articulates a gentle argument that Clare was a holy woman before she met Francis. Ingrid traces the development of Clare's mirror imagery and the manner in which Clare integrated her faith with the reality of her time. Contemporary seekers of divine intimacy will discover a well-documented text that encourages them to accompany Clare on her journey.

Clare Centenary Series

Eight volume series - Franciscan Institute Publications
St Bonaventure University - St. Bonaventure, NY 14778

+ Volume VI - *A Compendium of Resources for a Study of St. Clare*. The lifelong work of Sr. Mary Frances Hone OSC. A helpful guide to the history and spirituality of St. Clare, the Poor Ladies of San Damiano, and the Second Order.

+ Volume VII - *Clare of Assisi: Investigations* - Five lectures presented in Kalamazoo, MI. in May, 1992. 1. *Clare's Rule: Weaving together Law and Life* - Roberta McKelvie OSF. 2. *Clare of Assisi: The Eucharist and John 13* - Michael Blastic OFM Conv. 3. *Like a Beguine: Clare before 1212* - Ingrid Peterson OSF. 4. *The Legenda Versificata- Towards an official Biography* - Regis Armstrong OFM Cap. 5. *Elias and Clare: An Enigmatic relationship* - Michael Cusato OFM.

Clare of Assisi - A Heart Full of love

Ilia Delio OSF - St. Anthony Messenger Press

+ Clare, a resolute and loving saint whose life centers on the essence of human identity - Christ in each of us. Core tenets of Franciscan spirituality. Simple in its portrait of the human person as an image of God, yet profound in its theological implications.

+++

The number of fundamental source materials may initially be a bit overwhelming. We simply invite you to continue reading the source texts of the lives and spirit of St. Francis and Clare of Assisi. Reading source material about these two saints is a life-long pursuit. There is more material than we shared in this chapter. These readings stimulate us to a continued exploration of the spirit of Francis and Clare.

Our responsibility is to embrace their spirit and express it in 21st century language. Francis and Clare are important to us. Their spirit needs to be adapted to today's Church and world. That is our challenge - learning how to bring their gospel spirit to this century. As death drew near, Francis realized that he had done what was his to do. He encouraged his brothers to do what the Spirit called them to do. In a spirit of discovering Franciscan ideals, here are a few stories that illustrate elements of Francis' and Clare's spirit. Your own reading will find other stories about Francis and Clare. The following story of Francis and the wolf of Gubbio is a popular tale.

+ A ravenous wolf was terrorizing the town of Gubbio. People were afraid to go outside the walls of the city for the wolf had killed many people. When Francis came to the city they explained the situation. Francis immediately decided to go out and talk to the wolf. The townsfolk tried to deter him, but could not. They watched from the walls as the wolf and Francis came together. Dialoguing with the wolf, Francis was clear about the wolf's destructive actions, killing even human beings. If peace was to come, the wolf needed to cease and desist his killing spree.

Then Francis and the wolf entered the city and Francis talked to the people. He invited them to do penance and convert from their sinful ways. When he finished, the wolf promised not to kill and the people promised to feed the wolf. It is said in the story that the wolf then lived in Gubbio for two years and no one, not even the dogs, disturbed him. In turn, none of the people were harmed in any way. When the wolf died the people grieved at his loss since his presence reminded them of the holiness of St. Francis. (Cf. Francis of Assisi - The Prophet - Vol III - Page 601-603)

A number of qualities of Francis are illustrated in the story.

+ Francis shows his trust in God, willing to confront the evil in the wolf and invite him to change.

+ Francis required the wolf to change his ways if he wanted to live in peace with the people. Francis also required some sign that the wolf meant what he seemed to agree to.

+ Francis invited the people of Gubbio to change their ways if they wanted to live in peace with the wolf. Mutual changes were asked for by Francis.

+ Francis dealt with the causes of the wolf's killing spree, even killing people. He was hungry. When the people of Gubbio fed him he no longer brought fear and death to the town.

+ Both sides had to fulfill the requirements Francis invited them to embrace. When they did so they were able to live in peace with one another.

For us to create a spirit of peace among people requires these same qualities: trust in God / dialogue / willingness to change on the part of the participants / dealing with needs / following through on promises in order to live peacefully with one another.

+ Another story is about the Christmas celebration that initiated the celebration of the christmas crib. As Christmas drew near, Francis wanted to find a way to represent the poverty of the Savior on the night of His birth. He asked John, a man from Greccio, to provide a place, an ox and an ass. A cave in Greccio held the hay in a manger, and with the animals in place, the Christmas celebration began. It was like a new Bethlehem and everyone was amazed at how the Incarnation came alive. During the ceremony Francis was seen by a virtuous man to go to the empty manger and hold the figure of a child the man saw there. The child came alive in Francis' arms. As the story says:

It is therefore believed, and not without reason, that the Lord Jesus aptly revealed his infancy in this vision to the one who reflected on it. He who was asleep or dead in the hearts of many, owing to forgetfulness, was awakened and recalled to memory by the teaching and example of St. Francis. The solemnities were completed with great exultation, and everyone happily returned to their homes.

The Life of St. Francis by Julian of Speyer
Francis of Assisi - The Saint - Vol 1 - Page 405-407

Francis gives a new sense of the presence of God among us in Jesus. The Incarnation takes on new meaning with the visible image of the crib and this Franciscan Christmas.

+ The church of San Damiano, outside the walls of Assisi, is often mentioned as the place where Francis got direction for his way of life. It was a tumble-down chapel in need of repair. The *Legend of the Three Companions* speaks about Francis and this chapel.

A few days had passed when, while he was walking by the

church of San Damiano, he was told in the Spirit to go inside for a prayer. Once he entered, he began to pray intensely before an image of the Crucified, which spoke to him in a tender and kind voice: "Francis, don't you see that my house is being destroyed? Go, then, and re-build it for me." Stunned and trembling, he said:"I will do so gladly, Lord." For he understood that it was speaking about that church which was near collapse because of its age. He was filled with such joy and became so radiant with light over that message, that he knew in his soul that it was truly Christ crucified who spoke to him.

Legend of the Three Companions
Francis of Assisi -The Founder - Vol II - Page 76

As time passed, it became clear that the message applied to more than the church of San Damiano. Francis' life became filled with the desire to rebuild the Church through a return to gospel living and a deepened awareness of the words and example of Jesus.

One important lesson for us is the immediacy of the response Francis gave to the message. There were no long discussions, only an immediate search for stones and mortar to fix the church. It is Francis' immediate response to God's call that should touch us. Even if, like Francis, our first response to the Holy Spirit is not quite on target, it is a beginning.

And the Lord gave me such faith in churches that I would pray with simplicity in this way and say: "We adore You, Lord Jesus Christ, in all Your churches throughout the whole world and we bless You, because by Your holy cross You have redeemed the world."
The Testament - Francis of Assisi - The Saint - Vol 1 - Page 124-125

And after the Lord gave me some brothers, no one showed me what I had to do, but the most High Himself revealed to me that I should live according to the pattern of the Holy Gospel. And I had this written down simply and in a few words and the Lord Pope confirmed it for me.
The Testament - Francis of Assisi - The Saint - Vol 1 - Page 125

We are spouses when the faithful soul is joined by the Holy Spirit to our Lord Jesus Christ. We are brothers to Him when we do the will of the Father who is in heaven. We are mothers when we carry Him in our heart and body through a divine love and a pure and sincere conscience and give birth to Him through a holy activity which must shine as an example before others

Earlier Exhortation ... - Francis of Assisi - The Saint - Vol 1 - Page 42

Clare

The stories about Clare are perhaps less known than those of Francis. But they reveal the inner spirit of Clare and her response to the Spirit that called her to follow Francis.

At her canonization, witnesses came forward with stories about Clare. They can be found in the *Acts of the Process of Canonization of Clare of Assisi.* Giovanni di Ventura of Assisi gives his witness about Clare's life at home.

... although their household was one of the largest in the city and great sums were spent there, she nevertheless saved the food they were given to eat, put it aside, and then sent it to the poor. ... While she was still in her father's house, she wore a rough garment under her other clothes. He also said she fasted, prayed, and did other pious deeds ... and that it was believed she had been inspired by the Holy Spirit from the beginning.

The Acts of the Canonization of Clare of Assisi
Clare of Assisi - The Lady - Page 195

Sister Francesca, a nun of the community of San Damiano, recalled the time when Clare's prayer and courage saved both San Damiano and the city of Assisi from the Saracens who threatened it. Clare asked her sisters to help her get to the refectory of San Damiano and to bring a small box with the Blessed Sacrament inside. Then she prayed:

... "Lord, look upon these servants of yours, because I

cannot protect them." Then the witness heard a voice of wonderful sweetness: "I will always defend you!" The Lady then prayed for the city, saying: "Lord, please defend the city as well!" The same voice resounded and said: "The city will endure many dangers, but it will be defended."

Then the Lady (Clare) *turned to the sisters and told them: "Do not be afraid, because I am a hostage for you so that you will not suffer any harm now nor any other time as long as you wish to obey God's commandments." Then the Saracens left in such a way that they did not do any harm or damage.*

The Acts of the Process of Canonization of Clare of Assisi
Clare of Assisi - the Lady - Page 174-175

The heart of Clare was intimately linked to the heart of Jesus. She found ways and means to help the poor. People came to San Damiano to have Clare pray with them and often healings took place. While she focused on the prayerfulness of her community, she was open to the needs of others, especially the poor. She found ways to keep the link between prayer and care alive in her Franciscan life.

In her *Testament*, Clare shared these words:

I admonish and exhort in the Lord Jesus Christ all my sisters, both those present and those to come, to strive always to imitate the way of holy simplicity, humility and poverty and also the integrity of our holy way of living, as we were taught from the beginning of our conversion by Christ and by our blessed father Francis. From them, not by any merits of ours but solely out of the largesse of His mercy and grace, the Father of mercies has spread the fragrance of a good reputation, both among those who are far away as well as those who are near. And loving one another with the love of Christ, may you demonstrate without in your deeds the love you have within so that, compelled by such an example, the sisters may always grow in the love of God and mutual charity.

The Testament - Clare of Assisi - The Lady - Page 64

Finally, her *Second Letter to Agnes of Prague* contains some practical advice about listening to those who would guide her. Clare is both practical and engaged in mystical union with God.

In all of this, follow the counsel of our venerable father, our Brother Elias, the Minister General, that you may walk more securely in the way of the commands of the Lord. Prize it beyond the advice of others and cherish it as dearer to you than any gift. If anyone has said anything else to you or suggested any other thing to you that might hinder your perfection or that would seem contrary to your divine vocation, even though you must respect him, do not follow his counsel.

Second Letter to Agnes of Prague
Clare of Assisi - The Lady - Page 48-49

Readings/Questions for dialogue

The Testament
Francis of Assisi - The Saint - Vol 1
Pages 124 to 127

Chapter IV - *Dealing with Lepers*
Francis of Assisi - The Founder - Vol II
- Pages 74-75

The Blessing
Clare of Assisi - The Lady - Pages 66-67

1. Why is it important to have some acquaintance with the sources for the life and spirit of Francis and Clare?

2. How does the influence of your family stories reflect a similar influence to the stories of Francis and Clare? Explain.

3. Describe your present image of Francis and Clare through what you have learned. What qualities do they reveal through their words and stories?

4. What part or parts of this chapter made the most sense to you as you compare them to your own life?

5. List the things you learned in this chapter about Franciscan spirituality. Explain.

6. What motivation will move you to continue searching the Franciscan sources in order to grow in knowledge about Francis and Clare?

7. Scripture reflection: Colossians 1:9-14. How do the words of Francis and Clare reflect the spirit found in these words of St. Paul?

+++

Thus, there must be no doubt,
that we, who must speak
the message of God
who summoned Moses,
and whose mouth was opened
in Jesus of Nazareth,
and who keeps the Spirit alive
on behalf of justice
for so many centuries,
can only become advocates of the poor.

This is not to be simplistic,
to see all in black and white,
to be ignorant of economics
and the contributions of
other human sciences,
but in a profound sense
the choices are simple and stark:
+ death or life
+ injustice or justice
+ idolatry or the Living God

We must choose life.
We must choose justice.
We must choose the Living God. *(1975)**

**This Land is Home to Me (1975)*
At Home in the Web of Life (1995)
Catholic Bishops of Appalachia - Page 29

Chapter seven

A brief

History of SFO + Development of the Rule

Basilica of St Francis in Assisi

The SFO has over 800 years of history. The development of the SFO Rule of 1978 took several years of preparation. We will not cover each century nor each movement within the Secular Franciscan Order. This chapter has a few basic historical ideas. We will share thoughts on the development of the 1978 SFO Rule. We encourage you to do personal research into the history of the SFO.

Once upon a time there were no Franciscans in the Church or the world. That all changed with the coming of St. Francis and St. Clare of Assisi. They lived in a time of social upheaval and in a Church where power was often more important than the Gospel, in a world where class divisions of society were rampant. The 1100's to the 1400's were a time of change both in the Church and in society.

In the written history of the Franciscan Order scholars often hold differing opinions on dates and documents of the history of each branch of the Franciscan family. We will not research the many arguments about the beginnings of the Franciscan Family. There are fine books that offer resources about Franciscan history.

Once St. Francis attracted followers, the 1st Order blossomed rather quickly. As the numbers grew, so did differences of opinion about Franciscan life. By 1530 these differences had led to the development of three juridically independent branches of the 1st Order. These three branches are: the *Order of Friars Minor* (OFM); the *Order of Friars Minor, Conventual* (OFM Conv.); and the *Order of Friars Minor, Capuchin* (OFM Cap). The Church approved each branch as legitimate followers of St. Francis.

The Second Order of Poor Clares also experienced reforms and divisions. As with the friars following Francis' spirit, the various Poor Clare groups sought fresh ways to follow the spirit of Clare. That spirit, as well as the spirit of Francis, blossomed in many ways throughout the centuries.

The Third Order Secular began with laity who wished to embrace the penitential spirit of Francis in their lives. They did not intend to join a religious order but wished to show a penitential spirit in the world. *"Penitential / penance"* had a meaning different from many modern definitions.

Penance and penitential practices focus on *conversion, i.e.* moving from a self-centered, I-focused and selfish way of life to one in which doing God's will and desire becomes the focus of life. Conversion takes time, effort, and prayer.

There were many penitential groups in Francis' time and Franciscans appeared to be another penitential group. One group was led by Peter Waldo of Lyons, a rich man who sold his property, lived a poor life, and attracted followers. Pope Alexander III was asked to give approval. He did so, but forbade the group to preach unless the local clergy approved. Ignoring this directive and claiming the right to bless and consecrate (Claiming ordination was not needed), the *Waldensians* became heretical in some doctrinal areas.

Another group, the *Humiliati* in northern Italy, lived simply, worked hard and gained approval from the Church - but were forbidden to preach publicly. They disobeyed and became marginalized in the Church. In 1199 a number of the *Humiliati asked* Innocent III to accept them back into the Church. The Pope agreed.*

---

*Cf. St. Francis & the Third Order - Pazzelli - Page 95.

These and other penitential groups often caused more confusion than clarity. But they were attractive to ordinary people. Francis was guided through the minefields of penitential groups by Bishop Guido of Assisi. In 1209, Francis and his group of followers approached Pope Innocent III to receive approval for their way of life. Innocent III was concerned about yet another "penitential group" seeking his approval.

Initially, Innocent III leaned toward refusing Francis' request for approval of his "penitential" way of life. The story is told that Innocent III had a dream which showed Francis holding up the Lateran basilica which seemed to be falling apart. Encouraged by the dream, Innocent III was open to the words of Cardinal John of St. Paul who supported Francis. Cardinal John expressed the idea that to deny Francis would indicate that living the gospel was impossible. This would go counter to Jesus who expected his way of life not only to be possible but preferable.*

The Pope gave Francis and his group a verbal approval of their simple Rule in 1209. The approval by Innocent III gave Francis the freedom to follow the life to which the Spirit was calling him and his companions. Lay men and women would also follow Francis' vision of the gospel spirit in secular life. A new spirit was alive in the Church and among the People of God.

The Council of Lateran IV (1215) hesitated to create new lay groups of penitents in the Church. Francis escaped this decree because he had received approval before the Council. The Council also reformed pastoral practices. Many rural priests at this time were not well-educated. The Church had a need for doctrinal preaching. Training in theology became a requirement for preachers giving doctrinal sermons. However, preaching non-doctrinal sermons remained a possibility for lay preachers. Council decrees influenced Francis and the Franciscan Order.

---

*Cf. Francis of Assisi - Arnaldo Fortini - Page 301

All those who joined his group coming from various social strata were taught by Francis to live according to relationships in which they would be neither dominant nor dominated, where all are fraternally united and in which dialogue and mutual service was the only path to follow.

Francis of Assisi & the Laity of His Time
Prospero Rivi OFM Cap - Greyfriars Review - Supplement
Franciscan Institute, SBU - Vol 15 - 2001 - Page 50

The Franciscan Order grew after Innocent III's verbal approval for Francis' way of life. The text called the *Earlier Exhortation to the Brothers and Sisters of Penance* (1st version of the *Letter to the Faithful*) seems to have been written before 1215. It was addressed to the first lay penitents who came to share Francis' gospel way of life. (Cf. Francis of Assisi - The Saint - Vol I - Page 41ff). Though sometimes the title *The Letter to all the Faithful* is used, the title "*Earlier exhortation etc* ..." is more accurate.

The second version, *Later Admonition and Exhortation to the Brothers & Sisters of Penance* (Later *Letter to All the Faithful*) was probably written around 1220. It recalls Francis' earlier exhortation and incorporates teachings of Lateran Council IV. (Cf. Francis of Assisi - The Saint - Vol I - Page 45).

The Earlier Rule of the 1st Order developed as Francis and the friars had more experience in their Franciscan life. It was revised by the friars at the Pentecost Chapter of 1221. This *Earlier Rule* (1221) did not receive papal approval. Another text, *Memoriale propositi,* was written during this time period. It is more juridically oriented and seems to be co-authored by Cardinal Hugolino, a noted jurist, who was the Cardinal protector of the friars. Though Francis influenced the text, it is more juridical than Francis' ordinary style.* On November 19, 1223, Pope Honorius III gave his approval to the 1st Order *Rule of 1223.* (Cf. Francis of Assisi - The Saint - Vol 1 - Page 99ff).

---

*Cf. *"De Illis Qui Faciunt Penitentiam" - The Rule of the SFO: Origens, Development, Interpretation* - Robert M. Stewart OFM - Pages 183-199.

By 1221 there were about 3000 friars. By 1222 the numbers rose to 5000. By 1260 there were over 35,000 friars in Western Europe. The need for organization engaged the attention of the friars. The struggles beween structures and maintaining the vision of Francis created conflict within the First Order.

We should have recourse mainly to the fact that Francis made the people he met understand and see with their own eyes that God was their neighbor, because he had become incarnate, because he had been born like us, he had worked like us, he had suffered and died for all of us. He was able to present the human face of Christ, God made man, to share and bestow an incomparable meaning on ordinary, human life. In this way the profound value of everyday life was recovered for each person, which because of the incarnation, assumed in Christ and by Christ, the power of the eternal.

Francis of Assisi & the Laity of His Times - Rivi - Greyfriars Review - Volume 15 - 2001 - Supplement - Page 53

The 1st Order *Rule of 1223* (Called the *"Regular Bullata"*), approved by Honorius III, met organizational and "vision" needs for the friars. Lateran Council IV required a period of "novitiate" for religious groups. A written rule became a necessity both to reflect the requirements of the Council and the vocational needs of large numbers of friars.

Friars of the Order handled organizational elements at their chapters. The development of structures followed a common pattern of growth for large groups. The organizing efforts helped guide the Franciscan movement beyond the 1220's. Amid the turmoil, the Holy Spirit was at work.

But this process is always open-ended; love is never "finished" and complete; throughout life, it changes and matures, and thus remains faithful to itself.

God is Love *(Deus Caritas Est)* - Benedict XVI - Paragraph 17

More resources on the development of the First Order and the Third Order can be found listed at the end of this chapter - Page 81-82.

The Third Order of St. Francis

(Name of the Order until 1978)

This brief history of texts and the growth of the Franciscan First Order is linked to the growth of the Franciscan Third Order secular as well. The Third Order secular grew out of the willingness of lay people to follow the spirit of Francis in their life in the world. The development of a specific rule for seculars took time. Early on there were various texts that guided the lay followers of Francis.

The *Earlier Exhortation to the Brothers and Sisters of Penance* (Cf. "Prologue" to the 1978 SFO Rule) provided guidance in the early days of the Third Order secular. Nicolas IV became the first Franciscan Pope on February 15, 1288. At the request of several Franciscan penitent groups he approved the *Rule for Franciscan Penitents* on August 18, 1289. (The text of this Rule can be found in Robert Steward's book - Page 202ff). The papal document is named *Supra Montem*. There were misgivings among Penitents and friars about friars doing visitations to communities of lay penitents. On August 8, 1290, Nicolas IV issued another document, *Unigenitus Dei Filus,* re-asserting that friars would be the visitors. Eventually it received universal acceptance.

It can also be added that when speaking of the Order of Penitents this is not meant as a religious Order in the strict sense of the term, given that it implies neither life in community nor vows; but a religious Order broadly speaking, because it has a Rule approved by the Apostolic See, a novitiate (formation), *an irreversible profession, that is, a secular Order.*

Francis of Assisi and the Laity of his Time - Prospero Rivi OFM Cap
Greyfriars review - supplement - Vol 15 - Page 64

Examining the words which Francis addressed to the Penitents who were inspired by him, one can perceive his

---

Cf. + Francis of Assisi - The Saint - Vol I - Page 41ff / + *"De Illis Qui Faciunt Penitentiam" The Rule of the SFO: Origins, Development, Interpretation* - Robert Steward - Pages 199-201.

clear intention of proposing an ideal of Christian life which was wide-ranging and required great commitment. In substance, he proposed to the Penitents the same hard road which he asked of his friars: to follow the Lord with an ever increasing impetus, to let the spirit of the Lord and the paradoxical logic of the Gospel permeate their minds, their hearts and their lives.

Ibid - Page 70

The link between the First Order and the Brothers and Sisters of Penance initiated by Nicolas IV met with some initial resistance among both the friars and the penitents. But the document of Nicolas IV forms an ecclesial foundation for being one Franciscan family. Quotations from First Order/TOR Constitutions and Statutes below illustrate the present linkage between friars and Seculars.*

157 - The Secular Franciscan Order is closely related to the Order by common origin and heritage. The friars hold it in high esteem because they share with it the same Franciscan penitential charism. In union with their secular brothers and sisters, that charism is completely expressed.

TOR Constitutions - 1992 - #157

1. Within the ambit of the Franciscan family, the Secular Franciscan Fraternity or Order occupies a special place that both shares and promotes its authentic spirit. It should be esteemed as necessary for the fullness of the Franciscan charism (Cf. Ephesians 4:3). ... *4. Let the brothers, therefore, be eager to show from their heart a truly brotherly attitude for members of the Secular Order, nourish by their example of fidelity to the gospel life, and effectively foster the Order itself among the secular clergy and the laity.*

OFM Capuchin Constitutions - 1990 - #95.1, #95.4

1. The First Order has been entrusted with the care of the Secular Franciscan Order. This displays the spirit of

* First Order/TOR Constitutions and statutes may change to meet new needs and events of various times and places. The dates of the above First Order/TOR texts are given in the reference.

St. Francis in the world; it shares in the life, witness, and mission of the Franciscan charism and it makes its own necessary and complementary contribution to the fullness of that charism.

OFM Constitutions - 2004 - #60.1

1. All friars should consider the Secular Franciscan Order as the modern, necessary complement to their charism, esteem it highly, and foster it zealously. Therefore, the friars should be solicitous that the tertiaries, trained in the school of evangelical perfection, be a leaven in their own secular sphere and witnesses to poverty, love, joy, peace, marital fidelity, obedience to the Church, apostolic Christocentrism and sincere devotion to the Virgin Mary..

OFM Conventual Statutes - 1984 - #52.1

These words illustrate connections among the branches of the Franciscan family. The friars, Poor Clares, and the seculars help to maintain this common charism and assist one another to grow in Franciscan spirituality and gospel living. This *vital reciprocity* enables the Franciscan family to work together in bringing the Franciscan charism to the Church and the world.

In various ways and forms but in ***life-giving union with each other,*** *they intend to make present the charism of their common Seraphic Father in the life and mission of the Church.*

SFO Rule (1978) - article #1

The Rule of 1289 remained in force until 1883 when Pope Leo XIII promulgated a new rule for the *Brothers and Sisters of the Order of Penance.* Changes to the Rule of 1289 during the centuries were usually incorporated in statutes or constitutions. The *Rule of 1289* remained basically unchanged during these centuries. The "Penitents" of Francis, as a lay movement, continued to blossom. Some groups developed into religious Orders - men and women choosing to live in community and taking vows in a religious Order. (Cf. Robert Steward's book - Page 217-218)

These religious groups are part of the *Third Order Regular.* Franciscan communities of women have their origins in the Rule of the TOR. Likewise, it is during the period between 1289 and 1883 that the men's group known as the Third Order Regular (TOR) finds it origin. This period of growth saw the development of many Franciscan religious Orders.*

There is little doubt about Leo XIII's dedication to the Third Order of St. Francis. However his desire (in 1883) to bring all the faithful into the Third Order of St. Francis was a mixed blessing. Though initially successful in drawing many people to a dedicated Christian life, it ultimately lost its ability to inspire and empower Secular Franciscans (Cf. Robert Steward's book - Page 238-239). Its prescriptive legislation left little room for growth and inspiration. The Rule of 1883 would see a change in the next century with the writing of the Rule of 1978.

In the pope's zeal that the members of the Order "lead others by good example," he has diluted the original call to radical metanoia and transformed the "Rule of Life" to the simple praxis of the faith. ... Whereas Francis challenged people to the true spirit of penance, whereas Francis exhorted his followers to a radically different wisdom, struggle and sense of power in response to God's love, here the Rule of 1883 merely exhorts these same followers to the simple and "not too burdensome" praxis of Catholicism.

"De Illis Qui Faciunt Penitentiam" The Rule of the SFO Origins, Development, Interpretation - Steward OFM - Page 240

The Rule of 1978

November, 1965, saw the beginnings of a revision of the Rule of 1883. The four Franciscan Commissaries General (now known as the General Assistants to the SFO) wrote to their ministers General to initiate a reform or revision of the SFO Rule of 1883, plus the Constitutions of the SFO and SFO

---

* *Cf.* *St. Francis and the Third Order* - Pazzelli - Page 152.

Ritual. By March 9, 1966 they received approval. They wrote to friar provincials and commissaries, SFO spiritual directors (sic) and tertiaries (SFO members) in the world seeking worldwide suggestions and ideas for this renewal.

Most respondents called for a complete, radical reform of the Rule of 1883. They stated that the Rule of 1883 did not express the Franciscan charism. The next step was a gathering of male Franciscan religious in Assisi in January, 1968. They put together a text of a rule and in July of 1968 sent it to tertiaries and directors throughout the world.

The response to this first draft was basically negative. The response called for greater collaboration with the Secular Franciscans themselves. This led to an international gathering in Assisi in October of 1969. Three committees were established to explore the following aspects:

1. The Secular Franciscan Order and its characteristic in the world today.
2. The essential elements of a Franciscan spirituality for the laity.
3. The fundamental laws of government of the Order.

After ideas were concretized and reported back to the assembly, an International Congress produced a number of motions relating to a new rule - motions on defining the nature of the SFO; motions on essential elements of the spirituality of the SFO (17 essential elements - Cf. Page 103-104 in this book); motions on the government of the SFO.

It became clear that more time was needed in order to produce a rule reflecting these ideas. A Praesidium and Commission were established to develop a rule. Finally, after three drafts, a fourth draft of a rule was presented to the international commission. They suggested more changes. These were incorporated into a draft of the Rule in 1974.

On April 30, 1975 the text was sent to the National Councils of the SFO throughout the world for study and comment The responses were especially focused on the failure of this rule to adequately present a "secular" spirituality.

A new redaction of the rule was developed and once again sent throughout the Franciscan world. The response varied greatly, so a commission, composed of five lay people and two religious, was asked to review it and submit another redaction. It was then reviewed by experts in canon law, history, theology, and Franciscan spirituality. The International Commission reviewed the text and asked for a commission to "polish" it.

It was approved by the Ministers General who incorporated the *Earlier Exhortation to the Brothers and Sisters of Penance* as a prologue. The Rule was finally submitted to the Sacred Congregation for Religious and Secular Institutes for approval. After some dialogue, the Rule was **approved by Pope Paul VI on June 24, 1978**.

This is the SFO Rule that replaces all previous rules. It is offered by the Church as the way of fulfilling God's will as Secular Franciscans. If you wish to research extended documentation, copies of all the rules and the various texts can be found in Robert Steward's book.

Some resources on the history of the SFO and the First Order.

* *Francis & His Brothers* - Dominic Monti OFM - St Anthony Messenger Press (1st Order History)

* *Franciscan History* (The Three Orders of St Francis) - Lazaro Iriarte OFM Cap - Franciscan Press - Cf. Franciscan Institute at St. Bonaventure University (SBU), St. Bonaventure, NY 14778

* *St Francis and the Third Order* - Raffaele Pazzelli TOR - Franciscan Herald Press. - Cf. Franciscan Institute at SBU.

* *"De Illis Qui Faciunt Penitentiam" The Rule of the SFO: Origins, Development, Interpretation* - Robert Stewart OFM - Cf. Franciscan Institute at St. Bonaventure University for information on this book.

* *Francis of Assisi and The Laity of His Time* - Prospero Rivi OFM Cap - Greyfriars Review - Vol 15 - 2001 - Supplement - Franciscan Institute - SBU.

* *Francis of Assisi* - Arnaldo Fortini - Crossroad Publishing Co.

* *A History of the SFO in the United States* - *William Wicks SFO* - Volume one (1917-1942) - Further volumes are in process - Smokey Valley Printing - Box 189 - Lindsborg, KS 67456

+++

Readings/Questions for dialogue

Earlier Exhortation to the Brothers & Sisters of Penance
Francis of Assisi - The Saint - Vol I - Pages 41-44

The Later Rule (of the First Order - 1223)
Francis of Assisi - The Saint - Vol I - Page 99-106

The Life of St Francis - Chapter 4 - Julian of Speyer
Francis of Assisi - The Saint - Vol I - Page 383-387

1. Please read *The Earlier Exhortation* ... (*Prologue* to the 1978 Rule) and share a brief, personal understanding of the text.

2. What quotes in this chapter were most helpful for your understanding of the SFO way of life? Why?

3. What is the nature of the commitment you will make to live the SFO Rule? How long? How strong? How lived?

4. Why is the SFO Rule of 1978 so important for this time of history in the Church and the world? What is our gift to the Church?

5. Describe the nature of the relationship between the friars (1st Order / TOR) and the Secular Franciscan Order.

6. Scripture reflection: Matthew 5:13-16. How do these biblical words relate to Franciscans and the way they follow the Rule they profess?

Chapter eight

Scripture in SFO Life

Following the Gospel is important to our Franciscan way of life. In this chapter we will explore backgound elements to assist us in our relationship to Scripture. These elements for reading and implementing Scripture support a faith-filled Franciscan spirit in "listening" to Scripture.

One day the gospel was being read in that church about how the Lord sent out his disciples to preach. The holy man of God (Francis), *who was attending there, in order to understand better the words of the gospel, humbly begged the priest after celebrating the solemnities of the Mass, to explain the gospel to him. The priest explained it all to him thoroughly line by line. When he heard that Christ's disciples should not possess gold or silver or money, or carry on their journey a wallet or a sack, nor bread nor a staff, nor to have shoes or two tunics, but that they should preach the kingdom of God and penance,* (Mt 10:6-10 - Lk 9:2-3) *the holy man, Francis, immediately exulted in the spirit of God. "This is what I want," he said, "this is what I seek, this is what I desire with all my heart."*

Life of St Francis (1st Book) - Thomas of Celano
Francis of Assisi - The Saint - Vol I - Page 201-202.

And after the Lord gave me some brothers, no one showed me what I had to do, but the Most High Himself revealed to me that I should live according to the pattern of the Holy Gospel.

The Testament - Francis of Assisi - The Saint - Vol I - Page 125

2. Rule 4.3 *The Secular Franciscans, committed to following the example and teachings of Christ, must personally and assiduously study the Gospel and Sacred Scripture. The fraternity and its leaders should foster love for the word of the Gospel and help the brothers and sisters to know and understand it as it is proclaimed by the Church with the assistance of the Spirit.*

Constitutions - article 9.2

3. Ongoing formation - accomplished by means of courses, gatherings and the sharing of experiences - aims to assist the brothers and sisters:

+ Rule 4 ***in listening to and meditating on the Word of God, "going from Gospel to life and from life to Gospel;"***
+ *in reflecting on events in the Church and in society in the light of the faith, and with the help of the documents of the teaching Church, consequently taking consistent positions;*
+ *in discerning and deepening this Franciscan vocation by studying the writings of Saint Francis, Saint Clare and Franciscan authors.*

Constitutions - article 44.3

[We] forcefully and specifically exhort all the Christian faithful ... to learn the "surpassing knowledge of Jesus Christ" (Philippians 3:8) *by frequent reading of the divine scriptures. "Ignorance of the Scriptures is ignorance of Christ"* (St. Jerome). *Therefore, let them go gladly to the sacred text itself, whether in the sacred liturgy, which is full of the divine words, or in devout reading, or in such suitable exercises and various other helps which, with the approval and guidance of the pastors of the Church, are happily spreading everywhere in our day. Let them remember, however, that prayer should accompany the reading of sacred Scripture, so that a dialogue takes place between God and man. ...*

United States Catholic Catechism for Adults - USCCB - Page 32-33

But as for you, continue in what you have learned and firmly believed, knowing from whom you learned it, and how from childhood you have known the sacred writings that are able to instruct you for salvation through faith in

Jesus Christ. All Scripture is inspired by God and is useful for teaching, for reproof, for corrections, and for training in righteousness, so that everyone who belongs to God may be proficient, equipped for every good work.

2 Timothy 3:14-17

These texts give some idea of the role of Scripture in the life of a Franciscan. We are gospel people, committed to making the Gospel known by our words and our lives. The Gospel is precious to us. Gospel texts are living words from the living Christ. The need to accompany our scriptural reflection with prayer is important. Being present to the scriptural words is at the same time a prayerful time.

We read scripture texts that are translated into our language from the original languages. Linguists are aware that translations cannot offer the full flavor and nuances of the original languages. Our reliance on translations is not absolute. Translations are not always totally accurate and our English language keeps changing as well.

There are numerous translations by different scholars and groups of scholars. They try to determine how to put the original ideas and cultural meanings into another time and place and language. We understand that translations are not perfect - and that is acceptable in our human situation. The Holy Spirit can work through that limitation. We realize that English translations may not capture every nuance of the original texts nor enable us to recognize all the cultural influences in the text.

The Bible is a library of books written by different authors. Understanding the author's mind-set, their personal back-ground and the times in which they lived helps in understanding the text. St. Paul and King David do not have the same style nor the same growing-up background which influenced their writings. Paul's epistles and David's psalms require some understanding of these two people to better explore their texts. Our understanding improves as we get a "feel" for their way of writing and their perspectives.

We believe **the Bible is inspired by the Holy Spirit.** The revelations Scripture offers are precious to us. But not every word (especially in a translation) has the same impact and value. Words about the passion, death, and resurrection of Jesus or his teachings are more important than words about bird droppings in *Tobit* or talk about the number of soldiers killed on a given day in some of the stories about battles in war. These lesser words are not useless. But they need to fit into the bigger picture to understand the teaching of which they are a part. Context is important.

Gospel parables often contain a "moral teaching." To over-analyze each word of a parable, for example, can cause blindness rather than clarity, E,g. The parable about the rich man (Luke 12:16-21). He had a harvest too big for his barns. He decided to build bigger barns and then celebrate - *relax, eat, drink, and be merry!* (Luke 12:19). Jesus warns his listeners to be wary of such arrogance. Death can take everything away. Understanding comes from the impact of the whole story rather than an analysis of each word. You don't need to be an expert on barns or what kind of crops the man harvested. The teaching comes in the punch line: *So it is with those who store up treasures for themselves but are not rich towards God* (Luke 12:21).

The fact is that truth is differently presented and expressed in the various types of historical writing, in prophetical and poetical texts, and in other forms of literary expression. Hence the exegete must look for that meaning which the sacred writers, in given situations and granted the circumstances of their time and culture, intended to express and did in fact express, through the medium of contemporary literary form. Rightly to understand what the sacred authors wanted to affirm in their work, due attention must be paid both to the customary and characteristic patterns of perception, speech and narrative which prevailed in their time, and to the conventions which people then observed in their dealings with one another.

Dogmatic Constitution on Divine Revelation - Vatican II - Paragraph 12

The *Catechism of the Catholic Church* (CCC) offers guidelines for reading and understanding Scripture. It speaks of seeing the unity of Scripture; reading Scripture as connected to the living Tradition of the Church; being attentive to the fact that the truths of Scripture are linked together in revealing the plan of salvation. (Cf. CCC - #112, #113, #114). *

Interpretation of the inspired Scripture must be attentive above all to what God wants to reveal through the sacred authors for our salvation. What comes from the Spirit is not fully "understood except by the Spirit's action." (cf. Origen, Hom. in Ex. 4, 5: PC 12, 320).

CCC - #137

Sometimes we search for a scripture text to support something we have already decided is right. We wander through Scripture to find a text that agrees with us. We will probably be successful. In that case we are not listening to Scripture but rather attaching the scriptural word to what we already decided it should say.

Franciscans do the opposite. We listen to scripture and apply what it says to our lives without twisting it to fit a pre-conceived idea. Scripture calls us to conversion, deeper dedication, and a readiness to learn the truth God teaches through Scripture, especially the Gospels. We do **not** manipulate Scripture to say what we want to hear!

In our time words like *fundamentalists, evangelicals, conservatives, liberals,* and other terms fill the religious air. A variety of meanings are attached to these words. Sometimes they are used to label and isolate people. At other times they are used as a positive quality for someone's ideas and opinions. Whatever way we use them there is a need for dialogue. Personal positions on the issues of life and faith come to us from many different sources.

---

* For further guidelines, read Article 3, #101 to #141, Pages 30-38 in *The Catechism of the Catholic Church* and Pages 26 to 33 in the *United States Catholic Catechism for Adults.*

Sometimes our beliefs are colored by what people close to us believe. Sometimes they are colored by opposition to people we believe are out of touch with present-day reality. Sometimes we lean to a liberal or conservative stance because we have searched and resourced issues that finally brought us to a particular way of viewing the world, the Church and our faith. Sometimes we embrace a particular stance because someone we trust has shared arguments that make sense to us. Sometimes we accept a perspective because it allays the fear that we or others might lack knowledge about our faith. The liberal or conservative perspective gives us assurance that we are safe in our beliefs. Sometimes it is an honest seeking that puts us somewhere on the continuum from conservative to liberal.

The "purity" of our stance may lack something as well as offering us a sense of security and correctness. Humanly we want to be secure and correct in our faith. Of course, most of us do not have much time to research theological documents; or engage in theological reflection to arrive at our faith stance; or to bolster our Catholic approach to political or eccelesial positions in the Church or the world. Humanly, we decide where we stand and our presumption is that the other side is wrong or un-catholic or foolish or stubborn or arrogant or are destroying the Church etc. etc.

Franciscans recognize that the differences between us need to be bridged. Dominating the other side or dismissing them out-of-hand does little to achieve unity. Franciscans, following a Trinitarian spirituality, do everything possible to maintain relationships with opponents, whether ecclesial or secular. We choose this approach when we profess a Franciscan way of life. We show respect and reverence for people who disagree with us. Even if we think we're right, we listen respectfully to other ideas and opinions. As we maintain relationships we also maintain the possibility of future sharing. Dialogue becomes the way we share. Indeed, we may come to conclusions neither side expected when the dialogue began. The spirit of openness allows us to learn from one another and share with others without dominance or arrogance.

... seeking out ways of unity and fraternal harmony through dialogue, trusting in the presence of the divine seed in everyone and in the transforming power of love and pardon.

SFO Rule #19

Arrogance and name-calling do not fit our Franciscan vision. Hence, whether we happen to have a *conservative* or *liberal* slant, we are open to the possibility that we can learn from one another. True dialogue (i.e. listening **and** speaking) is our pattern in conversations with one another. When we dialogue we are not certain where the conversation will lead us. We trust the Holy Spirit's guidance if we are reverent to and respectful of one another. If we need to take prayerful time to achieve a sense of unity, prayerful time will be taken. If the dialogue takes more time, we will invest more time because Jesus' call for unity will not be ignored. Scripture texts will not be used as a club but as an invitation for common reflection.

The more we do for others, the more we understand and can appropriate the words of Christ: "We are useless servants" (Luke 17:10). *We recognize that we are not acting on the basis of any superiority or greater personal efficiency, but because the Lord has graciously enabled us to do so.*

God is Love *(Deus Caritas Est)* - Benedict XVI - Paragraph 35

As knowledge of our faith becomes more clear, dialogue will not mean abandoning what we believe. Instead, we learn to share our faith in such a way that we create understanding between ourselves and people of other beliefs. We create a welcoming atmosphere that allows us to dialogue without violence, verbal or otherwise. A relational atmosphere allows us to work together even when we hold differing beliefs. In this atmosphere the Holy Spirit is free to achieve the work of conversion. Arrogant arguments and put-downs usually separate us and close the door to relationships. Catholics who are not Franciscans may follow different ways of sharing the faith. Franciscans avoid arrogance which adds little or nothing to maintaining relationships or attracting others to our faith.

Fundamentalist understanding of Scripture may ignore some good tools of Scripture scholars. They may have a literal approach, accepting the translated message just as they read it. This literalism leaves aside the work of responsible scripture scholars and centuries of interpretation of the Scriptures. Fundamentalists may rely on private interpretation to guide their lives. With only the authority of their own interpretation they may come to tenuous conclusions.

Fundmentalists can be faithful to what they believe is a proper interpretation of Scripture. If they find texts that seem to exclude people from God's love they also exclude them. Or an individual text may invite them to embrace people and they do embrace them. Since private interpretation has a priority, *fundamentalists* may have many theological differences among themselves. Whatever their interpretation, and recognizing their desire to be faithful to their interpretation of Scripture, Franciscans approach them with love, not insults.

In response to biblical literalism, the Church holds that "the books of Scripture firmly, faithfully and without error, teach that truth which God, for the sake of our salvation, wished to see confided to the sacred Scriptures" (Dei Verbum - Vatican II - No. 11). *At the same time, the Church recognizes that the interpreter of Scripture needs to attend to the literary forms - such as poetry, symbol, parable, history, song, or prayer - in which the Bible is written. The interpreter "must look for that meaning which the sacred writer ... given the circumstance of his time and culture, intended to express and did in fact express, through the medium of a contemporary literary form."* (Dei Verbum - Vatican II - No. 12)

United States Catholic Catechism for Adults - USCCB - Page 30

Evangelicals are not a monolithic community any more than fundamentalists are. There are many shades of difference among them. Some are strictly religious in their response to Scripture, basically concerned about private religious practices. Others develop a concern for social issues that need to be addressed. Concern for the poor and marginalized is growing among evangelicals.

Here again, try to understand the position of any individual or group of evangelicals when entering into dialogue with them. Just as Catholics certainly are not a monolithic group, neither are evangelicals. Know the people and the territory as you engage in dialogue. Assumptions and presumptions can be roadblocks to good dialogue.

Franciscans are called to a respectful approach to people. We can dialogue without becoming enemies. We can disagree without having to separate from one another. But achieving that attitude and perspective takes regular conversion - and work! We choose to attract others to our beliefs rather than winning arguments or trying to show how smart we are. Such attitudes we leave to others.

As the Father sees in every person the features of his Son, the firstborn of many brothers and sisters, so the Secular Franciscans, with a gentle and courteous spirit, accept all people as a gift of the Lord and an image of Christ.

SFO Rule #13

Franciscans desire to share the faith both by life and words. In doing so we recognize that such sharing is meant to build the Kingdom of God in the world. It means sharing our vision in a way that attracts others. The SFO Rule offers an insight into the goal of evangelization: *... to build a more fraternal and evangelical world so that the kingdom of God may be brought about more effectively* (SFO Rule #14).

There are many texts and workshops to help in this task. Make use of programs that can aid your skills in evangelizing.

In 1975 Pope Paul VI wrote an encyclical titled: *Evangelii Nuntiandi - On Evangelization in the Modern World.* It is worthwhile to read the entire text. But some quotations from Paul VI give a sense of what evangelization is about.

For the Church, evangelizing means bringing the Good News into all the strata of humanity from within and making it new. "Now I am making the whole of creation new." (Revelation 21.5). *But there is no new humanity if there are not first of all new persons renewed by Baptism and by lives lived according to the Gospel* (Ephesians 4:23-24 - Colossians 3:9-10*) The purpose of evangelization is therefore precisely this interior change, and if it had to be expressed in one sentence the best way of stating it would be to say that the Church evangelizes* (Romans 1:16 / 1 Corinthians 1:18, 2:4) *when she seeks to convert solely through the divine power of the message she proclaims, both the personal and collective consciences of people, the activities in which they engage, and the lives and concrete milieu which are theirs.*

Evangelization in the Modern World - Paul VI - Paragraph 18

Pope Paul VI goes on to reflect on the results of sharing the good news with others in an effective way.

... the person who has been evangelized goes on to evangelize others. Here lies the test of truth, the touchstone of evangelization: it is unthinkable that a person should accept the Word and give himself to the Kingdom without becoming a person who bears witness to it and proclaims it in turn.

... Evangelization, as we have said, is a complex process made of varied elements: the renewal of humanity, witness, explicit proclamation, inner adherence, entry into the community, acceptance of signs, apostolic initiative. These elements may appear to be contradictory, indeed mutually exclusive. In fact they are complementary and mutually enriching. Each one must always be seen in relationship with the others.

Evangelization in the Modern World - Paul VI - Paragraph 24

Franciscans are called to build or re-build the Church (The People of God). It would be counter-productive to become arrogant, to act as though we are individually infallible, or to find ways to make people feel ignorant or stupid. None of these actions establish better relationships. Franciscans consistently search for ways to have a meaningful dialogue. We avoid using tools that overwhelm and denigrate the people with whom we seek to have conversations (dialogue). *Messengers of perfect joy in every circumstance, they should strive to bring joy and hope to others* (SFO Rule #19).

Scripture is always present in our lives. God's word hovers in conversations about faith or biblical interpretations, or how to live, or how to develop a moral stance in life or how to get to know God and God's only Son, Jesus Christ, or why love is so important, or why the poor hold a special place in the heart of Franciscans.

Our faith would be barren and only human were it not for God's revelation in Scripture. *The local fraternity ... should be a privileged place for developing a sense of Church and the Franciscan vocation and for enlivening the apostolic life of its members* (SFO Rule #22). Our love for Scripture gives the Word of God a special place in our lives.

But this is not just about making shrines to "The Book." If there are shrines to be built they are built through our manner of living the Gospel. Otherwise it becomes a simple intellectual exercise with "no meat on the bones." The "meat" is in the life we live. When we "live the Gospel" we fulfill the goal ... *to present the charism of their common Seraphic Father in the life and mission of the Church* (SFO Rule #1). Franciscans are committed to that goal, grasping the spirit of St. Francis who addressed all of creation as "brothers and sisters."

I therefore, admonish all my brothers and encourage them in Christ to venerate, as best they can, the divine written words wherever they find them. If they are not well kept or are carelessly thrown around in some place, let them gather them up and preserve them, inasmuch as it concerns them, honoring in the words the Lord "Who spoke them." For many things are made holy by the words of God and the sacrament of the altar is celebrated in the power of the words of Christ.

A Letter to the Entire Order
Francis of Assisi - The Saint - Vol I - Page 119

We Hold a Treasure Not Made of Gold

A treasure.
What does one do with a treasure?
How does someone spend lottery winnings?
Do we just get more for ourselves?
Do we share our treasure?
Hoard it?
Invest it to get more?
Use it for security?
Build houses with it?
Establish foundations with it?
Bury it?

What if the treasure is a way of living?
What if the treasure is something intangible
like an inner contemplative spirit that guides life?
What if it is a common concern
that leads to community?
What if the treasure is praying together,
seeking to be faithful to the Gospel?
What if it means getting together regularly
to keep on course?
What if the treasure gives us peace
when things go haywire in life?

What if the treasure is Lady Poverty
who asks that we recognize our need of God?
What if the treasure is Jesus
and Jesus' Spirit dwelling in us?
The treasure could be someone like
Francis or Clare of Assisi.
It could be people next door
who show hospitality and compassion.

It might be folks down on their luck
and living on the streets.
It seems a poor place to
look for treasure.
But surprisingly, there it is!

In a world often lost in trying
to find happiness in accumulation,
Scripture offers the real treasure
in freedom from domination by things.
In a world where hope seems hopelessly out of reach,
here we are, offering hope through
communion with Jesus and his Gospel.

If we are sensible realists,
we willingly share what we find in Scripture.
We share our Franciscan heritage
with anyone who will dialogue.

We invite folks to our way of life.
We share stories with them.
We tell them of our values
and how we seek to create
peace, communion, and joy.
We answer their questions
and allow the Holy Spirit to touch them
with a call to join us, or at least
to follow the Gospel in some way.

Sharing what we love
is another part of living
our Franciscan life.
Every Franciscan is called to do it,
and is able to share his/her
story of wonder at God's call.
After all, our world needs lots of help.
Being faithful Franciscans
is one way of giving that help.
Who wouldn't want to widen
the circle of those who follow
Francis and Clare and Jesus
and the Gospel?

Sharing the treasure we have discovered
seems natural when we love one another.
And may God find new, dedicated disciples
who have discovered the treasure
and want to spread the "Good News." Amen

+++

Readings/Questions for dialogue

Interpretation of Scripture
United State Catholic Catechism for Adults
Page 27 to 31

On Evangelization in the Modern World
Paul VI - Paragraphs 21-22-23

The Praises of God
Francis of Assisi - The Saint - Vol I - Page 109

1. Why is the Bible important to Franciscans?

2. What insights did you get by reading this chapter on Scripture?

3. Why do Franciscans embrace a sense of openness and welcoming in dealing with others who may not agree with us?

4. Explain your understanding of what is needed for a good interpretation of Scripture. Why is this important?

5. What attitude should we show in conversations with people who think differently than we do?

6. What is the value of labeling someone e.g. as *conservative, liberal, fundamentalist, evangelical* etc. How do Franciscans deal with such labeling?

7. Name some "treasures" in your life. What value do they bring to you and the people in your life? Evaluate them to

see what is worth keeping and what can be discarded.

8. Scripture reflection: John 1:1-18. What truth(s) about Jesus are contained in this text? Explain how verse 18 relates to the our dedication to the Gospel?

+++

Very Good News

Francis believed the Gospel.
The WHOLE THING - Matthew, Mark,
Luke, John and all the rest.
Jesus said: "Do not worry over what to eat ..."
And Francis didn't.
Jesus said: "Whoever wishes to follow me,
let him deny himself"
And Francis did.
Jesus said: "... take nothing with you on the way."
And Francis didn't.

It sounds simplistic, even impossible,
or at best - ridiculous, wouldn't you say?
No matter what you say, it happens to be
the way Francis saw things.

It is Gospel living
according to Francis,
taking the whole Gospel seriously.
Not watered down, not interpreted away,
not ignored nor pushed aside,
but embracing
the whole GOOD NEWS called Gospel.

Chapter nine

Vatican II + SFO Rule and Constitutions

Vatican II may seem like a long-ago dream. It was a time when Christians around the world realized that something special was happening in the Catholic Church. Catholics had a variety of responses to the Council. Words, pro and con, flew around the world. Some people were not happy with the direction of the Council. Others were delighted with the direction the Council took to energize those who believed in Jesus. The struggle to accept the fresh insights of faith was difficult for many Catholics. For other Catholics it was as though a mummy had finally come alive.

The words of John XXIII give a gentle reminder of how he saw the work of the Council. As he said, and many interpreters said later, the Holy Spirit both prompted and continues the work of the Council. Franciscans are aware that the Council invites us to continue the re-building of the Church as Jesus asked of Francis. We do this out of love, seeking to share the treasure of the word of God in Scripture and the wonder of the Word-made-flesh in Jesus.

Our task is not merely to hoard this precious treasure, as though obsessed with the past, but to give ourselves eagerly and without fear to the task which the present age demands of us - and in so doing we will be faithful to what the Church has done in the last twenty centuries. So the main point of the Council will not be to debate this or that article of basic Church doctrine that has been repeatedly taught by the Fathers and theologians old and new and which we can take as read. You do not need a council to do that. But starting from a renewed, serene and calm acceptance of the whole teaching of the Church in all its scope and detail as it is found in Trent and Vatican I, Christians and Catholics of apostolic spirit all the world over expect a leap forward in doctrinal insight and the education of consciences in ever greater fidelity to authentic teaching. But this authentic doctrine has to be studied and expounded in the light of the research methods and the language of modern thought. For the substance of the ancient deposit of faith is one thing, and the way in which it is presented is another.

John XXIII - Shepherd of the Modern World
Peter Hebblethwaite - Page 431-432

Some people say that Vatican II is history. Too many changes have touched the world, the Church and people for Vatican II to be influential today. The Council no longer offers the stimulus within the Kingdom of God it originally offered. On the other hand, it is also true that ecclesial self-understanding has not yet borne all its possible fruit. The Council's desire for the Church to be a *community of love*, joined in a unity of love, and a sign of salvation for all people, is still a challenge. The consequences of the Council and their influence among us are not yet complete.*

Vatican II certainly opened Scripture to people. The Bible became much more important in Catholic life. We have much work to do. We need to do the work that will enable us to see the Spirit's influence in the texts of Vatican II and to discern the work of the Spirit in applying Vatican II (and the Gospel) to daily life - today!

Exploring Vatican II and its influence is a responsibility for all of us. The SFO Rule of 1978 would have been impossible without Vatican II. Opening the doors of the Church to dialogue also opened the door to many changes. Whether we approve or disapprove, that "spirit" gave voice to the laity of the Church. It provided a way to take charge

---

* Cf. The Reception of Vatican II - edited by Giuseppe Alberigo, Jean Pierre Jossua, and Joseph A. Komonchak - Catholic University of American Press / Also - cf. the article by: Hermann Pottmeyer - Page 29 in the same book.

of their gospel way of life in the world and the Church.

In the church, there is a diversity of ministry but unity of mission. To the apostles and their successors, Christ entrusted the office of teaching, sanctifying and governing in his name and by his power. Lay people too, sharing in the priestly, prophetical and kingly office of Christ, play their part in the mission of the whole people of God in the church and in the world. In the concrete, their apostolate is exercised when they work to evangelize people and make them holy; it is exercised, too, when they endeavor to have the gospel spirit permeate and improve the temporal order, going about it in a way that bears clear witness to Christ and helps forward the salvation of humanity. The characteristics of the lay state being a life led in the midst of the world and of secular affairs, lay people are called by God to make of their apostolate, through the vigor of their christian spirit, a leaven in the world.

Decree on the Apostolate of Lay People
Vatican II - Constitutions, Decrees, Declarations
Austin Flannery OP, editor - pages 405- 406 - Paragraph 2

All the people involved in writing the SFO Rule of 1978 took the direction of the Council seriously. The Secular Franciscan way of life is a particular way of living the Gospel. The new rule was meant to make Francis' spirit clear for our times. Secular Franciscans developed a rule that fits our times. The worldwide dialogue among Franciscans about the rule shows the truth of this belief.

The 1978 SFO Rule provides not only a balance between prayer and action, but also illustrates how prayer and action are partners. Social action is clearly spelled out in a number of articles in chapter two of the 1978 Rule. The Rule requires Secular Franciscans to approach people with gentleness, care, and compassion - recognizing in them the image of God. We recognize our personal need for radical conversion and seek it with a willing spirit. By our lives we show how it looks to live a kingdom/gospel life. It must be attractive rather than boring; inviting rather than separating; welcoming instead of excluding; forgiving rather than vengeful; prayerful rather than domineering; with a passion for justice rather than allowing injustice to grow; seeking ways of peace rather than planning for war and violence; developing a spirit of community rather than individualism; recognizing a need for God rather than arrogant independence; finding hope and guidance in the Bible rather than dependence merely on human knowledge.

These ideas developed from the reflections of Secular Franciscans as they wrote a new rule. The dialogue and the conversations of several years allowed the Rule to grow into the fine document that resulted. Vatican II created the atmosphere that made these things possible.

A Secular Spirituality

Words are funny things.
"Secular" sounds harsh.
It has overtones of the crashing noise
of construction at work,
or the traffic of an expressway,
sometimes the noise of a washing machine,
or a siren, or a street fight, or a dance.

"Spirituality" is almost as puzzling.
It brings up images of
burning tapers and dark churches,
monks reading their prayers,
or chanting their praise to God.
It rings of rules and regulations,
and prayers and fasting -
not always attractive.

"Secular" carries overtones of the world
of everyday life - reality in the raw.
It describes people's lives and how life is lived.
Add on the place of work, the occupation,
the time clock and shift,
and "secular" seems to fit well.

It describes you and me,
where we are, what we do,
how we earn a living.

Putting "Secular" and "Spirituality" together
seems odd at first.
But if God is in our reality
then there is no separation
but only a description of where God
enters our lives, i.e. wherever we are.
Love of Jesus stands
side by side with love of work.
Prayer to Jesus stands
side by side with conversations with friends.

"Secular" simply describes where your
"Spirituality" takes place and blossoms.
Not in a monastary or convent,
not necessarily in a church.

You live it wherever you go,
where you play or where you work,
where you worship or where you recreate,
where you suffer or where you celebrate.
It lives where you live, for God is there.
If this is not so, then you have
a spirituality that is artificial, unreal, suspect.

You, Gospel, Reality, Jesus, Love, Joy, Cross;
they gather together in a "secular spirituality."
Francis invites you to integrate them
in your daily life.
cross and hope together.

"Secular Spirituality" happens in
kitchens, shops, cars, malls, buses,
hospitals, walking, on merry-go-rounds,
airplanes, bedrooms, churches - all over!
Or it won't happen at all !

Exploring the articles of the SFO Rule of 1978 will be a task for *candidacy*. In *candidacy* we explore the implications of the Rule as well as examining the insights offered by the SFO General Constitutions.

The SFO has had only three SFO Rules in over 800 years. The Rule is not changed very often because it is meant to contain the spirit that Francis shares with us. The Rule changes when the times require it - i.e. to fit the times in which it is lived. That is not a frequent occurrence but it is an important one. The changes that brought about the Rule of 1978 are very important for the continued growth of the SFO in the times in which we live.

In the process of revising the Rule the participants developed seventeen points that were critical to the articulation of the the SFO way of life. These seventeen points served as guidelines for the revision. We list them here so you to see how they influenced the Rule of 1978. They developed at the Assisi Congress of 1969.

1. *To live the Gospel according to the spirit of St Francis.*
2. *To be converted continually (metanoia).*
3. *To live as a brother or sister to all people and of all creation.*
4. *To live in communion with Christ.*
5. *To follow the poor and crucified Christ.*
6. *To share in the life and mission of the Church.*
7. *To share in the love of the Father.*
8. *To be instruments of peace.*
9. *To have a life of prayer that is personal, communal and liturgical.*
10. *To live in joy.*
11. *To have a spirituality of a secular character.*
12. *To be pilgrims on the way to the Father.*
13. *To participate in the Apostolate of the Laity.*
14. *To be at the service of the less fortunate.*
15. *To be loyal to the church in an attitude of dialogue and collaboration with her ministers.*

16. To be open to the action of the Spirit.
17. To live in simplicity, humility, and minority.

These seventeen elements influenced the development of the 1978 Rule. They grew from statements of Secular Franciscans. Near the end of the process the Ministers General of the 1st Order/TOR added the *Earlier Exhortation of Saint Francis to the Brothers & Sisters of Penance* as a *prologue* to the Rule. The *Exhortation* gives a guide for interpreting the 1978 Rule as well as connecting the Rule of 1978 with previous documents.*

In the Rule *conversion* means more than moving from one religious tradition to embrace another religious tradition. We commonly call such people "converts."

The use of the word *conversion* in the Rule has a much wider meaning. It does not happen all at once. It is not some special religious experience, though that is possible. Rather, it is a free choice by which an individual embraces a fresh way of perceiving reality. Conversion is both an initial and ongoing decision. We move in a new direction; embrace a new way of interpreting reality; accept new values or revive good old ones; relate to God and people in new ways; develop qualities and virtues that may have been missing in our lives; develop a sharper awareness of where our lives need conversion. We proceed to the work of achieving personal conversion.

No part of life is neglected in this *radical conversion* required by the Rule (SFO Rule #4). The qualities attributed to the heart are touched. Our way of loving changes. The ways of the mind are changed. Our intellect searches for ways to enrich knowledge of the Gospel and to make that knowledge operable in daily life. It touches our morality and how we deal with life and people. It deals with a

---

* Cf. The source for information in this section of our text is: *"De Illlis Qui Faciunt Penitentiam" - The Rule of the SFO, Origins, Development, Interpretation* - Robert Steward - Page 250 and 321ff

religious conversion that accepts responsibility for understanding and living the Franciscan spirit. The Rule of 1978 invites us to choose ways of peace and justice as well as having a concern for the whole of creation. Prayerful contemplation finds itself at home in this Rule. We trust our heart to love with ever greater passion and delight.

This is no little conversion. The requirements of conversion continue throughout life. The process of conversion is ongoing and is supported by a community of people with the same goal and desire. The SFO Rule of 1978 spells out ways to implement conversion day after day after day. It helps us to be aware of our need for conversion.

The Rule approaches the sacrament of Reconciliation as a means to overcome old habits or face new challenges on the journey of conversion. The Gospel invites us to change our lives. *On this road to renewal the sacrament of reconciliation is the privileged sign of the Father's mercy and the source of grace* (SFO Rule # 7).

The 1978 Rule offers direction while allowing for personal needs and individual understanding. It spells out, in its text, the expectations Franciscans strive to achieve. It leaves an opening for individual ways of achieving a *radical conversion* of life. A Secular Franciscan assumes personal responsibility for following the Rule of 1978. He/she makes a public *profession* proclaiming the commitment to do so.

Where there is charity and wisdom,
there is neither fear nor ignorance.

Where there is patience and humility,
there is neither anger nor distrubance.

Where there is poverty with joy,
there is neither greed nor avarice.

Where there is rest and meditation,
there is neither anxiety nor restlessness.

Where there is fear of the Lord to guard an entrance,
there the enemy cannot have a place to enter.

Where there is a heart full of mercy and discernment,
there is neither excess nor hardness of heart.

Admonition XXVII (The undated writings)
Francis of Assisi - The Saint - Vol I - Page 136-137

The SFO Constitutions contain comments on the Rule and insights for understanding the Rule. The Constitutions point out structures to help the Rule come alive in community life. The Constitutions spell out things like canonical procedures and structural developments. They deal with issues of lukewarm members and the role of the servant-leaders of fraternity life (councils). The Constitutions present ways and means to deal with issues that may arise in fraternity life. In a sense, the Constitutions become a wide-ranging commentary on the secular Franciscan rule and life. During initial formation we expect you to become acquainted with the SFO Constitutions.

Statutes are specific documents that spell out governing details not contained in the Constitutions. E.g. *The Statutes for Spiritual & Pastoral Assistance to the SFO* contain guidelines for spiritual assistance to local, regional, national or international councils. Regions within a country may develop *Guidelines* for specific needs in their region. Guidelines deal with issues not spelled out in the Constitutions or Statutes or give guidance to local/regional councils and/or formation personnel.

... The unbreakable bond beween love of God and love of

Recommendation: Purchase a copy of: The Essential Documents of the SFO. The book contains documents you need as you live and minister within the Secular Franciscan Order. It contains: *The Rule of 1978 / the General Constitutions of the SFO (2000) / The Statutes of the National Fraternity of the SFO in the United States / The Ritual of the SFO / Statutes of the International Fraternity of the SFO / Statutes for Spiritual & Pastoral Assistance to the SFO.* Your formation director can give you information on where to purchase a copy.

neighbor is emphasized. One is so closely connected to the other that to say that we love God becomes a lie if we are closed to our neighbor or hate him altogether. ... love of neighbor is a path that leads to the encounter with God, ... closing our eyes to our neighbor also blinds us to God.
God is Love *(Deus Caritas Est) - Benedict XVI - Paragraph 16*

+++

Readings/Questions for dialogue

General Constitutions
Articles 17 & 18

The Remembrance of the Desire of a soul
Thomas of Celano - Francis of Assisi - The Founder
Vol II - Chapter XV - Page 259

The Minor Legend of St Francis - Sixth lesson
Francis of Assisi - The Founder - Vol II - Page 696-697

1. Having spent nine months with us, you may have discerned whether or not you have a vocation to the SFO. Dialogue with formation personnel and/or a spiritual director can assist this discernment. Share your conclusions.

2. Vatican II influences our Franciscan way of life. How would you describe that influence?

3. Describe the differences between the secular Franciscan Rule, the Constitutions, and Statutes as well as Guidelines. What purpose does each one serve?

4. Why is "secular spirituality" a good way to describe Franciscan life? Explain what it means to you.

5. Which of the seventeen points (Page 103-104) means the most to you? Why? Which one is most dificult for you?

6. How would you describe "conversion" as understood by Francis and used in the SFO Rule?

7. Scripture reflection: Hosea 14:1-9. How do the words of Hosea refer to "conversion" from God's point of view? As you feel ready, write out your personal definition of "conversion" as understood in our Franciscan life.

+++

For it is the weak things of this world
which seems like folly
that the Spirit takes up and makes its own.
The dream of the mountain's struggle,
and the dreams of simplicity and of justice,
like so many other repressed visions is,
we believe, the voice of the Lord among us.

In taking them up again, hopefully the Church
might once again be known as

+ *a center of the Spirit,*
+ *a place where poetry dares to speak,*
+ *where the song reigns unchallenged,*
+ *where art flourishes,*
+ *where nature is welcome,*
+ *where humble people and humble needs come first,*
+ *where justice speaks loudly,*
+ *where in a wilderness of idolatrous destruction, the great voice of God still cries out for Life.* *(1995)**

This Land is Home to me (1975)
**At Home in the Web of Life* (1995)
Catholic Bishops of Appalachia - Page 98

At the beginning of *candidacy* there is a
Rite of Admission.
This is a public acceptance
of the *inquirer's* request
to live the gospel life in the spirit of St. Francis.

The rite is in the *Ritual for the SFO.*
The *Rite of Admission* itself begins on Page 14.
A copy of the Rule *(The Little Red Rule Book)*
is given to each candidate
in the course of this ritual.

The rite takes place
without Mass, but in a celebration
of the Word of God,

The rite is simple and done
in the presence of the whole fraternity.

Read the guidance given in the *Ritual.*
You may adjust the rite to fit your fraternity.
Formation personnel assure that the rite
is well-prepared and meaningful.

... Just like the clay in the potter's hands, so are you in my hands.

Jeremiah 18:6

WELCOME TO CANDIDACY!

You are entering
the final stage
of *Initial Formation.*
+
May your
commitment to the
Franciscan way of life
blossom during
this time of
Candidacy.

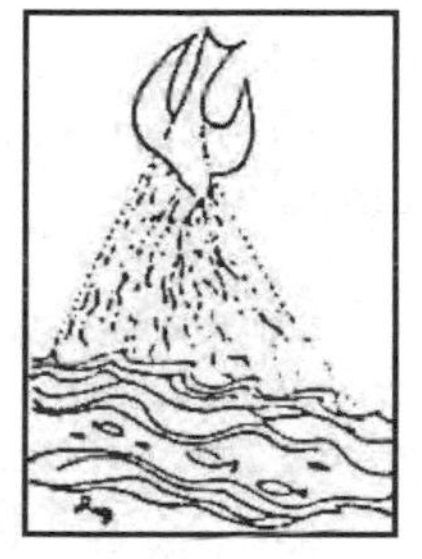

Chapter ten

Candidacy in the SFO

Candidacy lasts at least 18 months and no more than 36 months.

Candidacy is the final stage of *initial formation*. It is not the end of formation, but another step on the way. This period leads to your decision to make a permanent *profession* as a secular Franciscan. *Profession* opens the door to *ongoing formation* in Franciscan living. It is a time when you consecrate your gifts and skills to the service of the fraternity, the Church and the world. Your gifts and skills reach out beyond the fraternity. They bring the spirit of St. Francis to the Church and world.

The USA National Statutes (article 19.2b) determine that candidacy is not less than 18 months nor more than 36 months. *The length of candidacy* (between 18 and 36 months) is decided by the local council or by the regional council of the SFO. **This book has 24 chapters** for *candidacy*.

Candidacy will share information as well as implementation of the SFO Rule and Constitutions. Your task is not only to study and explore the Rule and Constitutions but to put them into practice. Information leads to ways of reforming your way of living. Putting the Rule and Constitutions into practice will enable you to make an informed decision about profession.

We live in the Kingdom of God where God is Lord and is recognized as Lord. The will of God is LOVE. It is not a place for judgment but an invitation to new life. In building the Kingdom of God we are called to offer our loving response to the Gospel. The desire of God is fulfilled when we love one another and show it in practical, everyday ways. The Rule of the SFO offers ways to love one another in a multitude of circumstances.*

The spirit of St. Francis invites us to deepen our relationship with Jesus. Prayers, rosaries, retreats, programs etc. are good. But if they become comfortable and not challenging, we can repeat them over and over again without any real conversion taking place in our lives. Conversion is a normal element of Franciscan life. We also recognize the importance of contemplative prayer that brings us to Jesus. He is the Beloved and the Lover. Jesus loves us. We are called "living stones" who build a community of believers (Kingdom of God). Formation must be liveable to be credible and it will show in our behavior.

Who is wise and understanding among you? Show by your good life that your works are done with gentleness born of wisdom. But if you have bitter envy and selfish ambition in your hearts, do not be boastful and false to the truth. Such wisdom does not come down from above but is earthly, unspiritual, devilish. For where there is envy and selfish ambition, there will also be disorder and wickedness of every kind. But the wisdom from above is first pure, then peaceable, gentle, willing to yield, full of mercy and good fruits, without a trace of partiality or hypocrisy. And a harvest of righteousness is sown in peace for those who make peace.

James 3:13-18

As we encounter the person of Jesus and grow in union with Him, the Holy Spirit transforms us. Prayer and action grow from this source. They assist our conversion to a Franciscan way of living. *Candidacy* explores ways and means to achieve intimacy with Jesus. In faith we discover ways to express love in daily life. Our Franciscan spirit enables us to share love in the Church and the world.

---

* Cf. The Monk & The World - Walter Dirks - Translated by Daniel Coogan - David McKay Co. Inc - New York - 1954 - Page 59

The *Prologue* to the SFO Rule

The Exhortation of St. Francis to the Brothers and Sisters of Penance serves as an introduction to the Rule of 1978. The dating of this *Exhortation* is uncertain, but the vision it creates for us is quite clear. Francis points out things that happen both when we do penance and when we don't. Our understanding involves both what Francis meant by the words and the meaning of the text for the 21st century.

Concerning those who do penance

In the first verses of the *Exhortation* Francis addresses the issue of love. The biblical words are straightforward and clear - love God with everything we have. Love neighbor in the same way. Love ourselves with an honest love. Avoid the selfishness that moves us to vices and sins. Recognize the importance of Eucharist as Jesus comes to us under the simple appearances of bread and wine. There is a call to *produce worthy fruits of penance.* Looking at life this way leads to decisions that reveal how well we understand the idea of "penance."

Penitents know how easy it is to follow a selfish way of living. It is easy to seek one's personal needs rather than thinking about the neighbor and the ways of God. Francis speaks of this (in his testament) as *"when I was in sin."* It wasn't simply individual sins that disturbed him. It was the self-centeredness that prompted the sins. It was the desire to have things his own way. It was his obvious need to be somebody and forget about other folks - *being in sin* - ignoring the ways of God. It was a self-centered life that ignored God and focused primarily on self-satisfaction. Such a way of living and choosing can also govern how we act and what we do - ignoring a gospel way of living.

The first lines of the *Exhortation* are a wake-up call about what a faith-stance looks like in daily life. If we find ourselves concerned about how everything touches us, and ignore neighbor needs, we may be *living in sin.* Recall that the *Exhortation* is among the first guidelines from Francis about how "penitents" would live. In this context we understand the perspective of Francis.

We are conditioned to think about *living in sin* as meaning we have committed some specific sin. That sin (or sins) becomes our focus. If our general status is a self-centered one that avoids loving God and neighbor as a first choice, than it is not the individual sins that hinder our growth. It is the fact that our inner spirit does not give God first place in our lives. We need a *conversion* that moves us to change that interior spirit.

If we embrace the *conversion* the Spirit calls us to make we find ourselves in a more peaceable stance. *The spirit of the Lord will rest upon them* (Cf. Isaiah 11:2) and God will make *his home and dwelling among them* (Cf. John 14:23). When we make our lives more Father-Jesus-Spirit-neighbor-centered we are children of the Trinity. *We will be spouses, brothers, and mothers of our Lord Jesus Christ* (Cf. Matthew 12:50).

Francis uses these terms to point out the spirit of a true penitent. Being a *spouse* symbolizes a relationship with Jesus. It is the work of the Holy Spirit to unite us to Jesus. We collaborate, but it is the Spirit that prompts and enables us to become intimate with Jesus. Joy, too, becomes a stable quality in our lives.

It is a portion of what is meant by *conversion*. We not only avoid individual sins, but we root out the radical sources of sin. Getting to the root of sinfulness makes us aware of where conversion is needed. Inner conversion influences the external actions of life. Our lives reveal more positively the gospel values that we embrace through baptism and *profession*. We learn that we can easily "miss the boat" in some of our priorities or values. To be a *spouse* reminds us that a personal relationship with Jesus is important in our lives. As that relationship grows we find ourselves better able to do *"the will of the Father who is in heaven"* (Matthew 12:50).

Being a *mother* is connected to spousal relationship. Our sex (male or female) is not what is being addressed. Rather it is our ability to be present to the Spirit dwelling within us. Through the Spirit we carry the presence of Jesus in our lives. This relationship prompts us to give birth to Jesus through our life and activity. We know Jesus and freely share his *way, truth, and life* with others. Our goal is to bring others to Jesus, giving birth to the same peace, compassion and joy that the Spirit creates in us. We give birth, in others, to a relationship with Jesus. Francis calls us to *"give birth to him through a holy life which must give light to others by example* (Cf. Matthew 5:16).

"Holy be Your Name:"

May knowledge of You become clearer in us
that we may know
the breadth of Your blessings,
the length of Your promises,
the height of Your majesty,
the depth of Your judgments.

A Prayer Inspired by the Our Father
Francis of Assisi - The Saint - Vol 1 - Page 158

We are *brothers (sisters)* when our lives reflect the model of our brother, Jesus. These terms (spouse, mother, brother) have to do with different dimensions of relationship. It is a relationship springing from Trinitarian spirituality. Brothers (sisters) are expected to fulfill *the will of our Father in heaven.*

Like Jesus, we embrace the way of the Father no matter what the cost. We imitate Jesus' compassion for the needy and concern for the poor and marginalized. As brothers, related to Jesus and one another, we are one family, concerned for the welfare of those we love. Francis expects us to imitate the dedication of God-made-flesh - Jesus. Contemplation is the soul of all we are and what we do.

Wherever the brothers may be and in whatever place they meet, they should respect spiritually and attentively one another, and honor one another without complaining. Let them be careful not to appear outwardly as sad and gloomy hypocrites; but show themselves joyful, cheerful and consistently gracious in the Lord.

The Earlier Rule - Francis of Assisi - The Saint - Vol 1 - Page 169

Having shared his ideas for being *spouse, mother and brother,* Francis goes further. The model for these relationships is God. We have a Father whose love is never-ending and who has consistent concern for the people God loves. To have such a *great and holy* Father is a glorious thing.

It is special to have a *spouse* like the Holy Paraclete. Without the Holy Spirit we would have no chance at holiness. Without the Holy Spirit there would be no Eucharist. We say over the gifts of bread and wine at Eucharist: *We ask you to make them holy* ***by the power of your Spirit,*** *that they may become the body and blood of your Son, our Lord Jesus Christ ...* (Eucharistic prayer #3). The Holy Spirit is the source of holiness and wholeness.

... the fruit of the Spirit is love, joy, peace, patience, kindness, generosity, faithfulness, gentleness, and self-control. There is no law against such things.

Galatians 5:22-23

When Jesus went to the synagogue, he stood up and read what the Spirit said in the prophet Isaiah:

The Spirit of the Lord is upon me,
because he has anointed me
to bring good news to the poor.
He has sent me to proclaim release to the captives
and recovery of sight to the blind,
to let the oppressed go free,
to proclaim the year
of the Lord's favor.

... Then he began to say to them,
"Today this scripture has been fulfilled in your hearing."
Luke 4:18-19, 21

The Holy Spirit builds up, animates, and sanctifies the Church. He prepares us to go out and bring others to Christ. He opens our minds to understand Christ's death and Resurrection. He makes present for us the mystery of Christ, especially in the Eucharist, and brings us to communion with God that we may bear much fruit. (Cf. CCC - no. 737)

United States Catholic Catechism for Adults - USCCB - Page 109

The final words of this part of the *Exhortation* find a compilation of Scripture texts that support Francis' words. Our relationship with the Father, Jesus, and the Holy Spirit moves us to proclaim the Gospel. This part of the *Prologue* illustrates the possibilities that embracing a life of penance and conversion can achieve.

Since the *Prologue* is an integral part of the SFO Rule, it calls us to accept the inner meaning of penance and conversion. It calls for a complete turn-around in our lives. It calls us to turn from self-centeredness that makes it *too bitter to see lepers* (*Testament* - Francis of Assisi - The Saint - Page 124). It calls for a total change of heart and life, not just the change of a few opinions or ideas. *What had seemed bitter to me was turned into sweetness of soul and body* (Ibid).

We go among lepers and show mercy to them. Kissing a "leper" changes that person from a "them" to a "brother or sister." The relationship changes us and invites us to relate to people in this new way. The relationship-conversion with a single leper calls us to make the same changes with all the people who enter our lives. No one is left out of this new way of living. More than a one-time change, it is a complete life-changing experience. The implications follow the pattern of relationships we embrace through accepting Trinitarian spirituality. Love becomes as vital to us as it does to the Trinity. It identifies us as Christians.

It calls us to follow the spirit of the seraphic lover, Francis of Assisi.

Concerning those who do not do penance

The first paragraph of this section finds Francis proclaiming the sad state of people who refuse to accept the call to conversion. Evil becomes normal for them. Eucharist is ignored. Promises are not kept. Negative influences dominate their lives. Anxiety becomes a normal stance.

Having rejected the way of Jesus, the light of the world, these people are blind. They ignore the Gospel and the light that is Jesus. Doing so they miss out on the wisdom Jesus brings from his Father. Francis minces no words in describing the sad state of these folks. *They see and acknowledge, they know and do bad things and knowingly destroy their own souls* (Prologue).

Since they walk in the dark, without the Christ-light, they are open to the temptations that a wickedly-wise devil brings to them. They are deceived by expectations that fail to fulfill. They forget that it will all cease. Death brings them to a sorry end, riddled with guilt and rejecting any hope of conversion or penance.

Francis uses extremes to make his point. Anyone who totally rejects Christ cannot hope for happiness. To choose self-centeredness rather than generous love leaves the doer in the dark, deceived by a selfish spirit that fails to bring life. Even when the opportunity to change is given, these people ignore the call. When death comes they still fail to change. Having rejected the wisdom that comes from God through Jesus, they lack resources at death.

Worst still, even their relatives and friends offer no support or consolation. The things they left to others in their will brings more rejection; *Cursed be his soul because he could have given us more, he could have acquired more than he did* (Prologue). When the body is buried the worms eat it and both body and soul are lost. They are forever separated from God.

Having written of the stark contrast between those who do penance and those who do not, Francis invites us to take this *Exhortation* seriously. He asks us to listen to the *fragrant words* of Jesus in Scripture. Not only read them, says Francis, but carry them out - *they are spirit and life.* To fail is to face judgment before Jesus Christ.

This *Exhortation* ... gives us insight into the passionate dedication of Francis. Having experienced the power of the Spirit; having built a strong relationship with Jesus; having a realization of the love of the Father for God's people, Francis cannot imagine that we would fail to do penance or accept the consequences of conversion.

And whoever observes these things, let him be blessed in heaven with the blessing of the Most High Father, and on earth with the blessing of His Beloved Son with the Most Holy Spirit, the Paraclete, and all the powers of heaven and with all the saints. And, as far as I can, I, little brother Francis, your servant, confirm for you, both within and without, this most holy blessing.

The Testament - Francis of Assisi - The Saint - Vol 1 - Page 127

Radical Conversion

Around and around we go.
We do stop, but then we're dizzy.
"Conversion, metanoia"
Almost sounds like a disease - but it's not!

It can be painful, but not like a toothache
or a headache. More like a heartache.
Francis didn't spend time on surface "stuff."
If your heart is right, the rest of you will be right.
If not, what good are all the externals?

"Someone has only as much knowledge
as he puts into action."
A fine defintion of wisdom.
So we cannot simply be intellecturals,
nor scholars, nor book-learners only.
Facts often fail to get below the surface of things.
We need to get a "feel" of conversion,
standing on our heads to see rightly.
Dependent on Jesus.

Metanoia is not a happening.
It is a process that goes on and on and on
as long as life lasts.
Some folks say it's not worth the work.
They need no one!
They can go it alone,
not touched by anyone, even the Lord.

Such folks may lack hope.
They may be deeply concerned with self.
Francis' way of life requires
BEING someone in love.
Warm, reaching out, serving, loving,
vulnerable and human.

We need to turn around in order
to BE someone like that (metanoia).
Franciscans pledge themselves to
keep turning around for life!
And life is never the same -
nor are they.

Readings/Questions for dialogue

The Sacrament of Charity *(Sacramentum Caritatis)*
Benedict XVI - Paragraph 71

Poverty & Joy - Wm Short OFM
Following the Footsteps of Jesus - Pages 74-75

Saved in Hope *(Spe Salvi)* - Benedict XVI
Paragraph 26

1. What most impressed you in reflecting on the *Exhortation* ... (Prologue)? Why?

2. How can *conversion* be a lifelong task? Explain.

3. How does the practice of penance give us insight into a gospel way of perceiving life in the world and the Church?

4. How does the study of the *Exhortation* give a foundation for the study of the SFO Rule?

5. Describe the qualities that Francis wants to see in those who follow his way of life.

6. What areas of your life are challenged by the *Exhortation*? What will you do about it?

7. Scripture reflection: 2 Timothy 1:8-14. What prompts St. Paul to write these words with such clarity? How did his conversion help him rely on God's *own purpose and grace*?

> *Without God man neither knows which way to go, nor even understands who he is. In the face of the enormous problems surrounding the development of peoples, which almost make us yield to discouragement, we find solace in the sayings of our Lord, Jesus Christ, who teaches us: "Apart from me you can do nothing." (Jn 15:5) and then encourages us: "I am with you always to the close of the age." (Mt 28:20)*
>
> Charity in Truth *(Caritas in Veritate)* - Benedict XVI - Paragraph 72

Chapter eleven

The SFO Rule

St. Francis in the stream of life
Anneta Duveen SFO

SFO Rule - Chapter one

1. The Franciscan family, as one among many spiritual families raised up by the Holy Spirit in the Church, unites all members of the people of God - laity, religious, and priests - who recognize that they are called to follow Christ in the footsteps of Saint Francis of Assisi.

In various ways and forms but in life-giving union with each other, they intend to make present the charism of their common Seraphic Father in the life and mission of the Church.

Being called a *family* requires a bit of explanation. We are not a blood family. We ordinarily do not grow up together. We do not have early childhood experiences together nor develop family relationships as life unfolds. We haven't all received similar educational opportunities nor have we attended family reunions together. We are not a *family* that reflects common cultural experiences before adulthood.

Having said that, we are a family because of our relationship to one another in the international Franciscan family. We experience common Franciscan formation programs. We are part of a local fraternity/family where relationships blossom. We are called to deepen our relationships with one another and show care and concern for one another. All of this is basically achieved in adult life. We are called by the Holy Spirit and choose to belong to the Franciscan family. It is good to see both the similarities and the differences when we use the term *family.*

Likewise, when we speak of *many spiritual families raised up by the Holy Spirit in the Church,* we recognize that most of these "families" are drawn together in adulthood. They experience growth patterns similar to our Franciscan development. Within the Church we experience adult relationships with these other families. It is normal to establish relationships as we work together to bring gospel ideals to the world. We recognize that many opportunities for ministry offer common cause for the various spiritual families in the Church and outside of it.

Within the Church, the Franciscan family draws together laity, religious, and clerics who recognize their call to follow the spirit of St. Francis of Assisi. The Franciscan family, of which the SFO is a part, is open to clerics, religious and laity alike.

The *Franciscan spirit* touches the lives of those who are called by the Holy Spirit to Franciscan living. Whether that call is to Franciscan religious life, clerical life or lay life, the *Franciscan vision* is the same. It has different expressions in the lives of priests, religious or laity, but the call is a common one. The *vision* is common to all of us. Structures may differ but our *spirit/vision* is the same.

As #1 of the SFO Rule puts it: *In various ways and forms but* ***in life-giving union*** *with each other* - we work together to offer the world and the Church an example of what the Franciscan charism looks like. Our contribution to the life and mission of the Church is to flavor it with our Franciscan spirit expressed in daily life.

It is obvious that we need to be aware of what a Franciscan charism looks like in people. This is one of the goals of formation. Formation personnel, and the people being formed, collaborate in achieving this goal. At the end of one of his parables, Jesus asked a question that seems appropriate to our situation:

"Have you understood all this?" They answered, "Yes." And he said to them, "Therefore every scribe who has been trained for the kingdom of heaven is like the master of a

household who brings out of his treasure what is new and what is old.

Matthew 13:51-52

2. The Secular Franciscan Order holds a special place in this family circle. It is an organic union of all Catholic fraternities scattered throughout the world and open to every group of the faithful. In these fraternities the brothers and sisters, led by the Spirit, strive for perfect charity in their own secular state. By their profession they pledge themselves to live the gospel in the manner of Saint Francis by means of this rule approved by the Church.

4. The Holy See has entrusted the pastoral care and spiritual assistance of the SFO, because it belongs to the same spiritual family, to the Franciscan First Order and Third Order Regular (TOR). These are the "Institutes" who are responsible for the "altius moderamen," referred to by Canon 303 of the Code of Canon Law

5. The Secular Franciscan Order is a public association in the Church. It is divided into fraternities at various levels: local, regional, national, and international. Each one has its own juridical personality within the Church.

Constitutions - article 1.4, 1.5

The term *altius moderamen* points to the responsibility that the First Order/TOR assume in relationship to the SFO. They receive, from the Church, the *vital life-giving union* with the SFO through accepting the *altius moderamen* (assistance, concern, and care) for the Secular Franciscan Order.

2. Their secularity, with respect to vocation and to apostolic life, expresses itself according to the respective state, that is:

+ *for the laity, contributing to building up the Kingdom of God by their presence in their life-situations and in their temporal activities.*

+ *for the secular clergy, by offering to the people of God the service which is properly theirs, in communion with the bishop and the presbytery.*

Both are inspired by the gospel options of St. Francis of Assisi, committing themselves to continue his mission with the other components of the Franciscan Family.

3. The vocation to the SFO is a vocation to live the Gospel in fraternal communion. For this purpose, the members of the SFO gather in ecclesial communities which are called fraternities.

<u>Constitutions</u> - article 3.2, 3.3

We have written about the Franciscan Order being a family. We have written about conversion and penance being an important part of our life. We have written that a continuing radical interior change is needed to fulfill our understanding of the meaning of conversion.

Article #2 of the SFO Rule has a little phrase that reiterates what we have been saying. It reads: ... *the brothers and sisters, led by the Spirit,* ***strive for perfect charity*** *in their own secular state.* It would be difficult to find a more demanding phrase.

It requires not just a little love now and then; or to show charity by writing checks to the poor; or an occasional show of charity to family or friends or the poor. It asks for *perfect charity*! Perfect charity requires a lot. It allows free reign for the Spirit to reveal the need for conversion in our personal lives. To achieve this goal requires self-knowledge and reflection and the power of the Holy Spirit.

"You have heard that it was said, 'You shall love your neighbor and hate your enemy.' "But I say to you, Love your enemies and pray for those who persecute you, so that you may be children of your Father in heaven; for he makes his sun to rise on the evil and on the good, and sends rain on the righteous and the unrighteous. For if you love those who love you, what reward do you have? Do not even tax collectors do the same? And if you greet only your brothers

*and sisters, what more are you doing than others? Do not even the Gentiles do the same? Be perfect, therefore, as your heavenly Father is perfect.**

Matthew 5:43-48

Luke repeats similar words in his Gospel.

But I say to you that listen, Love your enemies, do good to those who hate you, bless those who curse you, pray for those who abuse you. If anyone strikes you on the cheek, offer the other also; and from anyone who takes away your coat do not withhold even your shirt. Give to everyone who begs from you; and if anyone takes away your goods, do not ask for them again. Do to others as you would have them do to you. If you love those who love you, what credit is that to you? For even sinners love those who love them. If you do good to those who do good to you, what credit is that to you? For even sinners do the same. If you lend to those from whom you hope to receive, what credit is that to you? Even sinners lend to sinners, to receive as much again. But love your enemies, do good and lend, expecting nothing in return. Your reward will be great and you will be children of the Most High; for he is kind to the ungrateful and the wicked. Be merciful, just as your Father is merciful.

Luke 6:27-36

If you still think your charity is perfect you haven't been listening. This is demanding material. It is part of the Gospel we Franciscans profess to follow. If these texts are not enough commentary on perfect charity, consider these often quoted words of St. Paul.

If I give away all my possessions, and if I hand over my body so that I may boast, but do not have love, I gain nothing. Love is patient; love is kind; love is not envious or boastful or arrogant or rude. It does not insist on its own way; it is not irritable or resentful; it does not rejoice

---

* The Revised English Bible (REB) translation: *There must be no limit to your goodness as your heavenly Father's goodness knows no bounds.*

in wrongdoing, but rejoices in the truth. It bears all things, believes all things, hopes all things, endures all things. Love never ends.

1 Corinthians 13:3-8

Scripture is clear about the extent of *perfect charity.* We realize our need for the power of the Holy Spirit to keep striving for *perfect charity.* Profession in the SFO moves us to embrace a gospel way of life filled with *perfect charity.*

+++

3. The present rule, succeeding the "Memoriale Propositi" (1221) and the rule approved by the Supreme Pontiffs Nicholas IV and Leo XIII, adapts the Secular Franciscan Order to the needs and expectations of the Holy Church in the conditions of changing times. Its interpretation belongs to the Holy See and its application will be made by the General Constitutions and particular statutes.

This text gives an insight into authority within the Secular Franciscan Order. The Rule of 1289 (Nicolas IV) and 1883 (Leo XIII) found ways to adapt the SFO Rule to changing times. The Rule of 1978 (Paul VI) does the same. The Constitutions offer a commentary on the Rule of 1978.

1. The SFO is governed by the universal law of the Church, and by its own: the Rule, the Constitutions, the Ritual, and the particular statutes.

2. The Rule establishes the nature, purpose, and spirit of the SFO.

3. Rule 3 *The Constitutions have as their purpose:*
- *to apply the Rule;*
- *to indicate concretely the conditions for belonging to the SFO, its government, the organization of life in fraternity, and its seat* (office locale).

Constitutions - article 4.1, 4.2, 4.3

1. Rule 3 *The authentic interpretation of the Rule and of the Constitutions belongs to the Holy See.*

2. The practical interpretation of the Constitutions, with the purpose of harmonizing its application in different areas and at the various levels of the Order, belong to the General Chapter of the SFO.

3. The clarification of specific points which require a timely decision is the competency of the Presidency of the International Council of the SFO (CIOFS). *Such a clarification is valid until the next General Chapter.*

Constitutions - article 5.1, 5.2, 5.3

1. The international fraternity of the SFO has its own statutes approved by the General Chapter.

2. National fraternities have their own statutes approved by the Presidency of the International Council of the SFO.

3. The regional and the local fraternities may have their own statutes approved by the council of the higher level.

Constitutions - article 6.1, 6.2, 6.3

Then Jesus called the twelve together and gave them power and authority over all demons and to cure diseases, and he sent them out to proclaim the kingdom of God and to heal. He said to them, 'Take nothing for your journey, no staff, nor bag, nor bread, nor money - not even an extra tunic. Whatever house you enter, stay there, and leave from there. Wherever they do not welcome you, as you are leaving that town shake the dust off your feet as a testimony against them. They departed and went through the villages, bringing the good news and curing diseases everywhere.

Luke 9:1-6

Scripture points out that the authority to proclaim the good news comes from Jesus. It does not depend on how much bread we have, nor what we wear, nor how much money we have, nor our extra clothing. The power comes from Jesus and the Holy Spirit. Franciscans trust the Trinity to provide what we need. We have a sense of poverty, realizing our dependence on the Trinity. The authority we have is God-given and does not come from ourselves.

I did not come to be served, but to serve, says the Lord. (Matthew 20:28) *Let those who are placed over others boast about that position as much as they would if they were assigned the duty of washing the feet of the brothers. And if they are more upset at having their place over others taken away from them than at losing their position at their feet, the more they store up a money bag to the peril of their soul.*
Admonition IV - Francis of Assisi - The Saint - Vol I - Page 130

The connection between the various articles of the SFO Rule is important. The various articles of the Rule spell out our way of life. Though we may feel more comfortable with one or the other article, none can be neglected. *Profession* commits us to the whole Rule not just portions of it. *How* we implement particular articles may differ, but none of them can be neglected. Our vocation requires us to be faithful to the entire Rule.

+++

Readings/Questions for dialogue

Saved in Hope - (*Spe Salvi)*
Benedict XVI - Paragraph 27

The Church in the Modern World - (*Gaudium et Spes)*
Vatican II - Paragraph 34-35

Dogmatic Constitution on the Church - *(Lumen Gentium)*
Vatican II - Paragraph 42

1. How do you see yourself *striving for perfect charity* in your secular state? How does it look? What will you do that differs from any of your present practices?

2. What do you understand by the term "fraternity life?" How would you practice it at the regular gathering? Between gatherings?

3. Explain the various levels of authority in the SFO. What responsibilities do they have? (Cf. Chapter 2 - page 11ff)

4. Why is it important for Franciscans to realize their closeness to the Church? How does this show itself?

5. How did the scripture texts in this chapter challenge you?

6. Explain the role the constitutions and statutes play in the life of a secular Franciscan.

7. Explain how the three Franciscan Orders are a "family."

8. Scripture reflection: Ephesians 3:14-21. How do Paul's words flavor our Franciscan *striving for perfect charity?* Where does our power to love find its source?

+++

We need to respect the human dignity of every person. Governments and all other social institutions should serve and enhance the dignity of people. Society has the responsibility to create the conditions that favor the growth of virtues and of authentic spiritual and material values.

... Political authority should be used for the common good. "The common good comprises 'the sum total of social conditions which allow people ... to reach their fulfillment more fully and easily'" (CCC, no.1924, citing GS, no 26 paragraph 1).

... Just as governments and social institutions need to respect the unique human dignity of every individual, it is also the responsibility of every individual to do the same. Attitudes of prejudice and bias against any individual for any reason, as well as actions or judgments based on prejudiced or biased views, violate God's will and law.

<u>*United States Catholic Catechism for Adults*</u>
USCCB - Page 326

Chapter twelve

A focus on Christ

SFO Rule - Chapter two

4. The rule and life of the Secular Franciscans is this; to observe the gospel of our Lord Jesus Christ by following the example of Saint Francis of Assisi, who made Christ the inspiration and the center of his life with God and people.

Christ, the gift of the Father's love, is the way to him, the truth to which the Holy Spirit leads us, and the life which he has come to give abundantly.

Secular Franciscans should devote themselves especially to careful reading of the gospel, going from gospel to life and life to the gospel.

Thomas said to him, "Lord, we do not know where you are going. How can we know the way?" Jesus said to him, "I am the way, and the truth, and the life. No one comes to the Father except through me. If you know me, you will know my Father also. From now on you do know him and have seen him ... The words I say to you I do not speak on my own; but the Father who dwells in me does his works. Believe me that I am in the Father and the Father is in me."

John 14:5-7, 10-11

Jesus was frequently called a teacher (in Hebrew, Rabbi). Jesus taught about God as his Father and the Father of all human beings. He taught about his Father's mercy and forgiveness of sin. He taught about the Kingdom that his Father was establishing, a Kingdom where justice and love conquer injustice and hatred. He taught about himself as the Servant of God, sent by the Father to bring about conversion, even by the sacrifice of his own life.

Jesus also taught his disciples how they were to live in order to achieve the fullness of life and happiness that is God's will for all people. He did this by his own way of life and by his words. His teaching flowed from the tradition of ancient Israel but he also deepened that teaching and perfected it.

United States Catholic Catechism for Adults - USCCB - Page 307

Franciscans realize that Jesus Christ is the heart of our faith. Through Jesus we come to know the Trinity. Through Jesus we are given the way to live our lives. Through Jesus we find forgiveness. Through Jesus we find wisdom as he sends the Holy Spirit to us. Through Jesus we discover the wonder of a trinitarian relationship among all people. Through Jesus we learn the ways of the Father. Through Jesus we are saved. To say that Jesus has primacy in our lives is what I sometimes call a "throckmorton," i.e. *hot pursuit of the obvious.* Additionally, Jesus sought to bring people together in a community founded on love.

This communitarian character is perfected and fulfilled in the work of Jesus Christ, for the word made flesh willed to take his place in the human society. ... In revealing the Father's love and humanity's sublime calling, he made use of the most ordinary things of social life and illustrated his words with expressions and imagery from everyday life. He sanctified those human ties, above all family ties, which are the basis of social structures. ...

In his preaching he clearly described an obligation on the part of the daughters and sons of God to treat each other as sisters and brothers.

The Church in the Modern World *(Gaudium et Spes)* - Paragraph 32

Among other things, it is important for Franciscans to understand our theology about why Jesus came among us. The Incarnation, i.e. *God coming among us in Jesus*, was the result of God's love for us. Another theology in the Church speaks of this action of God as a result of the sin of Adam and Eve. Both theologies are legitimate. But Franciscans believe that since the nature of God is LOVE, the actions of God flow from that love. Hence, we believe that Jesus came among us because God desired to be with the people he loved and the earth God created. Sin does not dictate to God. We believe that God's love prompted his coming among us in Jesus.

Jesus is the human expression of God's love. Jesus makes visible the God who is always in love with us and wants to be with us. While it is true that Jesus also saves us from sin, Franciscans believe that the primary reason for the Incarnation is God's love, not people's sin.

We do not believe that sin is the catalyst for what God does. Rather we believe that love, the heart of the Trinity, is the reason for God sending Jesus to earth. God isn't a god waiting to catch us in sin. God is always looking for ways to bring us to gospel ways of acting if we sin. God is not patiently waiting to punish us for our sins. Rather, God looks for ways to free us from sin and experience the joy of unity with God through Jesus and the Holy Spirit.

We have Friar John Duns Scotus to thank for developing this theology. He believed that since God's nature is love, it would be impertinent on our part to give sin the power to dictate to God. Only God's love directs God's actions. Thus the Incarnation becomes the great act of God's love for us. For the same reason, God took the action of Incarnation to show what love can accomplish. Jesus did not back away from death on the cross. Love does not stop when the going gets tough. The cross becomes a clear sign of the extent of God's love for us. Francis recognized God's love in everything Jesus said and did.

It is a privilege to discover our way of life in the Gospel. Without a knowledge of the Gospel we could easily lose our way. The SFO Rule is clear about that. It calls for a careful reading of the gospel. How can we observe the Gospel unless we read it and absorb its spirit? Coupled with our reading is a sensitivity to the guidance of the community called Church. That is why Francis sought the approval of Pope Innocent III. Whatever Francis said and did he desired to proclaim the Kingdom of God and not the kingdom of Francis.

St. Jerome said: *Ignorance of the Scriptures is ignorance of Christ.* But when we read the Scriptures we are also listeners. It is imperative to listen to what the Bible is saying to us. We recognize Jesus as the *Word*-made-flesh as well as the *word*-revealed in scripture. Reading and listening are combined in one faith-action.

Our culture does poorly at teaching us to be good listeners. Talking is what we do well - on cell phones, and a plethora of technical tools that keep us "in touch." Television offers some of the same - people who talk at each other or at the same time while no one listens. There seems to be a sense that each speaker has the right ideas and opinions - and no one can shut them up and invite them to listen!

We are bombarded by advertisements about items we *must* buy *to be happy* - until we run out of money. But all this chatter may not help us learn how to listen with an open heart. Conversations are not always learning tools. We can be like railroad tracks, side-by-side but never together. I may prepare my rebuttal while someone is talking - and listening loses. Searching Scripture to support cemented opinions means we no longer listen but hear with a closed mind. We are selective in what we choose to hear.

To be a good listener is difficult when a speaker is boring, opinionated, or says the same thing again and again. Sharing the *good news* requires good content and passionate faith! Excitement about scripture/Jesus requires refreshing *ongoing formation.* We need a passionate love of Jesus and the Bible. Nor should our sharing be a monologue. We desire not only to share the *good news,* but also to establish some level of relationship with our listeners. One responsibility comes from our Trinitarian spirituality. The other comes from the richness and power of the scriptural word.

The Catholic Bible has 27 books in the New Testament and

46 books in the Old Testament (Sometimes called the Hebrew Testament). Protestant Bibles have only 39 books in the Old Testament. The seven books excluded from the Protestant Bible are *Tobit, Judith, 1 & 2 Maccabees, Wisdom, Sirach and Baruch* (apocrypha). More important, however, is the fact that the Bible offers God's word in the dialogue we have with God. Jesus teaches us what we need to know and do to achieve union with the Trinity and one another.

In October of 2008, 253 bishops gathered in Rome for a synod devoted to *The Word of God in the Life and Mission of the Church.* Cardinal Quellet of Quebec, Canada, compared Mary's dialogue at the annunciation as a model of dialogue with God (Luke 1:26-38). After the dialogue with God's angel Mary responded to God's word with a faith filled "Yes." Her dialogue with God's messenger was friendly, confident and prayerful. She asked questions and was able to accept the answers. What God did in her life was agreeable to her no matter how difficult it came to be. The Cardinal invites us to regard the Bible not as a textbook but as communication from God worthy of reflective time. (Cf. Catholic News Service - 10-9-2008)

I know what it is to have little, and I know what it is to have plenty. In any and all circumstances I have learned the secret of being well fed and of going hungry, of having plenty and of being in need. I can do all things ***through him who strengthens me.***

Philippians 4:12-13

As we focus on the biblical word it reminds us of the path we are called to walk. The Gospels speak to us of Jesus' words and works. They call us to follow the words and the Word as our way to build the Kingdom of God. To ignore the Gospel would be to miss the message and person of Jesus. We explore the letters of Paul, James, Peter, John, Jude and other writers to find reflections on Jesus, his words and works, and what the message means for us.

Blessed be the God and Father of our Lord Jesus Christ,

who has blessed us in Christ with every spiritual blessing in the heavenly places, just as he chose us in Christ before the foundation of the world to be holy and blameless before him in love. He destined us for adoption as his children through Jesus Christ, according to the good pleasure of his will, to the praise of his glorious grace that he freely bestowed on us in the Beloved In him we have redemption through his blood, the forgiveness of our trespasses, according to the riches of his grace that he lavished on us. With all wisdom and insight he has made known to us the mystery of his will, according to his good pleasure that he set forth in Christ, as a plan for the fullness of time, to gather up all things in him, things in heaven and things on earth.

Ephesians 1:3-10

The Franciscan Rule points the way for us to fulfill God's desire for us. The SFO Constitutions point out the importance of gospel study.

2. Rule 4.3 *The Secular Franciscan, committed to following the example and the teachings of Christ, must personally and assiduously study the Gospel and Sacred Scripture. The fraternity and its leaders should foster love for the word of the Gospel and help the brothers and sisters to know and understand it as it is proclaimed by the Church with the assistance of the Spirit.*

Constitutions - article 9.2

Hence, in sacred scripture, without prejudice to God's truth and holiness, the marvelous "condescension" of eternal wisdom is plain to be seen, "that we may come to know the ineffable loving-kindness of God and see for ourselves the thought and care he has given to accomodating his language to our nature." Indeed the words of God, expressed in human language, are in every way like human speech, just as the Word of the eternal Father, when he took on himself the weak flesh of human beings, became like them.

On Divine Revelation *(Dei Verbum)* - Vatican II - Paragraph 13

Franciscans face the task of linking scripture and the life and words of Jesus to their own lives. Moreover, we rely on the Holy Spirit to continue to teach us what we need to know. *When the Spirit of truth comes, he will guide you into all the truth ...* (John 16:13). We cannot escape the message of scripture nor the model that Jesus gives. Francis understood the primacy of Jesus and sought to imitate what he saw in and heard from Jesus.

The people of God believe that it is led by the Spirit of the Lord who fills the whole world. Impelled by that faith, they try to discern the true signs of God's presence and purpose in the events, the needs and the desires which it shares with the rest of humanity today. For faith casts a new light on everything and makes known the full ideal which God has set for humanity, thus guiding the mind towards solutions that are fully human.

The Church in the Modern World *(Gaudium et Spes)*
Vatican II - Paragraph 11

The Church believes that Christ, who died and was raised for the sake of all, can show people the way and strengthen them through the Spirit so that they become worthy of their destiny; nor is there given any other name under heaven by which they can be saved.

Ibid - Paragraph 10

You will notice, as we go through the SFO Rule, that Jesus is pointed out again and again as the model to be followed. Franciscans have no trouble in seeing that Jesus Christ is important for us. Jesus teaches us about the Father and the Holy Spirit. Jesus guides our way through his sharing of words and works. Jesus shows both a tender compassion and a faith-filled strength in responding to his Father's will. Jesus chooses his Father's way even when he is free to make other choices. The relationship with the Father and the Spirit is too vital to allow any choice to diminish the relationship. The impact of Jesus continues to guide us in the truth, the way to live and the path to follow.

Unless there had been something extraordinary in what

happened, unless the person and the words of Jesus radically surpassed the hopes and expectations of the time, there is no way to explain why he was crucified or why he made such an impact. As early as twenty or so years after Jesus' death, the great Christ-hymn of the Letter to the Philippians (Cf. Phil 2:6-11) *offers us a fully developed Christology stating that Jesus was equal to God, but emptied himself, became man, and humbled himself to die on the Cross, and that to him now belongs the worship of all creation, the adoration that God, through the Prophet Isaiah, said was due to him alone.* (Cf. Isaiah 45:23)

Jesus of Nazareth - Benedict XVI - *Foreword* - Page xxii

St. Paul's words to the Philippians (Philippians 2:6-11) might have been written by Francis. The poverty and humility of the crib and the cross meant that Jesus chose to come among us in an ordinary, human way. He does not have a retinue preparing the way like a king might have. In his death he does not appear powerful and domineering. In both cases he is faithful to the will of the Father and the guidance of the Holy Spirit. The trinitarian relationship called forth a faithfulness in Jesus that reveals what poverty is all about, i.e. a willingness to be faithful to a relationship no matter the cost. *Christ, the gift of the Father's love, is the way to him, the truth into which the Holy Spirit leads us, and the life which he has come to give abundantly* (SFO Rule #4).

Jesus welcomes sinners. Francis did the same. Jesus did not let man-made laws interfere with the mission he received from his Father. Francis moved ahead when human laws tried to confine him. Jesus invited his disciples to avoid getting bogged down with "things" that could hinder their ministry. Francis made the same choice through his love for Lady Poverty. Jesus preached forgiveness of enemies. Francis invited his followers to do the same. Jesus often went to quiet places to pray. Francis went to his caves and La Verna to spend time with God. Jesus could be strong in the face of authorities who abused God's plan. Francis followed a similar path in inviting his beloved Church to show a gospel face. Through his death and resurrection

Jesus gives us hope that new life is possible. Francis gave a similar example with a spirit that welcomed Sister Death.

When Jesus speaks in his parables of the shepherd who goes after the lost sheep, or of the woman who looks for the lost coin, or the father who goes to meet and embrace his prodigal son, these are no mere words: they constitute an explanation of his very being and activity. His death on the Cross is the culmination of that turning of God against himself in which he gives himself in order to raise man up and save him. This is love in its most radical form.
God is Love *(Deus Caritus Est)* - Benedict XVI - Paragraph 12

As we continue reflecting on the SFO Rule, keep in mind what we wrote here. Building the Kingdom of God takes planning and faith, courage and gentleness, understanding and compassion. Our task is to offer the world an example, in our lives, of what the Kingdom of God looks like. To achieve that goal draws us to Scripture and to Jesus. The values and qualities that Christians should imitate require the energy and power that the Holy Spirit brings to our lives. It becomes obvious that we cannot achieve the goal without the Holy Spirit ... *for the Mighty one has done great things for me and holy is his name* (Luke 1:49).

+++

Seeking to encounter
the living and active person
of Christ

"May they all be one, Father,
may they be one in us as you are in me
and I am in you. So that the world
may believe that it was you who sent me."
This is one sign that Christ-is-with-us.
That we are one with Jesus,
and one with each other,
always!

We are back to fundamentals -
Francis and the Gospel and the words:
"Without me you can do nothing!"

Unity with Jesus is important.
It is as important as
volunteer organizations, day-care centers,
new cars, political organizations,
big churches, well-knit fraternities,
two TV sets, the latest technology,
a new hair-do or fine clothes,
a motorcycle or a great date,
or other friends, or more possessions.

Franciscans know
deep inside where it counts,
that Jesus is #1 in their lives.
"Without me you can do nothing"
for you, for your brother or sister,
for your world, for anyone.

So, your response
to encountering Jesus
and being united with him
is a wholehearted
Franciscan "YES!"

Readings/Questions for dialogue

SFO Constitutions
Articles 10 & 11

Dogmatic Constitution on the Church
Lumen Gentium - Paragraph 42

Francis of Assisi - The Saint - Vol 1
Admonition 1 - Page 128-129

1. Why is Jesus important in the life of a Franciscan? What motive brought Jesus to earth in the Incarnation?

2. What attitude/spirit are we expected to have when we read or listen to readings from the Bible?

3. List the qualities a good listener needs to have. What qualities should she/he avoid?

4. Why does the profession of a Franciscan life take priority in the lives of Franciscans?

5. How can fraternity members assist in building up a vibrant fraternity life? List the ways and means!

6. Why did Jesus feel so strongly about unity within the people of God? How can it be achieved?

7. Name some of the qualities of people who live in the Kingdom of God. Illustrate some of the contrasts between these qualities and the qualities we often see in the world around us (or in ourselves?).

8. Scripture reflection: Philippians 2: 1-11. What do these words of St. Paul mean to you? How do they apply to a Franciscan's idea of poverty and humility?

Chapter thirteen

Encounters with Jesus

5. Secular Franciscans, therefore, should seek to encounter the living and active person of Christ in their brothers and sisters, in Sacred Scripture, in the Church, and in liturgical activity. The faith of Saint Francis, who often said: "I see nothing bodily of the Most High Son of God in this world except his most holy body and blood," should be the inspiration and pattern of their Eucharistic life.

We must always give thanks to God for you, brothers and sisters, as is right, because your faith is growing abundantly, and the love of every one of you for one another is increasing. Therefore we ourselves boast of you among the churches of God for your steadfastness and faith during all your persecutions and the afflictions that you are enduring.

2 Thessalonians 1:3-4

In our prayers for you we always thank God, the Father of our Lord Jesus Christ, for we have heard of your faith in Christ Jesus and of the love that you have for all the saints, because of the hope laid up for you in heaven. You have heard of this hope before in the word of the truth, the gospel that has come to you. Just as it is bearing fruit and growing in the whole world, so it has been bearing fruit among yourselves from the day you heard it and truly comprehended the grace of God.

Colossians 1: 3-6

No longer is it a question, then, of a "commandment" imposed from without and calling for the impossible, but rather of a freely-bestowed experience of love from within, a love which by its very nature must then be shared with others. Love grows through love. Love is "divine" because it comes from God and unites us to God; through this unifying process it makes us a "we" which transcends our divisions and makes us one, until in the end God is "all in all." (1 Corinthians 15:28)

God is Love *(Deus Caritas Est)* - Benedict XVI - Paragraph 18

In order *to encounter the living and active person of Christ* we need to be intimate with Jesus. If our connection to Jesus is minimal or weak, seeing Christ in others will be difficult. If our relationship with Jesus is fragile, it will be difficult to maintain a consistent awareness of Jesus' presence in others. This article of the rule connects to article #8 which speaks of *prayer and contemplation as the soul of all they* (we) *are and do*. It is difficult to see the person of Christ in others without awareness of his presence in us. Our awareness may not be perfect but it must be growing.

Article #5 of the Rule invites us to encounter Christ:
+ in our brothers and sisters;
+ in Sacred Scripture;
+ in the Church;
+ in liturgical activity.

Let's examine what each of these encounters might require.

... in our brothers and sisters. We understand that this simple statement leaves no one out of the circle of people in whom we recognize the *living and active person of Christ*. Our more difficult task is to discover "how" to recognize Christ in everyone.

Many of us do not necessarily fit the image of the *living and active person of Christ*. Self-knowledge tells us about our imperfections. We are not perfect and it may be difficult for others to recognize Christ in us. Other people may have similar faults and failings that fuzzy the image of Christ in them. Sometimes it seems to be totally hidden. Sometimes people may look more evil than good; or more disgusting than attractive; or more criminal than law-abiding; or do things that are more puzzling and crude than understandable and gentle. Any one of us could tell stories about how difficult it can be to recognize Christ in someone.

Our task is to find a way to override the disguises that hide the image of Christ. Perhaps we are looking in the wrong direction. Perhaps it is not achieved by looking at the person in front of us. Instead, we may need to look at ourselves.

St. Francis recognized how much God loved him. The more this became clear to him the more his whole person responded to the movement of the Holy Spirit in his life. Francis, in this sense, was never alone. God infiltrated the whole of Francis' life. As Francis grew intimate with Jesus and the Father and the Holy Spirit he came more readily to an acceptance of others.

It may be that seeing Christ in others begins by our awareness of Christ in us. As this becomes our natural situation the Holy Spirit prompts us to recognize the Christ in others no matter how well it is hidden. If all of creation is made in the image of God our experience of this loving God within us will move us to recognize the hidden Christ in others.

Francis was grounded in Christ. Francis identified with Christ. Francis put on the mind of Christ. Nothing and no one could diminish Francis' ability to recognize his beloved Jesus in robbers and sinful friars and men and women who were dominated by desires contrary to God's love. From his heart of compassion and love, Francis saw their deep need of God. He reached out with God's love, which dwelt within his own heart, to touch the unknown yearning in the heart of the other.

In the beginning was the Word, and the Word was with God, and the Word was God. He was in the beginning with God. All things came into being through him, and without him not one thing came into being. What has come into being in him was life, and that life was the light of all people.

The light shines in the darkness, and the darkness did not overcome it.

... And the Word became flesh and lived among us, and we have seen his glory, the glory as of a father's only son, full of grace and truth. ... From his fullness we have all received, grace upon grace. No one has ever seen God. It is God's only Son, who is close to the Father's heart, who has made him known.

John 1:1-5, 14-18

Henri Nouwen, in his book, *Reaching Out* (Image books - Page 66), offers a simple direction. When we meet the "other" in our lives, and label him/her as an enemy, our heart must change from suspicion to welcoming, from hostility to hospitality. Creating an atmosphere of hospitality offers the "other" a safe place to speak about what is in his or her heart. The enemy becomes a guest. Our attitude (love) creates a place where brotherhood and sisterhood can be experienced. If it takes persistent hospitality over a long period, that is what we offer.

This is not easy to do. But we do not empower ourselves to complete this task. Rather, we become more and more aware that our personal conversion is the work of the Holy Spirit. Our task is to respond to the Holy Spirit who, in these cases, inspires us to show the kind of hospitality needed by this "other" who stands before us.

For all who are led by the Spirit of God are children of God. For you did not receive a spirit of slavery to fall back into fear, but you have received a spirit of adoption. When we cry "Abba, Father!" it is that very Spirit bearing witness with our spirit that we are children of God, and if children, then heirs, heirs of God and joint heirs with Christ - if, in fact, we suffer with him so that we may also be glorified with him.

Romans 8:14-17

This perspective offers one way to develop a welcoming spirit for our brothers and sisters. Establishing this kind of atmosphere allows us to hear the "other" and allows them to experience acceptance. As the relationship grows, we influence each other. We recognize the living and active person of Christ in others. It is realistic rather than naive.

Prayer and contemplation are a resource for developing this spirit. Personal experiences with people we consider an "enemy" make it clear that we need the help of the Holy Spirit to be hospitable. As Henri Nouwen puts it, hospitality should not be limited to welcoming the stranger. It is a fundamental attitude towards "others" that can be expressed in many ways *(Cf. Reaching Out* - Page 66-67). In our world the stranger can be more threat than friend. Our fear and hostility can touch us not only when someone is a threat but also when he/she is a competitor. The reasons for hostility and suspicion are multiple.

The motivation for hospitality is not in order to change people. It offers a space where change can take place but it is not agressively pursuing conversion in the other. Friendship offers the other a safe space of freedom and acceptance. It diminishes the dividing lines between us. Options are possible for the "other" when we create this atmosphere. It is no easy task and success is not guaranteed. It requires personal growth and the recognition of the wide parameters of love. The Holy Spirit is the change agent.

The word that came to Jeremiah from the Lord: "Come, go down to the potter's house, and there I will let you hear my words." So I went down to the potter's house, and there he was working at his wheel. The vessel he was making of clay was spoiled in the potter's hand, and he reworked it into another vessel, as seemed good to him.

Then the word of the Lord came to me: "Can I not do with you, O House of Israel, just as the potter has done?" says the Lord. "Just like clay in the potter's hand, so are you in my hand, O house of Israel."

Jeremiah 18:1-6

... in Sacred Scripture. Finding the active person of Jesus

Christ in Scripture is faith-filled. We accept the inspiration of Scripture. We accept the Gospels as a record of Jesus' life and teaching. We are dedicated to the Bible as the word of God. In Scripture God speaks to us. We respond by implementing biblical teaching in our lives.

The Church recognizes two senses of Scripture, the literal and the spiritual. In probing the literal meaning of the texts, it is necessary to determine their literary form, such as history, hymns, wisdom sayings, poetry, parable, or other forms of figurative language.

... The spiritual sense of Sacred Scripture derive from the unity of God's plan of salvation. The text of Scripture discloses God's plan. The realities and events of which it speaks can also be signs of the divine plan. There are three spiritual senses of Scripture:

1. *The allegorical sense. We can acquire a more profound understanding of events by recognizing their significance in Christ; thus the crossing of the Red Sea is a sign or type of Christ's victory over sin and also of Christian Baptism.*
2. *The moral sense. The events reported in Scripture ought to lead us to act justly. As St. Paul says, they were written "for our instruction."* (1 Cor 10:11).
3. *The anagogical sense. ... We can view realities and events in terms of their eternal significance, leading us toward our true homeland: thus the Church on earth is a sign of the heavenly Jerusalem* (CCC, no. 117).

The Church's Scripture scholars are expected to work according to these principles to develop a better understanding of Scripture for God's people. Interpretation of Scripture is ultimately subject to the judgment of the Magisterium, which exercises the divine commission to hold fast to and to interpret authoritively God's Word.

United States Catholic Catechism for Adults - USCCB - Page 27-28

Faith tells us that Jesus Christ is the fulness of revelation. The Gospels, in a special way, reveal the witness, preaching and writing for all people to hear, guided by the Holy Spirit. Our response to the revelation of Scripture is faith, giving ourselves entirely into God's hands.

The linkage between the way human authors express themselves and what God wants to express is important. Jesus Christ is at the center of the scriptural words. We keep this in mind as we interpret the Scriptures. Ralph Hodgson put it this way: *Some things have to be believed to be seen!*

We approach, with faith, our exploration of Scriptural texts. Faith opens the door to trusting God's word. When we need an official interpretation we approach the magisterium of the Church. The Scriptural words may bring a meaning very real to us individually. But personal interpretations must be in accord with faith and not contrary to it. We do not become solitary "experts" in interpreting Scripture.

We declare to you what was from the beginning, what we have heard, what we have seen with our eyes, what we have looked at and touched with our hands, concerning the word of life - this life was revealed, and we have seen it and testify to it, and declare to you the eternal life that was with the Father and was revealed to us - we declare to you what we have seen and heard so that you also may have fellowship with us; and truly our fellowship is with the Father and with his Son Jesus Christ. We are writing these things so that our joy may be complete.

This is the message we have heard from him and proclaim to you, that God is light and in him there is no darkness at all. If we say that we have fellowship with him while we are walking in darkness, we lie and do not do what is true; but if we walk in the light as he himself is in the light, we have fellowship with one another and the blood of Jesus his Son cleanses us from all sin.

1 John 1:1-7

Seeing Christ in Scripture requires listening to the words of Scripture and letting them speak to us of Jesus Christ.

... in the Church. Searching for the face of Jesus in the Church can be a demanding task. Since the Church has such large numbers of people, the human situation is strongly felt. Within the Church are people of all kinds of opinions, practices and ideas. Establishing a relationship with all of them can be problematic. Catholics are not a monolithic group with only one way of seeing things. Differences are common among us.

Our differences come from a variety of influences. A catholic home influences the way we think about faith and authority and prayer and many other issues. We may accept familial ideas and guidance or rebel against what seems to be arbitrary. We may be influenced by friends with acceptable religious ideas different from our own. We may be influenced by professors or editorials or security needs or lack of time to pursue issues surrounding our faith.

We are loyal to the hierarchy and do not feel free to think for ourselves. Scandals about church leaders or good catholic friends may sour us on the Church. Some educational institutions speak clearly about the faith while other institutions are judged as adversarial to our faith. Religious TV and radio programs can attract us because we agree with their theological opinions. But they proclaim only one of many opinions expressed within the Church.

You might add more situations in which you find yourselves in disagreement with "others" in the Catholic Church. The SFO Rule invites us to *encounter the person of Christ* in all these folks. Whether these people are in positions of authority or ordinary Catholics, Franciscans seek ways to relate to them. Instead of finding ways to prove the "other" wrong or misguided or practically non-catholic, or who are ignorant of church doctrine, Franciscans continue the effort to accept people where they are at. We seek a relationship through acceptance of the person whose opinions we find difficult to accept. That is not the same as agreeing with them. Rather, it is a way to create space for dialogue.

If I presume I am infallible I do not need dialogue - I act with arrogance. I may have a good memory for quoting "experts." That does not necessarily make my opinions completely true. It only means someone else agrees with me or I with them. Only a few dogmas have been infallibly proclaimed throughout the 2000 years of Church history. They are not frequently the topics of ordinary conversations.

Our goal is to create unity among the People of God. Even should we disagree we shall not make it a cause for separation. Franciscans desire to build relationships so that we can dialogue about differences without separating from one another. Dialogue may lead to conclusions more appropriate to our beliefs. Our ability to engage in dialogue leaves the way open for a common understanding that enhances our faith. At least that is our hope. Jesus prayed for unity among us (John 17: 20-21). Followers of Francis take Jesus' prayer seriously.

Father, the hour has come; glorify your Son that the Son may glorify you, since you have given him authority over all people, to give eternal life to all whom you have given him. And this is eternal life, that they may know you, the only true God, and Jesus Christ whom you have sent.

John 17: 1-2

In his *Earlier Rule* St. Francis shares these words with the brothers. They apply to the topic we are discussing and show how wide are the consequences of love.

Let them love one another, as the Lord says: "This is my commandment: love one another as I have loved you." (Cf. John 15:12). *Let them express the love they have for one another by their deeds, as the Apostle says: "Let us not love in word or speech, but in deed and truth"* (1 John 3:18}.

Let them revile no one. Let them not grumble or detract from others, for it is written: "Gossips and detractors are detestable to God (Cf. Romans 1:29). *Let them be modest by showing graciousness toward everyone"* (Cf. Titus 3:2). *Let them not judge or condemn.*

The Earlier Rule - Francis of Assisi - The Saint - Vol 1
Chapter XI - Page 72

... in liturgical activity. Liturgy is a particular portion of the Church's activity. It is meant to draw believers together in common praise of God, gratitude to God, petitions to God, and glory to God. It finds its most perfect expression in the Eucharist.

The sacred liturgy is not the Church's only activity. Before people can come to the liturgy they must be called to faith and conversion.

... Nevertheless, the liturgy is the summit toward which the activity of the church is directed; it is also the source from which all its power flows. For the goal of apostolic endeavor is that all who are made children of God by faith and Baptism should come together to praise God in the midst of the church, to take part in the sacrifice and to eat the Lord's supper.

Constitution on the Sacred Liturgy - Vatican II - Paragraph 9-10

Paragraph #12 of the *Constitution on the Sacred Liturgy* reminds us that the spiritual life is not limited to participation in the liturgy. Christians should pray with one another but they also need to pray to their Father in secret and pray without ceasing. Devotions should harmonize with the liturgical seasons and, in fact, lead people to liturgical prayer. (Cf. *Constitution on the Sacred Liturgy* - Paragraph 13). This goal recognizes that the heart of the liturgy is Jesus Christ. Devotions should lead believers to union with Jesus Christ. Jesus alone is our savior.

It seems natural that liturgical celebrations should deepen our relationship with Jesus. In turn, the power of the relationship (initiated by the Holy Spirit) should move us to gospel living in daily life. Liturgical celebrations are community actions that open us to God's love. While we certainly hope God is pleased with our liturgical prayer, weekday preface #4 gives us an insight into what happens.

Father, all-powerful and ever-living God, we do well always and everywhere to give you thanks.
You have no need of our praise,
yet our desire to thank you is itself your gift.
Our prayer of thanksgiving
adds nothing to your greatness,
but makes us grow in your grace,
through Jesus Christ our Lord.

The Rule acknowledges that we are in the presence of Jesus when we celebrate liturgical actions together. Our participation should be as dedicated as we can make it. What we receive at the Eucharistic liturgy is so rich that we do not keep it to ourselves. We become passionate to share the good news with everyone, always in appropriate ways.

The Spirit invoked by the celebrant upon the gifts of bread and wine placed on the altar is the same Spirit who gathers the faithful "into one body" and makes of them a spiritual offering pleasing to the Father.

Sacrament of Charity *(Sacramentum Caritatis)*
Benedict XVI - Paragraph 13

The mystery of the Eucharist inspires and impels us to work courageously within our world to bring about that renewal of relationships which has its inexhaustible source in God's gift. The prayer we repeat at every Mass: "Give us this day our daily bread," obliges us to do everything possible, in cooperation with international, state, and private institutions, to end or at least reduce the scandal of hunger and malnutrition afflicting so many millions of people in our world, especially in developing countries.

Ibid - Paragraph 91

A deepened relationship with Jesus is achieved through his presence in the Eucharistic liturgy, through the presence of

Jesus in the gathered community, and through his presence in the proclamation of the biblical word. Each contributes to an intimacy with Jesus inspired by the Holy Spirit. The final words of article #5 of the SFO Rule put it this way:

... *The faith of St. Francis, who often said, "I see nothing of the Most High Son of God in this world except his most holy body and blood," should be the inspiration and pattern of their Eucharistic life.*

SFO Rule - article #5

+++

Readings/Questions for dialogue

God is Love *(Deus Caritas Est)* - Benedict XVI
Paragraph 15

SFO Constitutions
Article 9.1 / 14.1

United States Catholic Catechism for Adults - USCCB
Pages 17-18 - *Doctrinal Statements / Meditation*

1. Please describe your personal experiences in discovering Jesus: in your brothers and sisters / in Scripture / in the Church / in liturgical activity.

2. What was most helpful in this chapter to assist your ability to fulfill article #5 of the SFO Rule?

3. Why do the requirements of article #5 of the SFO Rule also call for personal prayer?

4. What quality(s) did this chapter invite you to embrace in your relationship with the hierarchy of the Church?

5. What role does the believing community play in the Eucharistic liturgy?

6. What are some of the consequences for your life because

of your participation in the Eucharistic liturgy?

7. Scripture reflection: Hosea 2:6-20. How do these words in Hosea address issues that were part of this chapter? What does this text say to you about God's ways to draw people to himself and God's desire to relate to the lady in the text?

✚✚✚

The Church expects from
the Secular Franciscan Order,
one and only,
a great service in the cause of the
Kingdom of God in the world of today.
The Church desires that your Order
should be a model of organic,
structural and charismatic unity
on all levels,
so as to present itself to the world
as "a community of love."
The Church expects from you,
Secular Franciscans,
a courageous and consistent testimony
of Christian and Franciscan life,
leaning towards the construction
of a more fraternal and gospel world
for the realization of the Kingdom of God.

John Paul II - Address to the SFO
November 22, 2002

Chapter fourteen

a Rebuilding Task

6. They have been made living members of the Church by being buried and raised with Christ in baptism; they have been united more intimately with the Church by profession. Therefore, they should go forth as witnesses and instruments of her mission among all people, proclaiming Christ by their life and words.

Called like Saint Francis to rebuild the Church and inspired by his example, let them devote themselves energetically to living in full communion with the pope, bishops, and priests, fostering an open and trusting dialogue of apostolic effectiveness and creativity.

1. Rule 6 *Called to work together in building up the Church as the sacrament of salvation for all and, through their baptism and profession, made "witnesses and instruments of her mission," Secular Franciscans proclaim Christ by their life and words. Their preferred apostolate is personal witness in the environment in which they live and service for building up the Kingdom of God within the situations of this world.*

2. The preparation of the brothers and sisters for spreading the gospel message "in the ordinary circumstances of the world" and for collaborating in the catechesis within the eccelesial communities should be promoted in the fraternities.

3. Those who are called to carry out the mission of catechists, presiders of ecclesial communities, or other ministries, as well as the sacred ministers, should make the love of Francis for the Word of God their own, as well as his faith in those who announce it, and the great fervor with which he received the mission of preaching penance from the Pope.

4. Participation in the service of sanctification, which

the Church exercises through the liturgy, prayer, and works of penance and charity, is put into practice by the brothers and sisters above all in their own family, then in the fraternity and, finally, through their active presence in the local Church and in society.

Constitutions - article 17.1, 17.2, 17.3, 17.4

Baptism and profession are intimately connected. At baptism we are brought into the family of the People of God. Should parents be unable to do so, Godparents are given the responsibility to share the faith with their God-children. The Church considers parents the primary teachers of their children. Godparents offer a supportive role in sharing the faith and guiding children in that pursuit.

*In the ritual of baptism the community celebrates what God has done, is doing and will continue to do for the one who is being baptised.** God says to us: "You are my son or daughter." The Spirit touches the person being baptised and draws them to Jesus. Baptism is the first gift in a series of gifts by which God enters the life of the baptised. Baptism prepares us to to receive the loving touch of God called "grace." This free gift, and our readiness for the gifts that follow, reveals the love God has for us. It begins a spiritual journey that ends only when Sister Death calls us home.

There is a theology that focuses on baptism as freeing us from original sin. But it is of equal importance to realize that baptism also makes us a new creature loved by God. We might say it this way: *Not only does God freely give us grace but God also makes us a new creature. Being a new creature means that God has freely forgiven our sins.*** This theological view celebrates God's love in the baptismal action. God's love embraces us and thus frees us from sin. This fits our Franciscan theology about God's love and its power to touch and transform our lives.

To say *they have been united more intimately with the*

---

* *Sacramental Guidelines* - Kenan Osborn OFM - Page 47 / ** Page 58

Church by profession (SFO Rule - #6) carries the implication that we are called to deeper intimacy with Jesus through *profession.* We are loved by a God who gifts us with the call to follow the spirit of St. Francis of Assisi. It calls for a life that is faithful to the SFO Rule as our return gift to God, the Church, and the world.

A faithful response to this gift gives witness to God's love made present in Jesus Christ. Baptism and profession happen within the community of believers called "church." *Profession* reiterates the call to bring the good news to all people through our Franciscan lives. *Profession* entails an active, deliberate choice to be gospel persons, witnessing to the message of Jesus. The SFO Rule shows the way that Franciscans witness to God's call through their baptism and profession.

Why do you call me "Lord, Lord," and do not do what I tell you? I will show you what someone is like who comes to me, hears my words, and acts on them. That one is like a man building a house, who dug deeply and laid the foundation on rock; when a flood arose, the river burst against that house but could not shake it, because it had been well built. But the one who hears and does not act is like a man who built a house on the ground without a foundation. When the river burst against it, immediately it fell, and great was the ruin of that house.

Luke 6:46-49

The link between Baptism and profession shows that we are loyal people of the Church. We desire to belong to a church that reflects, in her actions, the values and ideals of the Gospel. When the Church (People of God) is faithful to her witness to the Gospel, our love for her blossoms. Should the Church fail to bear such witness, our love is even stronger. Francis and Clare illustrate this loyalty. They sensed the call of the Holy Spirit to follow a particular way of life. They would not be deterred from that call. They remained faithful to the call of the Spirit. Though it took decades to achieve, Clare finally received her "privilege of poverty" from the Pope. Clare remained respectful during this struggle with popes and bishops. She could not abandon the call of the Spirit without harming her relationship with God and his Son, Jesus. Francis acted likewise while seeking approval for his way of life. Their faithfulness to the call of the Holy Spirit brought new life to the Church.

The spirit of Francis and Clare illustrates how to live in *full communion with the pope, bishops, and priests.* But they also recognized the importance of *fostering an open and trusting dialogue of apostolic effectiveness and creativity.* They brought new life to the Church and helped to rebuild her by engaging in dialogue within the Church.

As is true in our personal lives, the human elements of the Church are regularly in need of renewal. I think both Francis and Clare intuitively understood that reality. Creative dialogue within the Church brings fresh insights and explanations to church life. Franciscans lovingly share fresh ideas about God's love. They share ways for people to understand the wonder of the Trinity's love for us and how to practice it in daily life.

I appreciate Benedict XVI's words in the foreward to his book: *Jesus of Nazareth.* He writes:

It goes without saying that this book is in no way an exercise of the magisterium, but is solely an expression of my personal search "for the face of the Lord" (Cf. Ps 27:8). *Everyone is free, then, to contradict me. I would only ask my readers for that initial* ***good will*** *without which there can be no understanding.*

Jesus of Nazareth - Benedict XVI - *Foreward* - Pages xxiii - xxiv

As we reflect the image of God in our personal lives, our attempts at renewal in the Church will show the same respect for one another that God shows towards us. Our approach to others in the Church, no matter who they may be, will be one of respect, reverence and love. It cannot be otherwise if we understand our trinitarian approach to life. Dialogue is our natural way to have conversations about common beliefs or common differences. Instead of creating a dominating atmosphere, Franciscans create a welcoming atmosphere of hospitality.

Franciscans engage in dialogue because they have much to learn. Dialogue means listening to people who hold similar or different ideas with a spirit of respect, reverence, and courtesy. Our understanding of the disagreement is clarified as we listen without being defensive. One gift we bring to dialogue is the realization that we are not infallible. We surrender manipulating the conclusion of the dialogue. We maintain a gentle, listening attitude that allows the conversation to develop in a healthy way.

If we still disagree when the dialogue is complete (for now), we will be true to our desire to maintain unity. Because the relationship remains firm we can engage in dialogue on another day. In the meantime we have been nourished by sharing ideas and opinions. It may prompt a change in our way of perceiving things or do the same in the "other."

When we engage in dialogue we surrender control of what the conclusion may be. Other Christians may approach differences in another manner. Franciscans accept the task of *fostering an open and trusting dialogue of apostolic effectiveness and creativity*. We do this with people in authority as well as with other people. The SFO Rule calls us to use this tool respectfully in conversations with others.

Done respectfully and with love, dialogue helps fulfill Christ's prayer for unity. It supports the attitude that trinitarian spirituality requires of Franciscans - to avoid actions that would separate us from one another. The book of Wisdom reflects on true wisdom. It offers reasons to seek the ways of Wisdom that comes from God.

I loved her (Wisdom) and sought her from my youth; I desired to take her for my bride, and became enamoured of her beauty. She glorifies her noble birth by living with God, and the Lord of all loves her. For she is an initiate in the knowledge of God, and an associate in his works. If riches are a desireable possession in life, what is richer than wisdom, the active cause of all things? And if understanding is effective, who more than she is fashioner of what exists? And if anyone loves righteousness, her labours are virtues; for she teaches self-control and prudence, justice and courage; nothing in life is more profitable to mortals than these. And if anyone longs for wide experience, she knows things of old, and infers the things to come; she understands turns of speech and the solution of riddles; she has foreknowledge of signs and wonders and of the outcome of seasons and times. Therefore, I determined to take her to live with me, knowing that she would give me good counsel and encouragement in cares and grief.

Wisdom 8:1-9

Jesus called himself *the light of the world* (John 8:12). This image reflects the wisdom image of the book of Wisdom. Jesus calls us to bond with him and receive the wisdom he received from the Father. Trinitarian wisdom (The Holy Spirit) guides us and is made known through Jesus.

Again Jesus spoke to them saying, "I am the light of the world. Whoever follows me will never walk in darkness but will have the light of life."

John 8:12

We keep returning to Jesus who is the love of God made visible among us. Jesus is the one who has the words of eternal life. Jesus is the one who deals with pharisees, tax collectors, lepers, the blind and adulterers, those in need of healing, a wedding couple needing to avoid embarassment, a good thief, his mother, the apostles, a Samaritan woman, his beloved John, Judas Iscariot, and Thomas who needed proof for his belief. He taught his message to crowds of people. He fed people who were hungry. He talked with Pilate, teaching him that Pilate's power came from God. In short, the gospels reveal Jesus' contact with ordinary people, with Roman authorities, with Jewish religious authorities and with his slow-learning disciples. In the midst of all this activity he spent time in solitude, communing with his Father.

For the moment, let us imagine the idea of re-building the church as a task of re-building faith in people, ourselves and others; rebuilding hope in people who feel betrayed and depressed (a not infrequent occurance); bringing love to people who only experience its shallow expression or are objects of hatred and violence by others.

In a spirit of hospitality we seek to diminish anger and resistence and sadness because we respect others. We break down barriers because we do not build personal walls to keep people out of our lives. We create a welcoming space so conversations can deal with tough issues without rancor, name-calling, disrespect, injustice, labeling people or a myriad of other things that keep us apart.

The more successful we are at creating hospitable space, the better we will be at re-building the Church. Respect and reverence are qualities that serve us well. That same hospitable space will welcome the Holy Spirit's inspiration.

... I pray that, according to the riches of his glory, he may grant that you may be strengthened in your inner being with power through his Spirit, and that Christ may dwell in your hearts through faith, as you are being rooted and grounded in love. I pray that you may have the power to comprehend, with all the saints, what is the breadth and length and height and depth, and to know the love of Christ that surpasses all knowledge so that you may be filled with all the fullness of God.

Now to him who by the power at work within us is able to accomplish abundantly far more than all we can ask or imagine, to him be glory in the church and in Christ Jesus to all generations, for ever and ever. Amen

Ephesians 3: 16-21

Readings/Questions for dialogue

Saved in Hope *(Spe Salvi)* - Benedict XVI
Paragraph 47

The Prayer Before the Crucifix
Francis of Assisi - The Saint - Vol 1 - Page 40

Imitation: Becoming what we love
Franciscan Prayer - Ilia Delio OSF
Page 147 - First two paragraphs

The goal of question #1 is to discover the conversion you need in your life as you "dialogue with a spirit of hospitality." How would you enter into conversations with others about issues important to you and them - even when you disagree? How would you maintain a good relationship?

1. Consider how you would find ways to dialogue with the following people (what YOU would do, not what you expect of others).

+ Traditionalists or Progressives.
+ Bishops or other hierarchical figures.
+ A pastor who functions poorly or well.
+ Legislators/heads of corporations/supervisors.
+ People who agree/disagree with you, even among family members.
+ Criminals.
+ Immigrants.
+ People whose theology differs from yours.
+ Stubborn and arrogant people.
+ People at work or people who question your passionate support of some issues.
+ Young people - Older people.
+ People who have hurt you in some way.
+ Add others as you wish.

2. How do you show loyalty to the Church, the People of God? Does it always look the same? If not, why does it change?

3. What qualities do Franciscans develop in order to open the door to good conversations/dialogue?

4. What insights about the Franciscan spirit did you learn in this chapter as you move toward *profession* in the SFO?

5. What is the connection between *baptism and profession*?

6. At present, how do you proclaim Christ by your life and words?

7. Scripture reflection. Isaiah 55: 1-11. What insights does this text offer you? How does this text relate to our call to be gospel people?

+++

You are called to give your own contribution, inspired by the person and message of St. Francis of Assisi, in speeding up the advent of a civilization in which the dignity of the human person, co-responsibility and love will be a living reality (Cf. Gaudium et Spes - 31ss). *You must deepen the true foundations of the world-wide fraternity and create everywhere the spirit of welcome and the atmosphere of brotherliness. Commit yourselves firmly against all forms of exploitation, discrimination, and marginalization and against all attitudes of indifference towards others.*

John Paul II - Address to the SFO 10th General Chapter
November 22, 2002

Chapter fifteen

Gospel, Conversion, and Reconciliation

7. United by their vocation as "brothers and sisters of penance," and motivated by the dynamic power of the Gospel, let them conform their thoughts and deeds to those of Christ by means of the radical interior change which the Gospel itself calls "conversion." Human frailty makes it necessary that this conversion be carried out daily.

On this road to renewal the sacrament of reconciliation is the privileged sign of the Father's mercy and the source of grace.

Let them love one another, as the Lord says: "This is my commandment: love one another as I have loved you" (John 15:12). *Let them express the love they have for one another by their deeds, as the Apostle says: "Let us not love in word or speech, but in deed and truth."* (1 John 3:18)

The Earlier Rule - Francis of Assisi - The Saint - Vol I
Chapter XI - Page 72

1. The Secular Franciscans commit themselves by their profession to live the Gospel according to Franciscan spirituality in their secular condition.

2. They seek to deepen, in the light of faith, the values and choices of the evangelical life according to the Rule of the SFO:

+ Rule 7 *in a continually renewed journey of conversion and of formation.*
+ Rule 4.3 *open to the challenges that come from society and from the Church's life situation, "going from Gospel to life and from life to Gospel."*
+ *in the personal and communal dimensions of this journey.*

Constitutions - article 8.1, 8.2

We have spoken of penance before. We have shared thoughts about conversion. And here again we are brought to these issues. The Gospel has dynamic power. Within this article of the Rule we face a challenge to continue what we have begun to do.

Recently I listened to a talk given by one of my Capuchin brothers, Bill Cieslak OFM Cap. He was speaking of penance. At one point, speaking about the "penances" we often choose during lent (or at other times), he said something like this, quoting a friend: *I am having trouble relating to an ornery neighbor. So I am going to give up chocolate for lent!* - - - Is something missing here?

I think it is clear that such "penances" miss the point of being *brothers and sisters of penance.* Instead of recognizing what is really needed we substitute something that makes us feel good and allows us to enjoy chocolate on Easter. But we change little in any permanent way. Neither do we achieve any *radical interior change* other than losing a few pounds and praising ourselves for not eating chocolate for a few weeks.

To acknowledge that my life has a need for conversion is a different task. Embracing a penitential lifestyle presumes that we accept the need for *a radical interior change which the gospel itself calls "conversion."* Embracing the light of Christ, there is little doubt that we will recognize areas of life that need conversion. The "light" that is Christ enlightens us about things that keep us from enriching our relationship with Jesus and other people.

Anyone who has washed windows can recognize this reality. After washing windows on a cloudy day, I thought I had done a fine job. The next day, when the light of the sun hit these "clean" windows, I was unpleasantly surprised to see all the streaks. It is only an image. But we will "see" our need for conversion more clearly as the light of Christ floods our lives. Our clearer "vision" will focus on our need for *radical interior* changes. *Whoever loves a brother or sister lives in the light, and in such a person there is no cause for stumbling* (1 John 2:10). Human nature shows the need for radical change every day. *Human frailty makes it necessary that this conversion be carried out daily.* (SFO Rule #7). This makes sense only if we recognize our need for change. We may feel that we have no need to change. We are "nice" people who have achieved perfection. There doesn't seem much need for a *radical* interior change. If there is, it certainly isn't needed *daily!*

The Rule has an answer for such thinking. It says: ... *motivated by the dynamic power of the gospel, let them conform their thoughts and deeds to those of Christ* ... This sentence contains a challenge. Secular Franciscans realize that the Gospel is not always the guiding force in their lives. We may even find it difficult to believe that the Gospel has *dynamic power*.

God is moved by love to embrace the people he loves. When God, then, chooses to be with us, Francis saw God deliberately and lovingly choosing to come among us in a situation of poverty. Not only the poverty of a crib, but deciding to come among us with none of the trappings of power. God makes a loving decision to forego the power of being God. God enters our world and becomes like us in all things but sin. Such poverty struck Francis as the greatest kind of love (Philippians 2:4-11).

And the Word became flesh and lived among us, and we have seen his glory, the glory as of a father's only son, full of grace and truth. ... From his fulness we have all received, grace upon grace. The law indeed was given through Moses; grace and truth came through Jesus Christ. No one has ever seen God. It is God the only Son, who is close to the Father's heart, who has made him known.

John 1:14-18

The dynamism of God becoming human is an unbelievable event. God's outgoing love attracted Francis. He realized, as he experienced God's love, that he could never give a sufficient response. All Francis could do was to try to be totally generous in response to God's love. Since this is a difficult task for unassisted humans, Francis knew it would be possible only through the Spirit sent by Jesus. Dynamic love thus enters people's lives. Francis understood that the source of our power is the Holy Spirit.

A journey through some Gospel stories can offer clues about radical change. These texts invite a radical change and illustrate the dynamic power of Jesus' words in the Gospel. Francis' favorite Gospel was the Gospel of John. We'll go to the Gospel of John for our texts.

GOSPEL STORIES

+ The story of a man paralyzed for thirty-eight years shows Jesus dynamic power at work (Cf. John 5:1-15). Jesus simply heals him. Many Jews believed that this should not be done on the Sabbath. They told the man that he is not allowed to carry his mat on the Sabbath. His response was to say: *The man who made me well said to me, "Take up your mat and walk."* (Cf. John 5:12). Jesus uses dynamic power but did not draw attention to himself. He sought new life for the paralyzed man. When they met again Jesus shared another important message. *"See, you have been made well! Do not sin any more, so that nothing worse happens to you."* Jesus reminded him and us of the importance of remaining faithful to his Father.

+ In his attempts to teach the apostles something about priorities, Jesus ignores man-made laws. The story of the Samaritan woman illustrates this (Cf. John 4:5-30, 39-42). Jews avoided Samaritans. The law required them to remain separate to maintain Jewish purity. In this story the outsider, the Samaritan woman, recognized the law. Jesus' action of asking for a drink initiates an interesting conversation. *How is it that you, a Jew, ask a drink of me, a woman of Samaria?* At least someone knows the law. Jesus responds with a bit of theology and self-disclosure - which brings more confusion to the woman. *"If you knew the gift of God and who is saying to you, 'Give me a drink,' you would have asked him and he would have given you living water."* Whatever that means! The woman is practical in her response: *Sir, you have no bucket!* That answers whatever he is talking about. Then Jesus adds to the confusion with his next response. *Everyone who drinks of this water will be thirsty again, but those who drink of the water that I will give them will never be thirsty. The water that I will give will become in them a spring of water gushing up to eternal life!*

The Samaritan woman has another practical response to this: *Sir, give me this water, so that I may never be thirsty or have to keep coming here to draw water.* As the story progresses she comes to see that earthly water is not the topic of conversation. The subject has changed and something new is happening in her. This Jewish man, who should be ignored, might be worth listening to. Water is no longer on her mind. The change to talking about her "husband" brings another topic that draws her to new insights about Jesus. She ultimately leaves her water jar and returns to town. She is perceiving things differently and asking a new question: *He cannot be the messiah, can he?*

The apostles and the woman had to deal with a new situation. Jesus has a simple conversation and surprises everyone by his words and actions. The apostles were concerned about lunch (food) and the woman about water. Jesus teaches them that the food and water that nourishes him is to do God's will. It shatters the ideas that initiated this event. Pretty dynamic situation! The Gospel invites us to a new viewpoint as we listen to the story - and apply it to people and situations in our lives.

+ The story of the man born blind (Cf. John 9) has a different flavor. But it is no less challenging. It prys loose some of our ideas about Jesus. Jesus is walking along when he encounters the blind man. The story reveals religious ideas of the disciples who follow the theology they learned in their Jewish training *Rabbi, who sinned, this man or his parents, that he was born blind?* They spoke from a religious belief that they had learned and believed.

Jesus wastes no time in challenging their perception of what is happening in the blind man's life. *Neither this man nor his parents sinned: he was born blind so that God's works might be revealed in him.* That is a new slant on things! Jesus challenges the disciples by changing the subject from judgment to opportunity. We experience similar situations. Jesus asks us to change from opinions that judge people to opinions that create new opportunities for them.

Jesus smears the man's eyes with mud and tells him to wash in the pool of Siloam. Obedient to Jesus' words, the blind man does as directed and is now able to see. Consider what is being taught in this story. Lots of things changed for the blind man because of obeying Jesus.

His friends weren't sure he was the one they had known. But the man is clear on who he was. Religious Jews were upset by a cure on the Sabbath. They brought the former blind man before the Pharisees. They were convinced that anyone who disregarded Sabbath laws (like Jesus) couldn't be from God. The blind man gives an honest account of what happened only to have his parents called to substantiate that he was their son. They came with fear because ... *they were afraid of the Jews; for the Jews had already agreed that anyone who confessed Jesus to be the Messiah would be put out of the synagogue (John 9:22).*

Please take note of the variety of changed relationships for the man-born-blind and others as well. This happens because Jesus touched his life. Notice that the man-born-blind tells the truth throughout his interrogations. Note that the authorities consider him a nobody. But the man-born-blind knew who he was. Finally he confesses his belief in Jesus. "*Do you believe in the Son of Man?" He answered: "Who is he , sir? Tell me, so that I may believe in him." Jesus said to him, "You have* <u>*seen*</u> *him, and the one speaking to you is he." He said, "Lord, I believe." And he worshipped him* (John 9:35-38).

✦

Read these gospel stories prayerfully to realize their power. They are dynamic and brought people to real penance. That is what they can bring to our lives as well. With that dynamism comes the call to a *radical interior change which the Gospel itself calls "conversion.*

RECONCILIATION

*On this road to renewal the sacrament of reconciliation is the privileged sign of the Father's mercy and the source of grace. (*SFO Rule #7)

This sacrament developed gradually within the Church.* It reflects the mercy and compassion of Jesus. Reconciliation is the action of an infinitely compassionate God. In this sacrament God's love is once again revealed.

God knows we fail on our journey of faith. This sacrament celebrates God's love and mercy through forgiving our sins. Jesus reminded Peter of the need to forgive others. It wasn't just seven times. *Jesus said to him, not seven times, but, I tell you, seventy-seven times* (Matthew 18: 22). We are captured again by the compassion and love God has for us. We celebrate that love in the sacrament of Reconciliation.

In our day and age we are surrounded by evil - torture, genocide, crime, unfaithfulness, revenge, anger, murder, sexual abuse and all manner of evil. This atmosphere contributes to minimizing our sense of sin. In the midst of sinful excesses our failures may seem minor.

Our personal lives need conversion. None of us is so perfect that we never sin. Intimacy with Jesus brings the light that reveals obstacles to growth. This sacrament connects to

---

* Resource for these pages; <u>*Sacramental Guidelines*</u> - Kenan Osborne OFM - Paulist Press - Page 90ff

conversion and conforming our *thoughts and deeds to those of Christ* (SFO Rule #7). We are consistently called to do better. There are many things in our lives that diminish our relationship with God and others. Sin plays a part in this sacrament. But primarily the sacrament is about God's love showing mercy to us and forgiving our sins.

Sin is not worth a celebration. We are not smart enough to confuse God about what is evil and what is not. Evil is evil! When serious sin puts barriers between ourselves, God, and others we acknowledge it for what it is - something sinful that diminishes unity.

In this process we acknowledge the holiness of God. God does not traffic in sin. When we confess our sins we acknowledge our belief in a God whose love and compassion will forgive us. While the sacrament of Reconciliation includes the idea of sin, its focus is on God's gracious love for us. No one has yet managed to commit a sin that is bigger than God's love and forgiveness.

We examine our lives to see where we have sinned. God's love and light reaches into every nook and cranny of our lives to make us aware of any unfaithfulness. God wants to bring peace and joy to us through an honest confession. Hence, our reaction to God's forgiveness is one of praise and thanksgiving.

The one who rejects me and does not receive my word has a judge; on the last day the word that I have spoken will serve as judge, for I have not spoken on my own, but the Father who sent me has himself given me a commandment about what to say and what to speak.

John 12: 47-48

Franciscans are gospel people. We reflect on the word of God when we come to the sacrament of Reconciliation. The biblical word helps us discover areas of our lives where we may be distant from God. We come to realize that the Gospel does not guide all our choices and actions.

And this is the judgment, that the light has come into the world, and people loved darkness rather than light because their deeds were evil.

John 3:19

It is important to uncover the roots of our sinful words or actions. We look within to see how a negative spirit may have dictated to us. Our examination is illumined by the light of God's love for us. This is not a guilt trip. Rather, we look at life to find where conversion is needed. There may be places where a *radical interior change* is needed. Our relationship with God is one of love, not fear. God is love. When God acts it expresses his love.

Spirituality is fundamentally a response to God's loving and forgiving presence. When we realize, even in our day-to-day life, that a person loves us and loves us deeply, we respond to that love by expressions of gratitude. We know that we cannot purchase or merit or earn someone's love. Love is always a gift. God's forgiveness is an even greater gift of love to us, and our only response can be one of wonder, amazement, and gratitude. If a person experiences the love of God and then turns around and offends God again and again through continued sin, has one really understood God's love? If in our day-to-day love we say that we are glad someone loves us, but turn around and offend that person again and again, have we really understood how much the other person loves us? Is not our acknowledgment of the other person's love mere lip-service? We cannot honor God by mere lip-service. We honor God by a life of holiness, which is a reflection in our life of the very holiness of God.

Sacramental Guidelines - Kenan Osborne OFM
Paulist Press - Page 101-102

Franciscans always return to God's love as the source of holiness. Over and over we recognize the power of God's love for us. Jesus' words and deeds reflect that love. The SFO Rule puts it well when it says that *the sacrament of reconciliation is the privileged sign of the Father's mercy and the source of grace* (SFO Rule #7).

On one occasion when Jesus was going to the house of a leader of the Pharisees to eat a meal on the sabbath, they were watching him closely. Just then, in front of him, there was a man who had dropsy. And Jesus asked the lawyers and Pharisees, "Is it lawful to cure people on the sabbath, or not?" But they were silent. So Jesus took him and healed him, and sent him away. Then he said to them, "If one of you has a child or an ox that has fallen into a well, will you not immediately pull it out on a sabbath day?" And they could not reply to this.

Luke 14:1-6

Just as Jesus sought to bring compassion in response to the laws that Pharisees and others had created, so he does in our lives. In the sacrament of Reconciliation we experience that same call. If you have been unjust, judgmental, hurtful, biased, created walls between people through your words and actions - CHANGE! Let the experience of God's love teach you the ways of love in your everyday life.

It seems that Francis spent
little time asking God: "Why?"
because he already knew the answer:
"I am with you always"
and that is the source of strength in adversity,
patience in trials, endurance in suffering,
love in the presence of hatred,
joy in celebration,
forgiveness in the face of hurt.
Christ's presence through the Spirit
can accomplish
"... more than we can ask or imagine."
Which can be a lot!
So Francis let God be God without strings
or demands or trying to tell God how to be God.

Surprisingly, Francis discovered freedom
unlike anything he had known before.

The words in John's gospel became his talisman:
"If you stand by my teaching,
you are truly my disciples;
you will know the truth,
and the truth will set you free!"
(John 8:31-32)

Francis stood by Jesus' teaching,
he knew the truth,
and he was free and he sang!
What more can be said?
Amen.

1. Rule 7 *Secular Franciscans, called in earlier times "the brothers and sisters of penance," propose to live in the spirit of continual conversion. Some means to cultivate this characteristic of the Franciscan vocation, individually and in fraternity, are: listening to and celebrating the Word of God; review of life; spiritual retreats; the help of a spiritual advisor; and penitential celebrations. They should approach the Sacrament of Reconciliation frequently and participate in the communal celebrations of it, whether in the fraternity, or with the whole people of God.*

2. ... The fruits of conversion, which is a response to the love of God, are the works of charity in the interactions with the brothers and sisters.

Constitutions - article 13.1, 13.2

+++

Readings/Questions for dialogue

Teachings of the Ordinary Magisterium
Sacramental Guidelines - Kenan Osborne OFM
Page 104-105

Recognize sin - Praise God's mercy
United States Catholic Catechism for Adults - USCCB
Page 242-243

God is Love *(Deus Caritas Est)* - Benedict XVI
Paragraph 25.b

1. How is the Gospel a dynamic power in your life?

2. How does our Franciscan vocation bring us to unity with people?

3. What is the focus of the sacrament of Reconciliation? Explain why this is so and what it requires of us.

4. At this point of formation how would you define "penance" as understood by the Brothers and Sisters of Penance?

5. What is the meaning of the phrase: *that radical interor change which the gospel itself calls "conversion?"*

6. How does the sacrament of Reconciliation set you free? How has this chapter changed your view of the sacrament of Reconciliation? Explain what is different for you.

7. Scripture reflection: Choose a scripture story from this chapter. Spend reflective time with it (paralyzed man / Samaritan woman / the man-born-blind). Share the insights that come to you.

+++

The scribes and the Pharisees brought a woman who had been caught in the very act of committing adultery; and making her stand before all of them, they said to him, "Teacher, this woman was caught in the very act of committing adultery. Now in law Moses commanded us to stone such a woman. Now what do you say?" They said this to test him, so that they might have some charge to bring against him. Jesus bent down and wrote with his finger on the ground. When they kept on questioning him, he straightened up and said to them, "Let anyone among you who is without sin be the first to throw a stone at her." ... When they heard it they went away one by one, beginning with the elders; and Jesus was left alone with the woman standing before him. ... "Neither do I condemn you. Go your way, and from now on do not sin again."

<u>John</u> 8:3-11

Chapter sixteen

When you pray ...

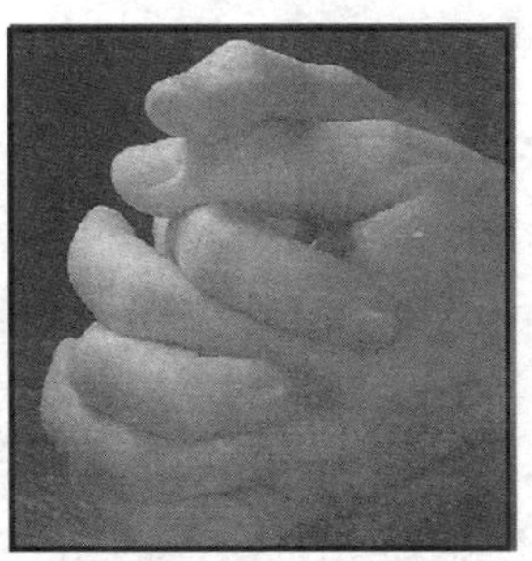

8. As Jesus was the true worshipper of the Father, so let prayer and contemplation be the soul of all they are and do.

Let them participate in the sacramental life of the Church, above all the Eucharist. Let them join in liturgical prayer in one of the forms proposed by the Church, reliving the mysteries of the life of Christ.

3. Rule 8 *The brothers and sisters should love meeting God as His children and they should let prayer and contemplation be the soul of all they are and do. They should seek to discover the presence of the Father in their own heart, in nature, and in the history of humanity in which His plan of salvation is fulfilled. The contemplation of this mystery will dispose them to collaborate in this loving plan.*

Constitutions - article 12.3

1. Aware that God wanted to make of us all a single people and that he made his Church the universal sacrament of salvation, the brothers and sisters should commit themselves to a faith-inspired reflection on the Church, its mission in today's world and the role of the Franciscan laity within it. They should take up the challenges and accept the responsibilities that this reflection will lead them to discover.

2. Rule 8 *The Eucharist is the center of the life of the Church. Christ unites us to himself and to one another as a single body in it. Therefore, the Eucharist should be the center of the life of the fraternity. The brothers and sisters should participate in the Eucharist as frequently as possible, being mindful of the respect and love shown by Francis, who, in the Eucharist, lived all the mysteries of the life of Christ.*

3. They should participate in the sacraments of the Church, attentive not only to personal sanctification, but also to fostering the growth of the Church and the spreading of the Kingdom. They should collaborate in achieving living and conscious celebrations in their own parishes, particularly in the celebrations of baptism, confirmation, marriage, and the anointing of the sick.

4. The brothers and sisters, as well as the fraternities, should adhere to the indications of the Ritual with respect to the different forms of participation in the liturgical prayer of the Church, giving priority to the celebration of the Liturgy of the Hours.

5. In all places and at all times, it is possible for true worshippers of the Father to give him adoration and to pray to him. Nevertheless, the brothers and sisters should try to find times of silence and recollection dedicated exclusively to prayer.

Constitutions - article 14.1, 14.2, 14.3, 14.4, 14.5

N.B. The Eucharist, celebrated with parish members, draws us to the Church. It keeps us in touch with the local parish and diocesan community. The fraternity may periodically celebrate Eucharist at their fraternity gatherings. This celebration is recommended for special occasions - e.g. Professions, jubilees of profession, a memorial Eucharist for the deceased of the SFO or other important occasions.. Cf. Benedict XVI's quote from *Sacramentum Caritatis* on page 184-185.

It is time to reaffirm the importance of prayer in the face of activism and the growing secularism of many Christians engaged in charitable work. Clearly, the Christian who prays does not claim to be able to change God's plans or correct what he has foreseen. Rather, he seeks an encounter with the Father of Jesus Christ, asking God to be present with the consolations of the Spirit to him and his work. A personal relationship with God and an abandonment to his will can prevent man from being demeaned and save him from falling prey to the teaching of fanaticism and terororism.

God is Love *(Deus Caritas Est)* - Benedict XVI - Paragraph 37

The Constitutions address a number of issues in regard to personal and public prayer.

+ Contemplation is a normal prayerful stance for Franciscans. We revel in the presence of God's love revealed in our hearts, in creation, in Scripture, and in the people God touches with love. They *should try to find times of silence and recollection dedicated exclusively to prayer.* (Constitutions - article 14.5)

+ Dedication to the Church should be a consequence of the prayer of secular Franciscans. The Trinity calls us to unity through our prayer.

+ Within the Church the Eucharist is the center of our lives. Attending a parish Eucharist is highly encouraged. We need to be consistently present at the gathering of the People of God. It reminds us of our union with the Church. Attending the parish Eucharist is a sign of our love for the Church as well as love for the Eucharist.

+ The *Liturgy of the Hours* unites us to the praying Church. Secular Franciscans may use it for their personal prayer or, at times, for fraternity prayer. Though it is given priority in the Constitutions, it may not fit everyone's prayer needs. Use it with sensitivity and a prayerful spirit.

+ The *Ritual of the SFO* offers models of prayer and rites for celebrations. It also tells us:

Except for the formula for profession or permanent commitment, which should be used basically in the form given, all the other formulae and prayers presented in the text are to be considered as models to guide those planning the ceremonies in providing a ritual expression that is both common to the whole SFO and suited to the local circumstances or to the particular people involved. ***The adaptation of the given texts is encouraged.*** (Cf. Ritual of the SFO - 4.21 - Page 7-8)

It may not be easy for us to be quiet in prayer. We tend to read prayers, somctimes a lot of them. We have many prayerbooks, novenas, rosaries, texts written by others, and numerous devotions to Jesus, Mary, and the saints. These things are good and can accomplish the purpose of drawing us to Jesus. But sometimes it feels like we are overwhelmed by someone else's words.

If we *let prayer and contemplation be the soul of all we are and do (Cf. SFO Rule #8),* we can be helped by dialogue about prayer at our gatherings. A conversation about silence may also be apropos. Shared ideas about Eucharist and the real presence could help our Eucharistic understanding. Trying to put these and other elements of prayer into one chapter is beyond what we could hope to accomplish.

In this chapter we want to stimulate love for a prayerful spirit. As we share ideas about prayer we hope to nudge you to search for more. Prayer is fundamental to Franciscan life.

Franciscan life focuses on the Trinity, especially on Jesus, the Word-made-flesh. The Incarnation brings the realization that God desires to relate to us. God came among us so we could be intimate not only with Jesus, but through him to the whole Trinity. Love is the basis for this relationship. Our prayerfulness is based on love and leads to loving actions. Francis *made Christ the inspiration and the center of his life with God and people* (SFO Rule #4).

Francis' conversion led him to dependence on Jesus and Jesus' Father and on the work of the Holy Spirit. Because of his awareness of God's love, Francis saw all of God's creation as good. Lady Poverty moved him to embrace the wonder of the created world without the need to "possess" it. His relationship to the Trinity brought him a sense of gratitude for all that God shares with us.

How do we achieve this intimacy? The simplest answer is through our relationship with Jesus. God's love, made visible in Jesus, is experienced as we take time to know and love Jesus. Relationships require time together and intimate conversations. In this case we call it prayer.

Jesus reveals God's love in multiple ways. From the humility of the crib to the vulnerability of the cross, Jesus shows that God's love is not dominating but approachable. Jesus is not distant from us, but close to us. Jesus does not waste words but offers words of life. Jesus is not a stern judge but a welcoming Son seated at the right hand of our loving Father. The Father is like the father of the prodigal son, welcoming us when we fail, delighted with our return to the family circle (Cf. Luke 15:11-32).

Francis, through his prayerful relationship with Jesus, grew in his love for everyone. Like Jesus, Francis is willing to give his life for the sake of other people. This is the ordinary result of a prayerful spirit. It seeks the spirit of Jesus and is responsive to the Holy Spirit.*

This loving response to Jesus moves us *to encounter the living and active spirit of Christ in their* (our) *brothers and sisters, in Sacred Scripture, in the Church, and in liturgical activity* (SFO Rule #5). We become more responsive as our prayerfulness blossoms. United with Jesus, we are moved to actions that embrace all people and all of creation.

Using Scripture for prayer is more than engaging in an intellectual exercise. Rather, we listen to God initiating a conversation with us. We need not enter scriptural prayer with needs and personal ideas that we want to talk about with God. Instead we recognize that we are encountering God in the living word through which God speaks to us. Our prayer is one of listening to the word with an open heart and without a personal agenda. Scripture is one manifestation of God. It is the initiative, on God's part, that is the heart of scriptural prayerfulness. In faith, we

---

* Cf. Franciscan Prayer - Ilia Delio OSF - Page 6 - Paragraph that begins: *Thomas of Celano provides etc ...*

believe that Scripture is God's word which has the power to transform our lives. With faith, trusting the word of God, we trust the biblical word to transform us. Our prayerfulness opens the door to hearing the message of the word.

In our prayers for you we always thank God, the Father of our Lord Jesus Christ, for we have heard of your faith in Christ Jesus and of the love that you have for all the saints, because of the hope laid up for you in heaven. You have heard of this hope before ***in the word of the truth, the gospel that has come to you.*** *Just as it is bearing fruit and growing in the whole world, so it has been bearing fruit among yourselves from the day you heard it and truly comprehended the grace of God.*

Colossians 1: 3 6

The Holy Spirit opens our lives to the desires God has for us. A personal relationship with the Trinity enables us to be faithful to the Gospel. Prayer responds to the scriptural word. This prayer is sometimes called *lectio divina.*

Lectio divina uses scripture as a foundation. It invites us to quiet space and can be prayed both privately and in a group. Simple directions for both private and group *lectio divina* can be found in the book: *An Invitation to Centering Prayer** *Lectio divina* gives God freedom to speak openly to us. It may be a word for yesterday's issues, for today, or for some time in the future. Trust God! Allow God's word to speak freely to your heart and your life.

But now more than ever the word about Jesus spread abroad; many crowds would gather to hear him and to be cured of their diseases. But he would withdraw to deserted places and pray.

Luke 5: 15-16

The forms of prayer are many. Francis' own words can stimulate prayer. Devotional prayer can assist us in coming

---

* Cf. *An Invitation to Centering Prayer* - M. Basil Pennington O.C.S.O. - Liquori - Liquori, Missouri - Pages 49-52 / 52-54 / 73-74

close to Jesus. The *Liturgy of the Hours* can bring us to scripture in a common recitation of psalms and readings. *Lectio divina,* or some form thereof, can lead our prayerfulness. The Eucharist is a community prayer of praise and thanksgiving. Reflecting in the quiet and beauty of creation can gentle our spirit. Whatever form our prayerfulness takes, our goal is intimacy with Jesus and fulfilling his words in our lives.

But be doers of the word, and not merely hearers who deceive themselves. For if any are hearers of the word and not doers, they are like those who look at themselves in a mirror; for they look at themselves and, on going away, immediately forget what they were like.

James 1:22-24

The "Magnificat" is a beautiful form of prayer. Reflection on the *Magnificat* (Luke 1:46-55) helps us praise and trust God. Our normal response to God's love shows itself through our actions in the world.

My soul magnifies the Lord,
and my spirit rejoices in God my Saviour,
for he has looked with favour
on the lowliness of his servant.
Surely, from now on all generations
will call me blessed;
for the Mighty One has done great things for me,
and holy is his name.

His mercy is for those who fear him
from generation to generation.
He has shown strength with his arms;
he has scattered the proud
in the thoughts of their hearts.
He has brought down the powerful from their thrones,
and lifted up the lowly;
he has filled the hungry with good things,
and sent the rich away empty.
He has helped his servant, Israel,

in remembrance of his mercy,
according to the promise he made to our ancestors,
to Abraham and to his descendants forever.

EUCHARIST

It is very much the wish of the Church that all the faithful should be led to take that full, conscious, and active part in liturgical celebrations which is demanded by the very nature of the liturgy, and to which the Christian people. "a chosen race, a royal priesthood, a holy nation, a redeemed people" (1 Peter 2:9) have a right and to which they are ***bound by reason of Baptism.***

In the restoration and development of the sacred liturgy ***the full and active participation by all the people is the paramount concern****, for it is the primary, indeed the indispensable source from which the faithful are to derive the true Christian spirit. Therefore, in all their apostolic activity, pastors of souls should energetically set about achieving it through the requisite formation.*

Constitution on the Sacred Liturgy - Vatican II - Paragraph 14

The Church, therefore, spares no effort in trying to ensure that, when present at this mystery of faith, Christian believers should not be there as strangers or silent spectators.

Ibid - Paragraph 48

The Eucharist is a time for common praise and thanks to God. God's word moves us to solidarity with the world's poor. We develop an openness to the needs of the world around us. We recall that the Holy Spirit prompts us to work at building God's Kingdom within the world and its people. Our welcoming attitude calls us to change structures of society that betray human dignity. We develop programs that supply the needs of all people. People with power are called upon to use their power to promote human dignity and to work for the common good.

The Eucharist, celebrated with dignity and sensitivity,

welcomes all people to the table of the Lord. It sends those gathered around the table to create a world where love and compassion are signs of society's care for people. Eucharist reminds us of the presence of the Holy Spirit to transform us - just as bread and wine are transformed by the Spirit.

By the power of the Holy Spirit, Christ is present in the proclamation of God's Word, in the Eucharistic assembly, in the person of the priest, but above all and in a wholly unique manner in the Eucharist. "This presence is called 'real' - by which is not intended to exclude other types of presence as if they could not be 'real' too, but because it is presence in the fullest sense: that is to say, it is a substantial presence by which Christ, God and man, makes himself wholly and entirely present" (CCC, no. 1374, citing Pope Paul VI, *Mystery of Faith,* no. 39)

United States Catholic Catechism for Adults - USCCB - Page 223

✦ *The fruits of Holy Communion include a deeper union with Christ, a closer identity with all the faithful, a commitment to the poor, and a pledge of future glory.*

Ibid - Page 229

Underlying the strength of a Eucharistic spirituality is the development of a loving Christian community. The Eucharist is not an isolated moment. It flows from the love with which the Trinity empowers the commmunity gathered in praise and gratitude. It flows back into the community to support its way of loving within the world. It enables the Christian community to continue its loving ways in the world, especially with compassion and justice, expressions of God's love - given to the community and its members.

In regard to **the issue of small group celebrations**, Benedict XVI offers guidance.

... While acknowledging the formative value of this approach (small groups), *it must be stated that such celebrations should always be consonant with the overall pastoral activity of the Diocese. These celebrations would*

actually lose their catechetical value if they were felt to be in competition with, or parallel to, the life of the particular Church. In this regard the Synod set forth some necessary criteria: small groups must serve to unify the community, not to fragment it; the beneficial results ought to be clearly evident; these groups should encourage the fruitful participation of the entire assembly and preserve as much as possible the unity of liturgical life of the individual families.

Sacrament of Charity - *(Sacramentum Caritatis)*
Benedict XVI Paragraph 63

Franciscans will regularly be present at their parish Eucharist. The Eucharist is a unifying, communal celebration. Courtesy invites us to conform to the ritual actions of the celebrating community, i.e. kneeling, bowing, standing, receiving communion. We are *"one-with"* and do not *"stand-out"* by personal ritual choices at Eucharist. We are sensitive to the unifying role of the Eucharist. This attitude also guides decisions we make about attending Eucharistic celebrations that do NOT encourage active participation in the Eucharist (Called for by Vatican II).

Franciscans recognize that in the Eucharist Jesus continues to fulfill God's desire to be with us. Through his *real presence* Jesus is with us. God chooses to remain close to us. Active participation in Eucharistic celebrations are second nature to us. If that response calls for a change in us, then we change! *Ongoing formation* can help us enrich our understanding of the Eucharist.

Dear brothers and sisters, the Eucharist is at the root of every form of holiness, and each of us is called to the fullness of life in the Holy Spirit. ... This most holy mystery thus needs to be firmly believed, devoutly celebrated, and intensely lived in the Church. Jesus' gift of himself in the sacrament which is the memorial of his passion tells us that the success of our lives is found in our participation in the trinitarian life offered to us truly and definitvely in him. The celebration and worship of the Eucharist enable us to draw near to God's love and to persevere in that love until we are united with the Lord whom we love. The offering of our lives, our fellowship with the whole community of believers, and our solidarity with all men and women are essential parts of that 'logike latreia,' spiritual worship, holy and pleasing to God (Cf. Rom 12:1) *which transforms every aspect of our human existence, to the glory of God.*

Sacrament of Charity *(Sacramentum Caritatis)*
Benedict XVI - Paragraph 94.

Readings/Questions for dialogue

Contemplation: Seeing and loving
Franciscan Prayer - Ilia Delio OSF - Page 127 to 129 - up to: *"Because identity ..."*

A Letter to the Entire Order
Francis of Assisi - The Saint - Vol I
Page 118 - #26-29 - Prayer: *"Let everyone be struck ...*

God is Love *(Deus Caritas Est)* - Benedict XVI
Paragraph 41- Mary's prayerfulness

1. What do you consider to be most important in seeking to become more contemplative in your life? What are some personal obstacles to developing a contemplative spirit?

2. What is the practical result of taking time for contemplation? How does it help you live your Franciscan life?

3. Give your definition of the purpose of prayer.

4. Explain why the Eucharist is so important in the life of a Christian who is also a Franciscan.

5. What is the value of using the *Liturgy of the Hours* or *Lectio Divina* as part of your prayer life?

6. Please share the form of your prayerfulness in your daily

life. How does it help in your transformation?

7. Please evaluate your ability to *let prayer and contemplation be the soul of all you are and do (SFO Rule #8)* - and share the results.

8. Scripture reflection: Psalm 67. How does this psalm model a form of prayer? What call from God do you discover in praying this psalm?

Resources for Franciscan contemplative prayer: "*Francis and Bonaventure* - Paul Rout - Triumph (Liquori Publications) - Page 61ff. / *The Journey of the Soul Into God* - St Bonaventure. / Ilia Delio's books: *Franciscan Prayer* (St Anthony Messenger Press) and *Simply Bonaventure* (New City Press). / Angela of Foligno - Classics of Western Spirituality - Paulist Press

Father, you are holy indeed, and all creation rightly gives you praise. ***All life, all holiness comes from you through your Son, Jesus Christ our Lord, by the working of the Holy Spirit.*** *From age to age you gather a people to yourself, so that from east to west a perfect offering may be made to the glory of your name.*

And so, Father, we bring you these gifts. We ask you to make them holy ***by the power of your Spirit****, that they may become the body and blood of your Son, our Lord Jesus Christ, at whose command we celebrate this Eucharist.*

Eucharistic Prayer #3

Chapter seventeen

The Mother of God ... and our Mother

9. The Virgin Mary, humble servant of the Lord, was open to his every word and call. She was embraced by Francis with indescribable love and declared the protectress and advocate of his family. The Secular Franciscans should express their ardent love for her by imitating her complete self-giving and by praying earnestly and confidently.

1. Rule 9 *Mary, Mother of Jesus, is the model of listening to the Word and of faithfulness to vocation; we, like Francis, see all the gospel virtues realized in her.*

The brothers and sisters should cultivate intense love for the most holy virgin, imitation, prayer and filial abandonment. They should manifest their own devotion with expressions of genuine faith, in forms accepted by the Church.

2. Mary is the model of fruitful and faithful love for the entire ecclesial community.

Secular Franciscans and their fraternities should seek to live the experience of Francis, who made the Virgin the guide of his activity. With her, like the disciples at Pentecost, they should welcome the Spirit to create a community of love.

Constitutions - article 16.1, 16.2

Francis saw Mary as a model responding to God's word with love. Her faith gave life to the Son of God. Within her body the Word became flesh. Her faith-filled willingness to trust God serves as a model for all of us. She trusted God whose love is always faithful. Francis speaks of Mary with great love.

Hail, O Lady,
Holy Queen,
Mary, holy Mother of God,
Who are the Virgin made Church,
chosen by the most Holy Father in heaven
whom he consecrated with His most holy beloved Son
and with the Holy Spirit the Paraclete,
in whom there was and is
all fullness of grace and every good.

Hail His Palace!
Hail His Tabernacle!
Hail His Dwelling!
Hail His Robe!
Hail His Servant!
Hail His Mother!

A Salutation of the Blessed Virgin Mary
Francis of Assisi - The Saint - Vol I - Page 163

Mary is the *virgin made church*. She is the dwelling place for Jesus, just as the Church is his dwelling place. She carried Jesus in her body. The Church, too, carries Jesus in his mystical body, the Church. We are members of that mystical body called "Church."

Outstanding among the saints is Mary, Mother of the Lord and mirror of all holiness. In the Gospel of Luke we find her engaged in a service of charity to her cousin Elizabeth, with whom she remained for "about three months" (Lk 1:56) *so as to assist her in the final phase of her pregnancy. "Magnificat anima mea Dominum," she says on the occasion of that visit, "My soul magnifies the Lord"* (Lk 1:46). *In these words she expresses her whole program of life: not setting herself at the center, but leaving space for God, who is encountered both in prayer and in service of neighbor - only then does goodness enter the world. Mary's greatness consists in the fact that she wants to magnify God, not herself.*

God is Love *(Deus Caritas Est)*
Benedict XVI - Paragraph 41

Mary is a partner in the saving love of God at work in the world. Her attraction to so many people throughout history is made clear through her role as "mother." She brings to the story of salvation a feminine face. Her power comes from a confident faith in God.

Mary is not a passive woman simply being nice to everyone. She initiates a ministry to Elizabeth, pregnant in her old age. She is no wilting lady when she becomes a refugee in Egypt. She is no silent wallflower at the wedding at Cana. Seeing a need she invites her son to handle the situation, ready or not. She lives a quite ordinary life as wife and mother. She does not collapse when her son is arrested nor does she hesitate to be with him when he is criminalized on the cross. She makes a firm decision about where to live when she and John are named mother and son by Jesus. She is part of the community who experience the Holy Spirit on Pentecost. Her faith in the God she knew so well gave her strength to live a faith-filled life.

Mary has a strong faith. In Jesus' earliest years as a child, both in Egypt and Nazareth, Mary and Joseph help form his character just as Mary had formed his body in her womb. She dealt with ordinary chores. During the centuries her visits to earth show her concern for us, transforming lives and bringing them to her son. Mary's role balances but never supercedes that of Jesus. She is intimately connected to Jesus' ministry of salvation.

Her ability to deal with life in its various demands makes her an attractive model to follow. She is virgin made church - a model of how to respond to God's call. Francis dedicated his Order of Penitents to her guidance and protection.

Devotion to Mary in no way replaces Christ. Rather, her role is to bring us to Christ, as is illustrated in Mary's admonition at the wedding feast of Cana, "Do whatever he tells you." (John 2:5).

<u>Popular Devotional Practices</u>
U.S. Conference of Catholic Bishops - Page 12

Devotion to Mary leads to intimacy with Jesus and through him to the Trinity. Should it fail to accomplish this goal it needs a re-evaluation. Mary plays an important role in salvation history but she is not the savior. Francis saw her as a dynamic model taking action in response to God. From her call to be mother of God; to being a refugee in a foreign country; to worry when her son stayed behind on a trip to Jerusalem; to his public ministry and his death on the cross, she tackled problems with faith and love.

Her Magnificat (Cf. Pages 182-183) offers a look at how God cares for the poor and marginalized. She reveals a trust that God will fulfill what He said He would do. Faith and hope freed her for dedication in serving the Lord and reaching out to the needy. Her day-to-day decisions came from a heart in love with God. She takes part in sharing God's love for people through the decisions she made. Francis loved her poverty, i.e. trusting God in all things. She is a good person to protect his Order.

Francis received his original message from the crucifix in San Damiano. But another church is special to him - the "cradle" of the Order - a church he repaired about three years into his conversion. It is the church of *Our Lady of the Angels,* commonly known as the *Portiuncula* (The Little Portion). He loved this church more than any other church. He asked his friars never to abandon it. The Portiuncula is "home" to the Franciscan pilgrims who visit it. Its quiet dignity made it special to Francis. He sought and received the favor of a plenary indulgence for those visiting the Portiuncula on August 2 (later extended to all Franciscan Churches).*

An approved Franciscan devotion to Our Lady is the *Franciscan Crown Rosary* of seven decades. Its origin is in the early part of the 15th century. Apparently a young man who entered the Order received a vision from our Lady. She instructed him to meditate daily on the seven joys of our Lady to remind him of the joy of the Franciscan

---

* Cf. Francis of Assisi - The Prophet - Vol III - #4 - Page 810-812.

spirit. It spread throughout the Order and was officially approved in 1422.*

The words of the SFO Rule do not speak of any particular devotion by which we show love for Mary. Instead it says, quite simply: *The Secular Franciscans should express their ardent love for her by imitating her complete self-giving and by praying earnestly and confidently* (SFO Rule #9).

Complete self-giving (profession) requires that we embrace the journey of conversion. Conversion moves beyond self-interest and selfishness. It opens us to a sharing, God-centered spirit in our relationship to God, to people and all of creation. This loving response demands our personal surrender to God. Franciscans assess the value of their devotion to Mary by the quality of their personal self-giving and prayerfulness.

In the words of the apostle there is but one mediator "for there is but one God and one mediator between God and humankind, the man Christ Jesus, who gave himself a redemption for all." (I Tim 2:5-6). *But Mary's function as mother of humankind in no way obscures or diminishes this unique mediation of Christ, but rather shows its power. All the Blessed Virgin's salutary influence on men and women originate not in an inner necessity but in the disposition of God. It flows from the superabundance of the merits of Christ, rests on his mediation, depends entirely on it and draws all its power from it. It does not hinder in any way the immediate union of the faithful with Christ but on the contrary fosters it.*

Dogmatic Constitution on the Church *(Lumen Gentium)* - Paragraph 60

---

* The Franciscan Crown rosary begins immediately with the first decade. After the seventh decade two Hail Mary's are added, making a total of seventy-two Hail Mary's in honor of a traditional belief in Mary's 72 years of life on earth. In conclusion, an *Our Father, Hail Mary* and *Glory be* are recited for the intentions of the Pope.

The joys of our Lady are as follows: 1) The Annunciation. 2) The Visitation. 3) The Birth of Christ. 4) The Adoration of the Magi. 5) Finding Jesus in the Temple. 6) Meeting Christ after the resurrection. 7) The Assumption and Coronation of Mary.

Some of the following words could readily be connected to the spirit of Mary: *Mindfulness / Acceptance / Gratitude / Inclusiveness / Compassion.** We do well to make them part of our spirit as Franciscans and lovers of Mary, the mother of God.

* Cf. Thomas Fox - East & West - NCR - Page 1a - October 31, 2008.

Readings/Questions for dialogue

Mary as the Full Image of Humanity
Poverty & Joy - Wm Short OFM
Page 55-57

The Cult of the Blessed Virgin in the Church
Dogmatic Constitution on the Church - *Lumen Gentium*
Paragraph 66 & 67

God's Plan for Mary - etc
United States Catholic Catechism for Adults- USCCB
Page 143-148

1. What is Mary's role in our lives and in the life of the Church?

2. Spell out personal attitudes and practices that would show your *complete self-giving* as a way to show your love for Mary.

3. What qualities of Mary are especially attractive to you? Why?

4. What is the goal of devotion to Mary? What criteria do you use to evaluate whether your devotion to Mary is supportive of complete self-giving in your Franciscan life?

5. Why is the little church of the Portiuncula (Our Lady of the Angels) important to Franciscans?

6. Share your ideas as to how the following words apply

to Mary: *Mindfulness / Acceptance / Gratitude / Inclusiveness / Compassion.* How do they apply to your own life?

7. What is your favorite devotion to Mary? How does it bring you closer to Jesus?

8. Scripture reflection. Acts 1:14. Why do you think it was important to Luke (and to us) to include Mary in the group gathered together after Jesus' ascension?

+++

**Francis' words about the Portiuncula,
St. Mary of the Angels.**

See to it, my sons, that you
never abandon this place.
If you are driven out from one side,
go back in from the other,
for this is truly a holy place
and the dwelling place of God.
Here the Most High increased our numbers
when we were only a few;
here he enlightened the hearts of his poor ones
with the light of his wisdom;
here he kindled our wills
with the fire of His love;
here all who pray wholeheartedly
will receive what they ask,
while offenders
will be severely punished.
Therefore, my sons,
hold this place, God's dwelling,
as worthy of all honor
and here praise God
in cries of joy and praise
with your whole heart.

The Life of St. Francis by Thomas of Celano
The second book
Francis of Assisi - The Saint- Vol I
Page 275

Chapter eighteen

Being Faithful

If I forget thee, O Jerusalem, let my right hand wither. ... (Ps.137:5-6)

10. United themselves to the redemptive obedience of Jesus, who placed his will into the Father's hands, let them faithfully fulfill the duties proper to their various circumstances of life. Let them also follow the poor and crucified Christ, witness to him even in difficulties and persecutions.

2. Rule 10 *With Jesus, obedient even to death, they should seek to know and do the will of the Father. They should give thanks to God for the gift of freedom and for the revelation of the law of love. In order to carry out the will of the Father, they should accept the help which is offered them through the mediation of the Church by those who are constituted as authority in her and by their confreres. They should take the risk of courageous choices in their life in society, with decisiveness and serenity.*

Constitutions - Article 12.2

In the Gospels, we see and hear Jesus summon others to accept, live and share the Kingdom of God. The proclamation of the Kingdom of God was fundamental to Jesus' preaching. The Kingdom of God is his presence among human beings calling them to a new way of life as individuals and as a community. This is a Kingdom of salvation from sin and a sharing in divine life. It is the Good News that results in love, justice, and mercy for the whole world. The Kingdom is realized partially on earth and permanently in heaven. We enter this Kingdom through faith in Christ, baptismal initiation into the Church, and life in communion with all her members.

United States Catholic Catechism for Adults - USCCB - Page 79-80

Should the Franciscan tradition teach people to recreate the experience of a Francis or Clare? Certainly not. The attempt would be fruitless and frustrating. And even if it could succeed, then, like Francis and Clare themselves, it would have to be dead. It continues to be a living tradition today because others have carried on the tradition, in new times and places in their own words and example. Francis presents us with one example, a moving and inspiring example, but the tradition does not stop with him. In his words, "I have done what was mine to do, may Christ now show you what is yours." Francis wished that his whole life would point to Christ. To stop at Francis would be to frustrate the intention he had for his followers. Clare also pointed away from herself, holding up the Mirror who is Christ, and indicating Francis as the one who showed her that Mirror. But both Clare and Francis, in their words and gestures, reveal to us, sometimes clearly, sometimes obscurely, intuitions about God-become-human that still remain profoundly challenging. That is the only reason for writing a book like this in our day; to express those intuitions in a language understandable to today's sincere Christian believer and religious seeker.

Poverty and Joy - Wm Short OFM - Page 127-128

It is our firm Franciscan belief that all Christians are **called to build the Kingdom of God.** Jesus came among us to proclaim how that kingdom would look. What is valuable for Franciscans is to have a Rule that describes our part in the building process. We are Catholics who assist in building the kingdom by following the Rule of 1978. We don't do everything. We do what we are called to do by our vocation to the Franciscan family. The better our knowledge and implementation of the SFO Rule, the better our contribution to building the Kingdom of God in the world.

Which brings us to obedience. The word generally is based on the idea of listening i.e. *ob-audire - to listen to*. Listening is a vital quality. It includes a sense of self-surrender while we listen. Our desire is to hear what another person is saying. Sometimes the words may be emotionally disturbing; sometimes uplifting; sometimes informative; sometimes boring; sometimes exciting; sometimes helpful;

sometimes useless, etc. The key to active listening is to hear what the other is trying to communicate. Attentive listening helps us understand what the conversation is about. Emotions and moods and perspectives may color the words. We listen to the entire mode of expression.

Obedience requires us to listen to God's words inviting us to move in a certain direction. To list some ways to discover God's desire for us, we might include the following:*

Prayer - listening to God's word in our heart and mind - recognizing elements that might influence our present situation or choice. In prayer we are open to the call of the Holy Spirit. Being faithful to prayerfulness helps us grow in sensitivity to the movement of the Spirit.

Friends - Competent friends can help us reach decisions about God's desire for us. People who know us well often perceive things we may miss. Seeing us from the "outside" they help us avoid the blindness that often colors our personal perceptions. By their support, friends can give us courage to take the difficult steps that may be needed.

Community - people who share a common vision, or have a common ministry, or a particular calling, are helpful in making important decisions and choices. Common scriptural reflection may shed light on what we are called to do. Other forms of prayerfulness in community can open the door to supportive dialogue.

Personal experience - good or bad experiences can influence our decisions. As we evaluate experiences, our awareness of others and their needs develops within us. Experiences that challenge our comfortability can invite change as well as strengthening our desire to achieve it. Changes can happen regularly at any age. Fresh ideas and ideals influence decisions we once considered impossible.

---

* Cf. Engaged Spirituality - Joseph Nangle OFM - Page 77-81

Signs of the times - as we develop a sensitive spirit, alert to God-at-work in our lives, our Church, and our world, we recognize what the signs of the times are telling us. Sickness can lead to a particular mind-set. Financial growth and the ability to live in luxury can blind us to the needs of others less fortunate. Conflict can require a fresh look at our words and actions. An honest look at the signs of the times invites creative and critical thinking in order to maintain a Franciscan spirit. The "times" keep changing and they call for Franciscans to make *a radical interior change the Gospel itself calls "conversion"* (SFO Rule #7).

Spiritual direction - sharing the melody of our inner life with a qualified spiritual director can assist in knowing God's desire for us. Revealing ourselves to someone we trust gives us courage to deal with personal qualities that either need enhancement or deletion - or somewhere in between. Spiritual directors are not answer machines. You remain in charge of your life. Spiritual directors offer alternatives, suggestions, or clarifications that recommend fresh choices as you decide what to do.

Each of these possibilities can help us discover what God desires of us. Sometimes we may need only one of them. At other times a combination can enlighten our choices and decisions. The key is our willingness to use the help that is available. Through a common-sense use of these helps we can be united *to the redemptive obedience of Jesus, who placed his will into the Father's hands ...* (SFO Rule #10).

As we grow accustomed to choices that reflect the Gospel, we develop ordinary and common-sense ways of responding to God. Gospel values and ideals influence our decisions. Little by little gospel ideals become a part of our personal identity. Our identity as Franciscans grows in its ability to influence daily life. The importance of this growth comes clear when we try to *faithfully fulfill the duties proper to their various circumstances of life* (SFO Rule #10). Each of us has a different ambiance in which we live. The variety of life situations are many. Each of them will require a fresh look to see how to fulfill the duties that are part of life. Consider some possibilities:

Married. Married with Children. Divorced. Divorced with children. Single. Joining a religious Order. Having a job. Being unemployed. Being retired. Being grandparents. Working for the Church. Having a political job. Having a chronic illness. Returning from war. In the midst of war. Working for peace and justice. Working to assist people in need. Doing volunteer work. Confined to bed. In a nursing home. Recovering from surgery. Having cancer. Being bored in school. Trying to earn a degree. Too poor to get a good education. Feeling hopeless and depressed. Being homosexual. Having a mental disease. Feeling isolated and alone. Excited about life's possibilities. Having two or more jobs to support a family. Facing crises on a daily basis. Marriage seems to be falling apart. Married love is growing. Having no friends. Uncertain about a good use of skills and energy etc. etc.

It is impossible to cover every possibility of life. When we look at the wide variety of people's experiences we understand that being faithful to the duties of life requires personal reflective time to put things in perspective. The goal is to develop a life that reflects the Franciscan spirit.

SFO Rule #10 has the audacity to ask us to witness to the poor and crucified Christ *even in difficulties and persecutions*. Because this requires persistent dedication we need a vibrant fraternity life to keep us on course. We are not alone in this struggle. We walk with other people whom God has called to bear witness to the *poor and crucified Christ*. It becomes obvious to us that we need the Holy Spirit and community support to fulfill our vocation.

For this reason, since the day we heard it, we have not ceased praying for you and asking that you may be filled with the knowledge of God's will in all spiritual wisdom and understanding, so that you may lead lives worthy of the Lord, fully pleasing to him, as you bear fruit in every good work and as you grow in the knowledge of God. May you be made strong with all the strength that comes from his glorious power, and may you be prepared to endure everything with patience, while joyfully giving thanks to the

Father who has enabled you to share in the inheritance of the saints in the light. He has rescued us from the power of darkness and transferred us into the kingdom of his beloved Son, in whom we have redemption, the forgiveness of sins.

Colossians 1:9-14

There is no need for us to create difficulties and persecutions. They usually come without asking them to show up. But it may happen that some of our ways of acting and speaking bring difficulties into our lives. Negative attitudes can create fertile soil for conflict. Our perspectives can be so stubborn or unfeeling that we are responsible for some of our difficulties and persecutions. We can be so domineering and arrogant that we lose friends through our attempts at creeping infallibility.

These areas of life need to be exposed for what they are. If we are the cause of difficulties and persecution then personal conversion is called for. One of my Capuchin brothers once sent me a card which read: *Are you helping with the solution or are you part of the problem?* It was sent in jest, but it invited me to an honest appraisal of how I would answer the question. Our Franciscan life requires personal honesty in these matters. It is easy to be blind to personal responsibility in many situations.

I am the vine, and my Father is the vine-grower. He removes every branch in me that bears no fruit. Every branch that bears fruit he prunes to make it bear more fruit. You have already been cleansed by the word that I have spoken to you. Abide in me as I abide in you. Just as the branch cannot bear fruit by itself unless it abides in the vine, neither can you unless you abide in me. I am the vine, you are the branches. Those who abide in me and I in them bear much fruit, because apart from me you can do nothing.

John 15:1-5

Strange as it may seem, our ability to be true to this article of the Rule (as well as the other articles) influences vocations to the SFO. When people see us consistently seeking peace; caring for the poor; forgiving enemies; praying for those who persecute us; opening ourselves to dialogue even with people who disagree with us; showing concern for the lonely and marginalized; giving life and flesh to the Beatitudes; showing integrity through our way of life; seeking justice; fulfilling duties required by our way of life; - the call of the Spirit will not go unheeded.

The witness of our lives has an influence on others. Our personal integrity as Franciscans should shine like stars in the night. If people are living in darkness we bring light. If people are isolated and marginalized we bring companionship. If people are sick and lonely we bring compassion. If people need to dance, we dance with them. If they want to break into song we harmonize in their singing. If they wish to proclaim the wonders of God's love, we join in the witness. If they proclaim the ways of peace and justice, we are at their side. We witness to Christ and his message in all the circumstances of life.

In addition, let us produce worthy fruits of penance.

And let us love our neighbors as ourselves. And if anyone does not want to love them as himself, let him at least not do them any harm, but let him do good.

Let whoever has received the power of judging others pass judgment with mercy, as they would wish to receive mercy from the Lord. For judgment will be without mercy for those who have not shown mercy

Later Admonition & Exhortation
Francis of Assisi - The Saint - Vol I - Page 47

What does it mean to be poor?
Jesus was poor.
But he had friends, places to sleep,
food to eat, friend's accomodations,
a donkey to ride on,
and an upper room for Passover.

He discussed things with Martha's sister
and his own disciples.
But no place was his own -
and he left his home behind when
his public ministry drew him away.

What does it mean to be poor?
Does it mean that time in not my own?
Life is not my own?
Ability and skills are not my own?

Francis discovered poverty and
she was a Lady and she was vital to him.
She was with Christ on the cross - naked.
Poverty is the seed.

For the seed to grow we must let loose of it.
Poverty is like seeing stars.
To see them we walk in the velvet darkness of night.
Poverty is pain actively accepted
so that the seed dies in order to live and grow.
Poverty is time spent in listening
when I want to get away.
Poverty is sharing a dollar
when my checking account is overdrawn.
Poverty is the gift of me to you
when I don't know what you might do with my gift.
Poverty is trusting God when there is
no human reason for doing so.

A gigantic crossword puzzle - that's poverty.
Touching corners of my life
I thought were safely hidden from Jesus.
Only after all the words are spoken
and life is lived
do I see how it makes sense.
It is faith, hope, and love
in and for Jesus alone -
POOR!

Readings/Questions for dialogue

Conclusion
Engaged Spirituality - Joseph Nangle OFM
Page 89-90

Saved in Hope *(Spe Salvi)* - Benedict XVI
Paragraph 31

The Franciscan Tradition Today
Poverty & Joy - Wm Short OFM - Page 127-130

1. Give your description of the meaning of *obedience*. Share some experiences where it is active in your life.

2. What are some duties of your life that may be changed because of article #10 of the SFO Rule? What moves you to change them?

3. What is your understanding of the meaning of *poverty* in our Franciscan life? How does it look in your life?

4. How are *poverty* and *freedom* connected? Explain how one helps the other.

5. What sources of support can enable us to make decisions that may require difficult choices and decisions?

6. Indicate various helpful ways you would choose when making important decisions. How do they help?

7. How is *obedience* redemptive? Share some Jesus stories that show his freedom in obeying his Father.

8. Scripture reflection: Romans 12:1-21. How do the words of this text of St. Paul stimulate your ability to trust God? What does it say about a community's contribution to ministry and community?

Chapter nineteen

A Simple Way to Live

11. Trusting in the Father, Christ chose for himself and his mother a poor and humble life, even though he valued created things attentively and lovingly. Let the Secular Franciscans seek a proper spirit of detachment from temporal goods by simplifying their own material needs. Let them be mindful that according to the Gospel they are stewards of the goods received for the benefit of God's children.

Thus, in the spirit of "the Beatitudes," and as pilgrims and strangers on their way to the home of the Father, they should strive to purify their hearts from every tendency and yearning for possession and power.

1. Rule 11 *Secular Franciscans should pledge themselves to live the spirit of the Beatitudes and, in a special way, the spirit of poverty. Evangelical poverty demonstrates confidence in the Father, creates interior freedom, and disposes them to promote a more just distribution of wealth.*

2. Secular Franciscans, who must provide for their own families and serve society by means of their work and material goods, **have a particular manner of living evangelical poverty.** *To understand and achieve it requires a strong personal commitment and the stimulation of the fraternity in prayer and dialogue, communal review of life, and attentiveness to the instructions of the Church and the demands of society.*

3. Secular Franciscans should pledge themselves to reduce their own personal needs so as to be better able to share spiritual and material goods with their brothers and sisters, especially those most in need. They should give thanks to God for the goods they have received, using them as good stewards and not as owners.

They should take a firm position against consumerism and against ideologies and practices which prefer riches over human and religious values and which permit the exploitation of the human person.

4. They should love and practice purity of heart, the source of true fraternity.

Constitutions - article 15.1, 15.2, 15.3, 15.4

When Jesus began the Sermon on the Mount, he proclaimed the eight Beatitudes as the ways to authentic happiness. The first of these stated that poverty of spirit would enable us to inherit the Kingdom of God. In other words, the first step on the road to joy begins with a healthy detachment from material goods. Later on in the same sermon, Jesus taught that building up wealth for its own sake is foolishness. We should be more interested in spiritual riches.

... The financial scandals that periodically occur in our culture remind us that greed is a constant threat to moral behavior. It leads many to conclude that money is the root of all evils. But in fact, "the love of money is the root of all evils" (1 Tim 6:10). *In the study of the Seventh Commandment, we dealt with the visible acts of stealing and injustice. The Tenth Commandment looks at the interior attitudes of greed and envy that lead us to steal and act unjustly.*

... On the positive side, the Tenth Commandment calls us to practice poverty of spirit and generosity of heart. These virtues liberate us from being slaves to money and possessions. They enable us to have a preferential love for the poor and to be witnesses of justice and peace in the world. They also enable us to adopt a simplicity of life that frees us from consumerism and helps us preserve God's creation.

United States Catholic Catechism for Adults - USCCB - Page 449-450

When we speak of a simple lifestyle we sometimes think of a house in the woods without running water or indoor plumbing, growing our own food and generally avoiding the consumerism that influences society. That pattern may be how some live a simple life, but it is not for everyone.

Article #11 of the SFO Rule offers some guidelines.

1. Jesus *valued created things attentively and lovingly.* This is reflected in the spirit of Francis. Far from running away from created things, Francis was drawn to them. He did not wish to possess them but to treat them with love and thanksgiving. They were God's gift, given for our use but not for our exploitation. Creation became a place of seeing God's love at work. Sensitivity to created things is obvious in the life of Francis. We, too, strive to grow in respect for and love of created things.

We need many things nature provides. Materials for building houses; plants and animals to provide food for eating; rivers and lakes to provide water for drinking and recreation. We use things according to need rather than desire. Recognizing that natural resources are limited, we use common-sense, avoiding actions that would deplete them. We all need the fundamentals of life. We do not "corner the market" nor deprive others of what they need. We do not create structures that would deny their use to those lacking financial resources. God's earth is given to support all people. Franciscans strive to achieve that goal.

2. A *poor and humble life* is built on the spirit of sharing and a spirit that avoids exploitation for financial gain. Our poverty does not require us to be deprived of necessities but to avoid being possessed by possessions. In fact, the Rule asks us to have *a proper spirit of detachment from temporal goods*. This spirit prompts us to realize that **we are stewards of material things.** Being stewards allows us to share material goods *for the benefit of God's children.* They are given to us to use both for our needs and to share.

Many years ago I worked for a project developed by a rich man. He got "religion" while reading the gospel text to sell what you have and give to the poor (Mt 19:16-22). His initial reaction was to give his wealth to the poor. Talking with a spiritual guide, he was invited to consider another option.

If you give away everything it may be initially satisfying. But the reality is that we will now have one more poor person. Consider that you might use your wealth to develop a program to help the poor. Thus you would embrace a sense of stewardship while helping the poor. Your wealth will become a gift that continues to share, but in a different way than you originally thought.

The man considered the advice and followed it. The result was a program that found ways to build houses and create jobs for the poor, bringing hope to many people. In his own spirit he came to recognize that being a steward has many faces. His sense of stewardship led him to create an ongoing program in which he shared *goods received for the benefit of God's children* - for a long period of time.

3. Not everyone can do this kind of sharing. But the spirit behind this story is open to all of us. Our Franciscan vocation calls us to develop this spirit. We need housing, food, means of transportation, education, and the money to pay for such things. We need work to help us support ourselves, our families and others. The SFO Constitutions put it well: *Secular Franciscans, who must provide for their own families and serve society by means of their work and material goods,* ***have a particular manner of living evangelical poverty*** (Constitutions - article 15.2).

Dialogue at fraternity gatherings can explore this *particular manner of living evangelical poverty.* There is not just one way to achieve this particular *manner.* Whatever solutions our conversations bring, they will need revision and tweaking as they are lived in daily life. What the Franciscan vision asks of us, however, is less changeable. Simplifying our lifestyle is part and parcel of Franciscan life. That goal is always before us. When we deal with our use of material goods we are directed by our desire to keep things simple.

There may be no one way to fulfill this article of the Rule. Consider the different situations Franciscans face. What kind of car do we buy? How much can we spend on transportation? How simple can our children's wedding be? Can we impose our vision on our children? What about housing, rent, or the kind of furniture we buy to make it a home? How much can we spend on our pets? What contributions do we make to the fraternity or for charitable causes? How do we pay for the education of ourselves and our children? What about our investment in clothes and shoes and overcoats and haircuts and permanents?

Once we list "things" that are part of life, detachment seems a secondary concern. Banks do not enjoy our simple lifestyle if we don't pay the mortgage. Stores want their money up-front. Credit card companies give few signs of compassion. Hospitals ordinarily want payment for services rendered. Companies want to make a profit even if we are laid off to achieve it. One accident or a single disease and hospitalization can destroy saving accounts. Health care can ruin us financially or deplete the savings that we put aside for education or retirement or whatever.

Detachment from things presumes that there are things to detach from. One way to learn detachment is to recognize how fragile things are. One fire, or flood, or tornado, or hurricane, or lightning strike and "things" are gone. The greater our attachment the greater our grief. To be free of attachment to material things (even while we use them) means we are free to move on without being owned by them. Detachment is a gift that frees us from dominance by "things" in our lives. Detachment brings the gift of freedom. We are stewards, responsible for our use of material things but not possessed by them.

4. The call *to be pilgrims and strangers on their way to home of the Father* doesn't seem too difficult. Pilgrims do have a certain freedom from things. When you travel a lot you learn to travel light. I have found that I usually take too much in my suitcase. I try to prepare for every eventuality. The trouble is that most of the eventualities

never happen. All of us could benefit from some honest dialogue about this article of the Rule.

Francis delighted in being a pilgrim.
He discovered the familiar in the foreign,
the wonder in the reflections of the holy ones.
So many things reminded him of the Father,
and the Spirit and Jesus.
People need connections,
to find traces of home
away from home.

We need to sense God's presence in our world,
in our country or elsewhere.
We feel a longing for our real home,
because of the wonders of our home away from home.
Francis traveled and made the world his home
because it belonged to his Father in heaven.
cared for by a loving God.
He was alert to the signs
of God's presence all around.

Such a spirit allows us to walk through the world,
taking care to wonder at
and delight in each gift.
To use them well and respectfully,
so everyone has what they need for life.
We love this world with all our heart
even when we know that our
final family reunion with God
will make it seem pale.

Pilgrims don't store up a multitude of things,
but empty their knapsacks
so others can live.
Life is important.
People are important.
And we are pilgrims together,
finding the gospel way to live.

5. These reflections remind us of our *Trinitarian spirituality.* Our primary call from God is to relate to people. We **proclaim the good news of the kingdom** to people. We invite people into our lives and care for their human rights. We look for the common good of people. Whatever the culture or color, we develop a loving attitude toward people and our lives give expression to that love.

6. Part of Franciscan growth comes through our efforts to purify our *hearts from every tendency and yearning for possessions and power.* Bombarded as we are by advertising, telling us how much we need a particular item, it seems safe to say that society doesn't support our efforts. We don't waste time condemning the values of society. Instead we use our creative imagination to discover ways to avoid accumulating too much "stuff." At fraternity gatherings our conversations can address ways and means to avoid the *tendency and yearning for possessions and power*.

Let us refer all good to the Lord, God Almighty and Most High, acknowledge that every good is His, and thank Him "from whom all good comes for everything." (Romans 1:25) *May He, the Almighty and Most High, the only true God, have, be given, and receive all honor and respect, all praise and blessing, all thanks and glory, to Whom all good belongs, He Who alone is good.*

Fragments - Francis of Assisi - The Saint - Vol I - Page 90

7. In *prayerful dialogue* we recognize that we relate to a loving God. God's message to us and love for us is shared with others without the *tendency and yearning* to cling to possessions and power. We discover our treasure and find ways to share it with others - freely.

8. Our attitude toward *power* is one of being a servant. Being elected or appointed to an office does give us power. Nothing bad about that. The difficulty comes if we yearn to have power so we can dominate people and groups. **Our Franciscan spirit is one of service to others.** Power is used to achieve the common good.

In fraternity life that means assisting each other in being faithful to the SFO Rule of life. Power offers us a variety of opportunities. On the one hand we can initiate programs that satisfy our own needs. We can use our position to push our pet ideas without regard for others. On the other hand, we can use power to serve people, creating an atmosphere where people are welcome to share gifts and ideas. We can work together to enhance the quality of fraternity-community life. The common good is our goal rather than self-centered attempts to get our own way.

You know that the rulers of the Gentiles lord it over them, and their great ones are tyrants over them. It will not be so among you; but whoever wishes to be great among you must be your servant, and whoever wishes to be first among you must be your slave; just as the Son of Man came not to be served but to serve and give his life as a ransom for many.

Matthew 20:25-28

9. The Beatitudes were not only preached to a select group of disciples but to crowds waiting to hear Jesus. Jesus proclaims many values for us to embrace in the words of the Beatitudes (Matthew 5:1-12 / Luke 6:20-26).

We have written about the *poor in spirit* from a Franciscan point of view. We use created things and we have personal opinions. The key for the *poor in spirit* is not to cling to them so tightly that they dictate to us or to others with no hope of change. On the contrary, as stewards, we share our gifts with one another. Being *poor in spirit* opens us to God's call and way of doing things. It brings us freedom to follow the path of conversion in our Franciscan life.

Blessedness in mourning is not some trick of Jesus to keep us from enjoying life. Rather, mourning can be understood in at least two ways. On the one hand, we do mourn when someone we love dies. That is human and natural. Jesus says that we will be comforted by his loving presence. On the other hand, we are called to mourn for personal and societal sinfulness and things we do that fracture relationships or deny human rights. As we mourn these actions or words, we begin to find comfort by changing our ways of acting or that of society. Discovering our mistakes in relationships helps us seek ways to correct such mistakes. Initiating the process of conversion brings comfort.

Gentle (meek) individuals have the strength to **see what needs to be done and to actually do it.** Gentleness allows us to touch people's lives without arrogance or dominance. It is a spirit that helps others retain their dignity. This spirit of acceptance ordinarily does not create opposition but gives us a glimpse of what good relationships can accomplish.

People *who hunger and thirst for righteousness* (justice) *will be filled.* This beatitude fits the SFO Rule (article #15) that invites us *to be in the forefront in promoting justice.* The fullness we receive may not be found through our success ratio. Working for justice does not always achieve the results we desire. However, our scriptural integrity in working for justice gives us a sense of peace even when we do not reach the desired goal. **We *hunger and thirst*, faithful to building a world where all people are treated with dignity.** *Only lovers of justice and truth can possess the Kingdom of Heaven, and to be children of God we must be lovers of justice and truth* (Venerable Solanus Casey OFM Cap).

The merciful will receive mercy. This is a fine slogan to follow. It reflects the spirit that Francis and Clare showed in their lives. No matter how often someone fails or hurts us, **we offer the hand of mercy.** It is who we are - merciful people. *Jesus is no crank! He knows we are no angels, but poor sinners, and He understands when we fail. After all, His mercy is above all His works and His patience is essentially one with His mercy* (Venerable Solanus Casey OFM Cap). What Jesus, Francis, and Clare did in their lives, we will do in our lives - **show mercy and seek reconciliation.** We are, after all, people of the Beatitudes!

The *pure in heart* are people who are not deceived by artificiality, lies or other tools people use to hide their inner lives or actions from others. *Purity of heart* is clear-sighted. There are no cataracts nor glaucomas in their seeing. The *pure in heart* see things as they really are. Even more, they are willing to deal with reality in a faith-filled way. Having clear vision means that they see the presence of God all around them. Francis certainly had such *purity of heart.* It enabled him to recognize the presence of God in the whole created world and its people. Check out articles #5 and #13 of the SFO Rule to discover who we should see in people and the world around us.

Peacemakers ... will be called children of God. When we bring peace to conflictual situations we imitate God in his deepest desires. We all experience conflict in different forms. It can happen - in our hearts; in our relationship with others; between competing groups; between countries; beween religions. The SFO Rule reflects this beatitude, inviting us to be *Mindful that they* (we) *are bearers of peace which must be built up unceasingly ...* (SFO Rule - article #19). This beatitude brings delight and confidence in our search for peace. We will be *children of God.* We seek ***both/and*** solutions (combining people's ideas) rather than seeking *either/or* solutions (which easily separates people into winners & losers).

The final beatitudes are a reality check. If you do what the Beatitudes require, you will find yourselves persecuted and reviled. Not to worry. That's the normal reaction of those who refuse the gospel vision. Actually *you can rejoice and be glad for your reward is great in heaven.*

There are numerous books on the Beatitudes. Each book contributes something to our understanding and implementation of Jesus' words. Search for them and use them wisely.

Owe no one anything, except to love one another; for the one who loves another has fulfilled the law. The commandments, "You shall not commit adultery; You shall not murder; You shall not steal; You shall not covet;" and any other commandment, are summed up in this word, "Love your neighbor as yourself!" Love does no wrong to a neighbor; therefore, love is the fulfilling of the law.

Romans 13:8-10

He also told this parable to some who trusted in themselves that they were righteous and regarded others with contempt: 'Two men went up to the temple to pray, one a Pharisee and the other a tax-collector. The Pharisee, standing by himself, was praying thus, "God, I thank you that I am not like other people: thieves, rogues, adulterers, or even like this tax-collector. I fast twice a week; I give a tenth of all my income." But the tax-collector, standing far off, would not even look up to heaven, but was beating his breast and saying, "God, be merciful to me, a sinner!" I tell you this man went down to his home justified rather than the other; for all who exalt themselves with be humbled, but all who humble themselves will be exalted.

Luke 18:9-14

+++

Readings/Questions for dialogue

Christianity & Social Progress *(Mater et Magistra)*
John XXIII - Paragraph 257

Conclusions
Engaged Spirituality - Joseph Nangle OFM - Page 15-17

Saved In Hope (*Spe Salvi*) - Benedict XVI
Paragraph 26

1. What spirit did Jesus have toward created things? How does that spirit express itself in your life?

2. Explain the value of detachment for a Franciscan. How does it help you in embracing the Franciscan way of life?

3. What basic spirit does a pilgrim need? Why?

4. Explain your understanding of what it means to be a

steward of God's gifts to us. Evaluate your ability to act as a steward in regard to material things or personal talents.

5. Which Beatitude do you find easiest to live? Which one is most difficult? How does the spirit of the Beatitudes show itself in your life?

6. Explain/share your understanding of *your particular manner of living evangelical poverty* (Constitutions - article 15.2) and how it looks in your life.

7. Scripture reflection: Ezekiel 37:1-14. How does this text give you hope when your best efforts fail to achieve the good things you set out to accomplish?

+++

God,
grant me
the SERENITY
to prioritize the things
I cannot delegate,

the COURAGE
to say NO
when I need to,

and the WISDOM
to know when to go
HOME.

+++

If you think you're too small to be effective,
you've never been in bed with a mosquito.

Chapter twenty

Freedom to Love

12. Witnessing to the good yet to come and obliged to acquire purity of heart because of the vocation they have embraced, they should set themselves free to love God and their brothers and sisters.

When we search for the meaning of life in general and our lives in particular, we can generally summarize the results of this search into three categories: beliefs, practices, and narratives. In other words, we find meaning in life when we are able to base our lives on truths bigger than ourselves, to articulate why we do what we do, and to share the stories that unite and motivate us. All religions must grapple with these concerns and provide an encouraging response to the searches of believers.

For Franciscan-minded people, narrative holds a place of priority not only because the early Movement is primarily handed down to us through stories but also because stories inspire us. Often enough, while beliefs and practices may differ among world religions, there are extraordinary similarities in their narratives, not in the details but surely in their sweep.

Build With Living Stones - Unit 8 - Page 7
St. Bonaventure University, St. Bonaventure, NY 14778

Freedom is a word that is tossed around a great deal. It seems to have many meanings, depending on who is using the term. Exploring this article of the SFO Rule requires us to spell out our understanding of the meaning of *freedom*.

Freedom is the power given by God to act or not to act, to do this or to do that, and so to perform deliberate actions on one's own responsibility. Freedom characterizes properly human acts. The more one does what is good, the freer one becomes. Freedom attains its proper perfection when it is directed toward God, the highest good and our beatitude. Freedom implies also the possibility of choosing between good and evil. The choice of evil is an abuse of freedom and leads to the slavery of sin.

Compendium - Catechism of the Catholic Church
USCCB - #363 - Page 108

Freedom makes people responsible for their actions to the extent that they are voluntary, even if the imputability and responsibility for an action can be diminished or sometimes cancelled by ignorance, inadvertance, duress, fear, inordinate attachments, or habit.

Ibid - #364 - Page 108

Since freedom has many mothers who give birth to a variety of definitions, Franciscans need to be clear about freedom. From the very beginning God did not want the praise of robots but the praise of people freely choosing to praise God. There was no value in creating robots. Instead God chose to give us the freedom to make choices. The early chapters of Genesis reveal that people did not do well at making good choices. Adam and Eve didn't do too well. Cain and Abel certainly left something to be desired. Reading the Bible stories, including the story about King David, the adulterer and murderer, help us understand that we are not always good at handling freedom.

Further reflection points to the reason why freedom functions best when it has borders within which to function. A look at team sports illustrates this fact. Games provide a framework in which to play. Rules and guidelines offer a space within which talent is shown. Knowing the rules enables us to focus our abilities to function within a certain framework. It also requires a respect for the "other," whether team-mates or opposing team members. Within that framework talent can blossom and grow. When the rules don't work, people change them so that competition is fair and the rules apply to everyone in the sport.

Without some framework personal freedom could go wild. The joy of watching competition would disappear. Instead of enjoyment we would have chaos, perhaps physical harm, impossible situations, no accountability and a sad commentary on unbridled and irresponsible freedom.

People in ordinary human life live within a framework of laws and regulations. Laws and structures are not infallibly helpful. But without the presence of good laws/structures society would break down into chaos and disrespect. Religion, though not necessarily law-oriented but gospel-oriented, needs law and structure to create an atmosphere of freedom for gospel living. This freedom allows us to respond to the Gospel according to the call of the Spirit.

Without law and direction we could wind up with all kinds of interesting, even misleading, ways of life. Structures create a framework within which to function. When the laws and structures interfere with or stymie the work of the Spirit we change them. We use freedom in order to dialogue about the influence provided by structures and laws. Dialogue, done with respect and reverence, can move us to change structures that hinder gospel goals.

But societies and churches are not the only law givers. People create their own laws. They decide how things will function within their own homes or among family members. Companies and corporations make laws to control how people work within that company or corporation. Generally, the goal is efficiency. This is certainly not evil. But when efficiency competes with the human rights of people it creates problems. Efficiency is generally needed to increase profits. For that reason it frequently wins the battle between profit and human need.

A reasonable profit is just that - reasonable. But extravagant profits and diminishing concern for employees is not so reasonable. This struggle touches Franciscans who own or work for a business, company, store, or corporation. An atmosphere of freedom is not always present. Sometimes coercion and threats become tools to force compliance with company policies. When dialogue is rejected, chaos, depression and violence can rear their ugly heads.

Families need rules to guide a healthy family life. Learning how to accomodate to the needs of others is a serious part of growing-up. Creating a safe environment within the family circle is helpful to all. But there are also times when guidelines or rules need to be changed. When they become a source of constant arguments, dialogue is required. The atmosphere created by structures is meant to support growth rather than interfere with it. Again, freedom functions best within a framework that is respectful. Changing domineering structures and rules is a common consequence of respect and reverence.

... they should set themselves free to love God and their brothers and sisters (SFO Rule #12).

None of us evades this task of being free. We try to free ourselves of structures that are controlling and have little or no other purpose. We free ourselves of opinions that label people, calling them evil or other names. Franciscans cannot tolerate anything that causes separation among people. Even when we passionately disagree, we try to do it in such a way that relationships are not broken.

This attitude calls for strong faith and a reliance on the Holy Spirit. It requires maturity and concern for the "other" (Love). It is not easily accomplished without the help of the Holy Spirit. In short, it is not easy to achieve gospel freedom without reliance on God's love for us.

We do not live to ourselves, and we do not die to ourselves. If we live, we live to the Lord, and if we die, we die to the Lord; so then, whether we live or whether we die, we are the Lord's. For to this end Christ died and lived again, so that he might be Lord of both the dead and the living.

Why do you pass judgment on your brother or

sister? Or you, why do you despise your brother or sister? For we will all stand before the judgment seat of God. For it is written, "As I live, says the Lord, every knee shall bow to me, and every tongue shall give praise to God." So then, each of us will be accountable to God.

Romans 14:7-12

So whether you eat or drink, or whatever you do, do everything for the glory of God. Give no offence to Jews or to Greeks or to the church of God, just as I try to please everyone in everything I do, not seeking my own advantage, but that of many, so that they may be saved. Be imitators of me, as I am of Christ.

1 Corinthians 10:31-33, 11:1

In many scripture texts we discover a framework in which we are called to live. It is an atmosphere that draws us together in Christ. Scripture proclaims qualities that are part of living in the Kingdom of God. Within the structure of the Kingdom our citizenship requires us to fulfill responsibilities arising from the Gospel. If we are to - witness *to the good yet to come and obliged to acquire purity of heart because of the vocation they have embraced* (Rule #12) - the values of the Gospel will be freely embraced. **We choose a gospel way of living before any others.** We may struggle to learn the ways of achieving the goal, but we will not evade the struggle. Faith, hope and charity will be bright lights in our lives.

Evangelizing is in fact the grace and vocation proper to the Church, her deepest identity. *She exists in order to evangelize, that is to say in order to preach and teach, to be the channel of the gift of grace, to reconcile sinners with God, and to perpetuate Christ's sacrifice in the Mass, which is the memorial of his death and glorious resurrection.*

On Evangelization in the Modern World - *(Evangelii Nuntiandi)*
Paul VI - Paragraph 14

- The Church is an evangelizer, but ***she begins by being evangelized herself.*** *She is the community of believers, the community of hope lived and communicated, the commu-*

nity of brotherly love; and she needs to listen unceasingly to what she must believe, to her reasons for hoping, to the new commandment of love. She is the People of God immersed in the world, and often tempted by idols, and she always needs to hear the proclamation of the" mighty works of God" (Acts 2:11 / 1 Peter 2:9) *which converted her to the Lord; she always needs to be called together afresh by him and reunited. In brief, this means that* ***she has a constant need of being evangelized****, if she wishes to retain freshness, vigor and strength in order to proclaim the Gospel.*

On Evangelization in the Modern World (Evangelii Nuntiandi)
Paul VI - Paragraph 15

The inter-connectedness of articles in the SFO Rule is obvious as we reflect on article #12 of the Rule. Our ability to live in freedom within the Kingdom is connected to our ability to dialogue about ways and means to live the Rule. Our freedom is given direction by the Rule. The Rule creates a structure which guides daily decisions.

The SFO Rule offers direction - on what to choose and what to reject; what to do and what to leave undone; how to deal with one another; when to support others in finding their way; how to move to contemplative prayerfulness; discovering the need to change in order to promote relationships. Franciscan growth surrounds us through the SFO Rule given us by the Church.

Profession is our free response to the call of the Holy Spirit to commit ourselves to the Franciscan spirit. We freely choose to live within the framework of Franciscanism. The freedom to follow Francis' spirit becomes part of our personal identity. Our trust in and love for God continues to grow and brings peace and joy in its wake. It moves us to love one another just as Jesus loves us.

Witnessing to the good yet to come and obliged to acquire purity of heart because of the vocation they have embraced, they should set themselves free to love God and their brothers and sisters (SFO Rule #12).

The Franciscan revolution means that we hold nothing back but share whatever gifts God has given us. Joy is present in our life where love for Jesus, the Father, and the Holy Spirit spills over into a love for all of creation.

... *to acquire purity of heart* requires us to cleanse our mind, heart, emotions and actions of anything that hinders the love of God working through us. As the Beatitude puts it, *Blessed are the pure of heart, for they shall see God.* This beatitude is an invitation to develop our sense of the presence of God in people whose lives we touch, even if they are far from God. We are not deceived by another's selfishness or violence or withdrawal. Rather, we discover God's presence and see into the heart of the "other."

Purity of heart is important in living our Franciscan life. We humans can be good at hiding our real selves. We have all kinds of excuses for refusing to change. We create attitudes that keep people from getting close to us. We rationalize behavior that has little or no connection to a gospel life. We silently bear hurts and grief that ought to be verbalized and addressed.

Purity of heart enables us to see the things that bind people. We initiate actions that will bring people to freedom. *Purity of heart* enables us to relate to people in ways that bring them to new life. It establishes a new dimension to our relationship with one another. We are wise enough to know when we need help from other people.

Being pure of heart means seeing clearly.
Being humble means understanding reality.
Being little means God pours blessings
on the little ones who know their need of God.
These are Franciscan traits.

Since nothing is ours,
we share ourselves and our gifts with others,
always yearning to be people of the Gospel.

We are Franciscans.
In tune with the needs of our brothers and sisters,
free of unnecessary baggage.
We enjoy living in our Father's world,
and among God's people.

Sometimes we wonder at God's love.
Sometimes we feel abandoned
in a dark night of fear.
But we know that we must follow the Gospel.
Sometimes we drown the gospel call
in a feverish burst of activity or addiction,
but silence calls again
and we answer.

Jesus' heartbreak at Peter's failure
is ours when a brother or sister
is hurting and refuses our help.
Yet, we rise to listen to another call
that cannot be put off.
Content in the task of giving.

Francis is our guide.
He leads us in the footsteps
of the crucified One.
To a Calvary where love proves itself.
Everything takes on meaning
because of Jesus.
Everyone is important
because of Jesus.

Lord, keep me faithful to being
a Franciscan in the world.

When we respond to the Spirit's call to follow Francis many decisions and choices are already made. The Franciscan spirit surrounds us within and without. We show the Franciscan spirit by the life we lead. Following the guidance of the SFO Rule our lives become visible models of

Franciscan life and Kingdom people. The formation of a Franciscan is ongoing and never ends.

Just as I have loved you, you also should love one another. By this everyone will know that you are my disciples, if you have love for one another.

John 13:34-35

Readings/Questions for dialogue

The Responsible Practice of Freedom
United States Catholic Catechism for Adults - USCCB
Page 310-311

Saved in Hope *(Spe Salvi)* - Benedict XVI
Paragraph 24, a and b

Decree on the Apostolate of Lay People - Vatican II
(Apostolicam Actuositatem) - Paragraph 4

1. Describe your understanding of "purity of heart." How does it assist your ability to live a Franciscan life?

2. Why is freedom so important to God? What is the highest form of gospel freedom? Explain.

3. What is the goal or purpose of structures and laws? What do we do if structures, inside or outside the SFO, fail to help us live the Franciscan life called for by the Church?

4. What role do structures/laws play in supporting freedom? How is freedom connected to dialogue?

5. Why is it often difficult to change laws/structures in any organization? What (who?) can initiate change?

6. Explain how a secular Franciscan's faithfulness depends on a commitment to live the entire SFO Rule? What would be missing if this is not done?

7. Scripture reflection: Luke 1:39-45. How do Elizabeth and Mary model an example of purity of heart in this text? How does this meeting hint at what happens when people are in tune with God?

+++

Poverty, for Francis,
was the key to love.
Although poverty played
a central role
in his way of life,
it is interesting that
he almost never explains it
in his writings.
Francis was not really interested
in the poverty of material possessions;
rather he was concerned
for the type of poverty that
would lead to interdependence
and the love of the brothers
for one another.
Thus he advocated that
his followers live 'sine propio' -
not without things
but without possessing things,
for when we possess things
we may think
that we do not
need other people or have
a responsibility of love
toward them.
Francis had profound insight
into the human person
and he placed poverty
in the context
of human relationships.

Franciscan Prayer - Ilia Delio OSF
Page 82-83

Chapter twenty one

How to Love People

13. As the Father sees in every person the features of his Son, the first-born of many brothers and sisters, so the Secular Franciscans with a gentle and courteous spirit accept all people as a gift of the Lord and an image of Christ.

A sense of community will make them joyful and ready to place themselves on an equal basis with all people, especially with the lowly for whom they shall strive to create conditions of life worthy of people redeemed by Christ.

1. Secular Franciscans are called to make their own contribution, ***inspired by the person and message of Saint Francis of Assisi, towards a civilization in which the dignity of the human person, shared responsibility, and love may be living realities.***

2. Rule 13 *They should deepen the true foundations of universal kinship and create a spirit of welcome and an atmosphere of fraternity everywhere. They should firmly commit themselves* ***to oppose every form of exploitation, discrimination, and exclusion and against every attitude of indifference in relation to others.***

3. Rule 13 *They should work together with movements which promote the building of fraternity among peoples: they should be committed to "create worthy conditions of life" for all and to work for the freedom of all people.*

Constitutions - Article 18.1, 18.2, 18.3

... we need to acquire the virtues of moderation in our possessions, justice in our treatment of others, respect for their human dignity, and solidarity with all peoples.

Moderation curbs our attachment to worldly goods and restrains our appetite for consumerism. Justice helps us respect our neighbor's rights and be interested in their human well-being. Solidarity opens our hearts to identifying with the whole human family, reminding us of our common humanity.

We should not steal from each other, pay unfair salaries, cheat in business, or exploit people's weaknesses to make money. Promises should be kept and contracts honored to the extent that the issues are morally just (Cf. CCC, no. 2410). *We need to safeguard property rights, pay our debts, and fulfill obligations freely incurred. The government has the right and duty to safeguard legitimate ownership of money and property and to protect people from robbery and injury.*

United States Catholic Catechism for Adults - USCCB - Page 419

Once again we are called to an examination of our perspectives on relationships. It moves beyond family and fraternity relationships. They are important and deserve consideration. But this article of the Rule moves us to decisions about relationships to all people and especially the decisions we make about the "lowly." That word is not the best one to use about people, but it is linked to the reality that many people consider themselves "lowly."

What is the spirit that guides our Franciscan way of relating to people? Article #13 of the Rule sets forth a number of qualities:

1. **A gentle spirit;**
2. **A courteous spirit;**
3. **Accept people as a gift;**
4. **Accept people as an image of Christ;**
5. **Place ourselves on an equal basis with people;**
6. **Recognize people's worth.**

A gentle spirit - understands that people are not perfect. In our personal lives, as well as that of other people, we recognize that not all our choices are life-giving. A gentle person understands this. Therefore, his/her reaction to other's poor choices is one of acceptance of the person without giving approval to poor choices. A gentle person creates a spirit of hospitality rather a spirit of condemnation. This choice opens the door to dialogue about choices rather than creating a site of judgment.

In our humanness this is no easy choice. We may be of the opinion that the "culprit" doesn't deserve another chance. Understand that a gentle person is not a pushover, "caving in" readily to others. The gentle person has a good grasp of reality and takes action that fits the situation. But the goal is supporting change without creating conflict that hinders a solution. The gentle person does not presume to have all the answers. Sometimes this entire event lasts for a long period. The gentle person does not give up or give in. Gentle people seek help when they recognize their inability to deal with a situation.

The gentle person does not allow the *other's action to dictate* their response. Instead of bowing to the various ways the "culprit" attempts to control or manipulate the situation, the gentle person focuses on the goal to be achieved. His/her actions and words stay in tune with that goal and are not detoured by the others' words and actions. These are often used to distract us from the goal.

These situations also help us recognize our need for the guidance of the Holy Spirit and a prayerful approach. We may be incompetent for this situation, or competent but fearful, or uncertain about our competency. A gentle person calls on the inspiration of the Holy Spirit and the inspiration of competent people as needed.

Let all the brothers who know that he (another brother) *has sinned not bring shame upon him or slander him; let them, instead, show great mercy to him and keep the sin of their brother very secret because those who are well do not need a physician, but the sick do.* (Matthew 9:12-Mark 2:17-Luke 5:31)
A Letter to a Minister - Francis of Assisi - The Saint - Vol I - Page 98

A courteous spirit - is built on a foundation of respect for other people. Courtesy is our human way of recognizing the dignity of another person. A gospel story gives an image of what it is like to be courteous.

While they were talking about this, Jesus himself stood among them and said to them, "Peace be with you." They were startled; and terrified, and thought that they were seeing a ghost. He said to them, "Why are you so frightened, and why do doubts arise in your hearts? Look at my hands and my feet; see that it is I myself. Touch me and see; for a ghost does not have flesh and bones as you see that I have." And when he had said this he showed them his hands and his feet. While in their joy they were disbelieving and still wondering, he said to them, "Have you anything here to eat?" They gave him a piece of broiled fish, and he took it and ate in their presence.

Luke 24:36-43

This group had hardly been loyal supporters of Jesus during his passion and death on the cross. Yet Jesus responds to their needs without judgment. These are the people who were going to build the Kingdom of God. Jesus kept his goal in mind and treated them with courtesy. Troubled as they were, Jesus' reaction to them opened the door to listening to Jesus' words. In that same text Jesus tells them: *And see, I am sending upon you what my Father promised; so stay here in the city until you have been clothed with power from on high.* (Luke 24:49).

Courtesy has more authority than politeness. Politeness can direct us in using the right fork or spoon or how to address people, or saying "please" and "thank you" at the proper time. Politeness has less to do with relationships than to acting correctly in social situations. Courtesy springs from our inner spirit of respect for all people. Politeness is one way to show respect but it can be merely external.

In his *Letter to Brother Leo*, Francis illustrates respect for Leo who was so close to him. Francis' words show his love for Leo while leaving Leo free to decide whether or not to speak to Francis about personal issues.

Brother Leo, health and peace from Brother Francis!

I am speaking, my son, in this way - as a mother would - because I am putting everything we said on the road in this brief message and advice. If, afterwards, you need to come to me for counsel, I advise you thus: In whatever way it seems better to you to please the Lord God and to follow his footprint and poverty, do it with the blessing of the Lord God and my obedience. And if you need and want to come to me for the sake of your soul or for some consolation, Leo, come.

A Letter to Brother Leo - Francis of Assisi - The Saint - Vol I - Page 122

Francis shows respect for Leo that springs from the courtesy that Francis embraced. Throughout his life Francis gave witness to courtesy. Perhaps his *Canticle of the Creatures* gives an exclamation point to his spirit of courtesy to all of creation. Courtesy was shown because all of creation reflects God's love. Francis' courtesy was not withheld from anyone who needed it.

Franciscans are called to have the same courtesy. The SFO Rule puts it precisely when it says: *accept all people as a gift of the Lord and an image of Chris*t.

Accept all people as a gift ... anyone who knows people knows that people do not always appear as a *gift!* That is true. So we're not addressing the issue out of some naive ideas about people. On the other hand, if we are serious about proclaiming the Kingdom of God, then we do need to embrace the idea that people *are a gift.* It nudges us to act toward them with this idea in mind.

We will not let people who are less than a gift dictate how we choose to act. Our identity as Franciscans teaches us how to act. It also touches us with plenty of opportunities for conversion. Since Franciscans commonly make use of such opportunities, it should be normal for us to accept a call to conversion.

None of us always give a fine example of being a gift to others. If we are made aware of this fact, we engage in the changes that can be called *conversion.* Our desire to be faithful to the Franciscan spirit will motivate us to walk the road to conversion as needed. With a whole world in need of some form of conversion, we need to show the way by example. The SFO Rule points a direction for us to follow. *Profession* will cement that choice by the permanent commitment to follow the SFO Rule and the consequences of baptism.

Jesus stood still and ordered the man to be brought to him, "What do you want me to do for you?" He said, "Lord, let me see again." Jesus said to him, "Receive your sight; your faith has saved you." Immediately he regained his sight and followed him, glorifying God; and all the people, when they saw it, praised God.

Luke 18:40-43

When we see with Franciscan eyes and recognize people as a gift of God and an image of Christ, we follow Christ and glorify God.

... *Accept people as an image of Christ* - will require a change in us. It's not like people suddenly look like Christ. Rather, we begin to search for the image of Christ in people. We will still have our initial impressions. People may bear little resemblance to Christ. Their ideas and actions may not reflect the love of Christ. Our task is to search for the image of Christ. Listening to people, whoever they may be, brings us some knowledge about who they are right now.

Sometimes, like peeling an onion, we must peel away layers of poor decisions that brought people to this point in their lives. It takes time. Trust is needed, so we must be trustworthy. Confidence in our love is needed, so we must be persistent in our love. A caring spirit must manifest itself, so we will need to care. Throughout this process change may be happening in both of us. If groups are involved, a great deal of patience will be required since it takes time for a group of people to change.

Without quickly discovering gold, we must persist in the process. Since success is not assured, we are brought once more to rely on the power of the Holy Spirit. We realize that we are earthenware jars that hold this treasure of love. As Jesus put it to his disciples:

The hour is coming, indeed it has come, when you will be scattered, each one to his home, and you will leave me alone. Yet I am not alone because the Father is with me. I have said this to you, so that in me you may have peace. In the world you face persecution. But take courage, I have conquered the world.

John 16:32-33

As Jesus knew that his Father was with him, so the Holy Spirit (and the Trinity) is with us and within us. We are not alone in facing relationship issues. That doesn't mean it is a smooth road. It does mean that inspired by the Spirit we will fulfill the Gospel in our daily lives and **persist in discovering the image of Christ in others.**

... ready to place ourselves on an equal basis with all people - this is a spirit we bring to conversations and contacts with people. Equality doesn't mean everything is exactly equal. Men are not women and vice versa. Educational development is not the same in everyone. Experiences have not brought everyone to the same point in life. Family traits differ among us. Cultural qualities bring different perceptions as people mature.

The common thread is that we are human. Being human and created in God's likeness, *male and female God created them* (Genesis 1:27), makes each of us an image of God. It is the basis of our equality. If we are true to the first part of article #13, equality will be a consequence.

The first man and woman were qualitively different from and superior to all other living creatures on earth. They were uniquely made in the image of God, as are all human beings, their descendants. What does this mean? God's image is not a static picture stamped on our souls. God's image is a dynamic source of inner spiritual energy drawing our minds and hearts toward truth and love, and to God himself, the source of all truth and love.

To be made in the image of God includes specific qualities. Each of us is capable of self-knowledge and of entering into communion with other persons through self-giving. ... To be made in God's image also unites human beings as God's stewards in the care of the earth and of all God's other creatures.

United States Catholic Catechism for Adults - USCCB - Page 67

This understanding keeps us in touch with all people. **Franciscans have a special love and concern for poor people and the marginalized.** This includes anyone whose human dignity is diminished by factors beyond their control or by negative personal factors they refuse to address. It is a choice and part and parcel of our Franciscan vocation. How we serve the poor may differ, but our spirit will always lean to the needs of poor people when choices can be made.

In addition, one of the things we will do, often together with other groups, *is to strive to create conditions of life worthy of people redeemed by Christ.* Other people often help in this attempt to create conditions worthy of people made in God's image. Their motivation may be different, but their passion for societal change and concern for the poor calls us to work together.

How we do this will depend on our situation in life. Differences are normal. Franciscans, because of their *profession,* have a common desire to relate to God, all people, and all of creation. We have chosen to accept this challenge as part of being Franciscans. Joined in a community life we bring joy to others through our common collaborative efforts.

But now thus says the Lord, he who created you, O Jacob, he who formed you, O Israel; Do not fear, for I have redeemed you; I have called you by name, you are mine ... Because you are precious in my sight, and honoured, and I love you. ... Do not fear, for I am with you.

Isaiah 43: 1, 4-5

If God has such sensitivity for us, we will show the same sensitivity to one another.

+++

Readings/Questions for dialogue

Created in God's Image
United States Catholic Catechism for Adults - USCCB
Page 67-68

Francis: 'Vivere Sine Proprio'
Poverty and Joy - Wm Short OFM - Pages 59-62

Fifth Lesson
The Minor Legend of St Francis - St. Bonaventure
Francis of Assisi - The Founder - Vol II - Page 691

Formation personnel and Candidates:

This session of formation will be longer than usual because of the questions. Please provide extra time so that all the material can be shared.

1. This is a time to review your growth in the Franciscan spirit and how it is affecting your life. Evaluate the following elements, not only for intellectual understanding but also for how you put the SFO Rule into practice.

+ Dialogue with one another in answering these questions +

+ How have your relationships with people changed? Give some examples.
+ What changes have you made in your prayer life?
+ What changes have you achieved in regard to serving the poor and growing in a sense of stewardship?

+ How have personal changes affected your family life? Church life? Fraternity life? Single life or married life? Work life?
+ What is your opinion regarding structures and law and their relationship to the Franciscan spirit? How can they help achieve the goal of a group?
+ At this point how do you feel about making profession in the Secular Franciscan way of life?
+ What qualities (spirit) are you developing in order to show a Franciscan spirit in dealing with other people?
+ What is the goal of a call to the SFO? How does profession affect society and the larger church?
+ How has the formation process helped you in preparing for profession? Are there any positive improvements we might make?

2. What are the qualities article #13 requires of Secular Franciscans? Share the ways in which you have absorbed these qualities and show them in daily life.

3. What effect does gentleness and courtesy have as we interact with one another? How can you develop these qualities if you already have negative ideas about people?

4. What would *conditions of life worthy of people redeemed by Christ* look like? How can you help achieve such conditions? What are you doing to achieve this goal?

5. What steps can you take *to accept people as a gift of the Lord and an image of Christ*? How can we help one another to achieve this spirit?

6. Scripture reflection: Matthew 21:28-32. What does this text say to us about the ability to change? What kept the chief priests and elders from believing in Jesus? Why would tax-collectors and prostitutes believe in Jesus?

+++

Christianity, if false, is of no importance,
and if true, is of infinite importance.
The only thing it cannot be is moderately important.

C.S. Lewis

Chapter twenty two

Foundations for the Kingdom

14. Secular Franciscans, together with all people of good will, are called to build a more fraternal and evangelical world so that the Kingdom of God may be brought about more effectively. Mindful that anyone "who follows Christ, the perfect man, becomes more of a man himself," let them exercise their responsibilities competently in the Christian spirit of service.

1. Rule 14 *Secular Franciscans should always act as a leaven in the environment in which they live through the witness of their fraternal love and clear Christian motivations.*

2. In the spirit of minority, ***they should opt for relationships which give preference to the poor and to those on the fringe of society,*** *whether these be individuals or categories of persons or an entire people;* ***they should collaborate in overcoming the exclusion of others and those forms of poverty that are the fruit of inefficiency and injustice.***

Constitutions - article 19.1, 19.2

1. Rule 14 *Secular Franciscans, committed by their vocation to build the Kingdom of God in temporal situations and activities, live their membership both in the Church and in society as an inseparable reality.*

2. As the primary and fundamental contribution to building a more just and fraternal world, ***they should commit themselves both to the generous fulfillment of the duties proper to their occupation and to the professional training that pertains to it.*** *With the same spirit of service, they should assume their social and civil responsibilities.*

Constitutions - article 20.1, 20.2

107. All are invited by Jesus to enter the Kingdom of God. Even the worst of sinners is called to convert and to accept the boundless mercy of the Father. Already here on earth the Kingdom belongs to those who accept it with a humble heart. To them the mysteries of the Kingdom are revealed.

108. Jesus accompanied his words with signs *and* miracles *to bear witness to the fact that the Kingdom is present in him, the Messiah. Although he healed some people, he did not come to abolish all evils here below but rather to free us especially from the slavery of sin. The driving out of demons proclaimed that his cross would be victorious over "the ruler of this world"* (John 12: 31).

Compendium - Catechism of the Catholic Church
#107 & #108 - Page 34

The SFO Rule gives motivation for building a more evangelical and fraternal world. Building that kind of world makes it possible for the Kingdom of God to grow there. An *evangelical* world would better reflect gospel values. A more *fraternal* world would help us live in caring and loving relationship with one another - a community.

This is not done in a corner of the world where everything works just right. Building a more evangelical and fraternal world takes place in the middle of a muddled world. We don't have universal agreement that such a world is what we want. We don't have universal approval of gospel ideas that might create such a world. We face opposition in our attempts to develop such a world. While we might talk about a "Christian" nation, none (or few) of them exist.

That might move us to cease our efforts. It seems like we are talking about a dream-world that sounds nice but never happens in real life. For Christians that is actually beside the point. Even if the full dream is never achieved we continue making inroads in society to make it responsive to human dignity and need. Though achieving a total transformation of society may not happen, it doesn't stop us from making improvements in the present situation.

Our ministries and work walk us into the heart of society. It is in the midst of that world where we proclaim our values by words, actions, and presence.

We live in a particular country and society. That is the starting place for building a fraternal and evangelical world. As our ability to recognize the gospel vision improves, we may expand our ministries to wider needs that require our attention. Community concerns will invite us to invest energy to seek solutions. Because of the inter-linking of people and needs, global ministries will also arise.

In meeting these needs we seek ways to collaborate with people even if they have different beliefs. Our talk about working together has to move beyond words. Words and actions combine to build a society that respects and supports the dignity of all people. It is no little task. But every step along the way can build a better way of dealing with economic and human dignity issues. Progress is slow and sometimes frustrating. If we can diminish greed, selfishness and the profit-only way of looking at things, progress is possible. Getting there will take persistent effort.

There are a variety of ways to go about this project. John XXIII lays out one way in Mater et Magistra.

The teaching in regard to social matters for the most part are put into effect in the following three stages: ***first, the actual situation is examined; then, the situation is evaluated carefully in relation to these teachings; then only is it decided what can and should be done in order that the traditional norms may be adapted to circumstances of time and place.*** *These three steps are at times expressed by these three words: observe, judge, act.*

Christianity & Social Progress *(Mater et Magistra)*
John XXIII - Paragraph 236

The SFO Rule teaches us about many qualities we need in dealing with personal relationships. Many of these same skills will be useful in our efforts to build a more fraternal and evangelical world. Some level of relationship creates an atmosphere where respect can flourish. It may also create the possibility of true dialogue in seeking solutions.

As you engage in dialogue it is important to LISTEN to the "other" without prejudice. Otherwise you only hear what you want to hear. When you speak it is expected that you accept responsibility for what you say. Don't blame others for your ideas and opinions. Be sensitive since we all have different ways of expressing ourselves. Try to give yourself time to think before you speak or respond. It helps us avoid words we wish we hadn't said. Check how you feel or what assumptions you make about the situation. Assumptions get in the way of understanding the issue. In some conversations it can be helpful to keep the conversation confidential. People need to know that their ideas and opinions in the dialogue won't be spread across the landscape. Ultimately the conclusion can be shared.*

Dialogue does not always end with a perfect solution. It may be ambiguous. Perfect solutions are rare. But when people, with a variety of faith beliefs (or no religious beliefs), dialogue and come to a conclusion, it is at least one step along the way. Further dialogue may be needed but progress is being made.

These suggestions do not exhaust the variety of tools that can help in any dialogue. The goal Franciscans wish to achieve is to build a more *evangelical and fraternal world*! When people are respected and treated with love and justice it helps us prepare ways to build the Kingdom of God.

The Kingdom of God thrives when people are shown respect and love; when people respond with respect and love; when people seek one another's welfare and build a society of concern and compassion. In this fraternal and evangelical world it is possible to live a gospel life with greater freedom and within an atmosphere that nourishes

---

* Cf. Kaleidoscope Institute - 840 Echo Park Ave - Los Angeles, CA 90026

the qualities called for by the Kingdom of God. In the Our Father, we pray: *Thy Kingdom come ...*

590. The Church prays for the final coming of the Kingdom of God through Christ's return in glory. The Church prays also that the Kingdom of God increase from now on through people's sanctification in the Spirit and through their commitment to the service of justice and peace in keeping with the Beatitudes. This petition is the cry of the Spirit and the Bride: "Come, Lord Jesus" (Revelation 22:20).

Compendium - Catechism of the Catholic Church
#590 - Page 173

In the process of projects that seek positive change in society, it is important to recognize our competencies. Personal self-knowledge helps us perceive where we can best contribute to the project. Sharing our personal gifts enables a fraternity to do together what one person could not accomplish alone.

Lay people ought themselves to take on as their distinctive task this renewal of the temporal order. *Guided by the light of the Gospel and the mind of the church, prompted by christian love, they should act directly in this domain and in their own way. As citizens among citizens they must bring to their cooperation with others their own special competence, and act on their own responsibility, everywhere and always they have to seek the justice of the kingdom of God. The temporal order is to be renewed in such a way that, while its own principles are fully respected, it is harmonized with the principles of the christian life and adapted to the various conditions of time, place and people. Among the tasks of this apostolate christian social action is preeminent. The council desires to see it extended today to every sector of life, including the cultural sphere.*

Decree on the Apostolate of Lay People - Vatican II - Paragraph 7

If social action is preeminent for all Christians, it is obviously important for Franciscans to participate. A fraternity may have people with a variety of skills who can assist the fraternity to choose a social action that fits the members. In fact, they may embrace more than one brand of social concern. The council/members develop a plan of action after the fraternity has an opportunity to discuss the issues involved. Common conversations about social issues will help to reveal the ideas existent in the fraternity and the motivation to do something. *Ongoing formation* about social issues is a way to begin the process. With good knowledge good decisions can be made.

The Rule addresses a rather important issue at the end of article #14. ... *let them exercise their responsibilities* ***competently*** *in the Christian spirit of service.*

It is wise to know what we are able to do competently and what we do poorly. In building an evangelical and fraternal world we ought to be competent at what we volunteer to do. Ignorance can lead us to volunteer for things beyond our competence. Of course, we can always learn. But it is good to fit your competencies to the ministry that you choose. Take time to consider how you can best contribute to the task. Talk with the leaders of the group. Recognizing your skills helps to clarify your role. It will assist you to serve with competence and enjoy what you do.

Finally, service in all situations calls for a *Christian spirit of service.* Whether we hold an office in the fraternity or are involved in other ministries and projects, we are servants. This is something that engages our inner spirit. Our imitation of Jesus calls for us to serve rather than seeking to be served. But gracious acceptance of service from others is also part of this call. If everyone chooses the way of service everyone will be cared for when the need arises.

Servant-leaders focus on meeting needs rather than on how they look in doing the task. We want to give competent service. People may overlook clumsiness when love is present - but clumsiness may also threaten the project! Healthy competence is a quality to look for in leadership.

The point is this: the one who sows sparingly will also reap sparingly, and the one who sows bountifully will also reap bountifully. Each of you must give as you have made up your mind, not reluctantly or under compulsion, for God loves a cheerful giver. And God is able to provide you with every blessing in abundance, so that by always having enough of everything, you may share abundantly in every good work.

2 Corinthians 9:6-8

The Rule inserts another item that links social action to Christ. It states ... *that anyone "who follows Christ, the perfect man, becomes more of a man himself."* Again, not the best translation but the idea is a good one. We have one savior and that is Jesus. When we are involved in social transformation our ability to persist will need union with Jesus and the prompting of the Holy Spirit. It will also require the help of people "who know the territory."

As idealistic as our social action may be, we need to be wise in its implementation. Many people with different, even opposing ideas, may be part of our working group. We have our dreams but we will also be realistic, aware of dangers and threatening possibilities in neighborhoods. Or aware of people who can and will block our efforts. It is Christ who prompts us to act. "Street smarts" help us to act with respect and common sense in particular situations.

Some social actions are simple and direct - visiting sick people; helping a needy person; providing transportation for physically challenged folks; writing to congress personnel about issues. At times social action may take us to places and people who could harm us. Common sense will be needed about our personal involvement. Decisions need to be made about demonstrations that support particular causes. Will I merely demonstrate? Will I act in ways that could get me arrested? Will my actions bring jail time? What is the goal of the demonstration or protest? Many christian groups offer workshops and prayer time to help people decide on the "how" of their participation. They take time to pray together. Franciscans, who unceasingly seek the ways of peace (SFO Rule #19) will avoid violence in these actions.

The following thoughts come from Walter Buhlmann OFM Cap in a talk given to Capuchins in Europe on May 5, 2005. His ideas and ideals speak to all of us.

As Franciscan people inspired by the Holy Spirit, we must believe that this secular world is and remains a world of God, that all human beings, without exception, are images and likenesses of God and that God accompanies them with his grace and love, and has patience with them because he knows that at the right time he will speak to their innermost being, draw them to himself and bring them home. Therefore, we must hold to the following: there is no godless human being, because: whoever gives up God will not be given up by God. And: no one can fall so deep that he or she falls out of God's love. So as pastors of souls who try to do all that is conceivable and externally have such insignificant results, we must give this encouragement; there is no need for more supplies, nor more commissions, nor more documents, not more hectic pace, but in truth more spirituality, faith, that in the end we do not save human beings, but God himself does it! We must do what we can and leave all the rest to God!

To this positive interpretation comes the second important element: the witness of one's life. We cannot impose the faith anymore. We can only offer it, set an example of it. We have moved from heritage to offering, from conquest to simple presence, from self-defense to public relations, so that for the many who are searching for the meaning of their life, we make it possible for them to meet God.

Section entitled: *Evangelical Presence in a Secular World*
Walter Buhlmann OFM Cap - May 5, 2005

This will be our way of preparing the way for the Kingdom of God. Our Franciscan spirit reaches out beyond ourselves to enable others to experience the friendship, peace, and justice of the Kingdom of God. Our profession calls us to this spirit in whatever way is possible for us.

In you, O Lord, I seek refuge; do not let me ever be put to shame; in your righteousness deliver me. Incline your ear to me; rescue me speedily. Be a rock of refuge for me, a strong fortress to save me. You are indeed my rock and my fortress; for your name's sake lead me and guide me, take me out of the net that is hidden for me, for you are my refuge. Into your hand I commit my spirit; you have redeemed me, O Lord, faithful God.

Psalm 31:1-5

Readings/Questions for dialogue

Practice the Church's Social Teaching
United States Catholic Catechism for Adults - Page 420-421

II. Action & Suffering as setting for learning hope
Saved in Hope (*Spe Salvi)* - Benedict XVI - Paragraph 35

Scientific, Technical etc ... / Respect for a hierarchy of values
Christianity & Social Progress *(Mater et Magistra)* - John XXIII
Paragraphs 163-165 and 175-177

1. Describe your understanding of how an evangelical and fraternal world would look in your neighborhood/city.

2. What is the purpose of building a fraternal and evangelical world?

3. List your competencies. How would these skills serve people in the fraternity, the church and the world? Why is it important to be aware of personal competencies?

4. What does it mean to be a "servant-leader? If you are elected/appointed, describe your spirit as a servant-leader.

5. What is the value of collaborating with other groups in seeking to change oppressive or unjust structures in society?

6. In your opinion, why does the Rule focus on social issues? How does it fit into secular Franciscan spirituality?

7. Scripture reflection: Mark 8:14-21. This story is tough on the disciples. In your opinion why were they failing to understand Jesus? For your own reflection: Do you ever find yourself in the same situation as the disciples? If so, how can you get past it?

+++

Here are a few suggestions for social involvement prepared by secular Franciscans involved in peace and justice issues.

Keep in touch with news about issues of peace and justice / volunteer to help in a soup kitchen, homeless shelter etc as you feel able / help youngsters with language or school problems because they do not speak English well / as you feel competent, mediate between people in conflict / get back in touch with someone who you lost touch with / write congress people about issues / attend programs for learning about social issues of various kinds / visit someone in prison / teach your children-grandchildren-friends etc about peace and justice / advocate for someone with mental, psychiatric or chronic physical problems / learn about where and under what conditions your clothes or other things are made / visit another country and learn about their culture / participate in non-violent demonstrations for peace and justice / help people find housing or financial resources / work with parish or neighborhood groups to diminish bias and prejudice against individuals or groups of people etc.

A boss tells people what to do
and expects that they simply do it.

A leader empowers people
to contribute what they have to offer
to the common enterprise. You are not leading
until you are empowering someone else to serve.

Keith Clark OFM Cap - Leadership: The Art of Empowering
Contact: Monte Alverno Retreat & Spirituality Center
1000 N. Ballard Rd - Appleton, WI 54911

Chapter twenty three

Justice and Franciscan life

15. Let them individually and collectively be in the forefront in promoting justice by the testimony of their human lives and their courageous initiatives. Especially in the field of public life, they should make definite choices in harmony with their faith.

1. Rule 15 *Secular Franciscans should "be in the forefront ... in the field of public life." They should collaborate as much as possible for the passage of just laws and ordinances.*

2. The fraternities should engage themselves through courageous initiatives, consistent with their Franciscan vocation and with the directives of the Church, in the field of human development and justice. They should take clear positions whenever human dignity is attacked by any form of oppression or indifference. They should offer their fraternal service to the victims of injustice.

3. ***The renunciation of the use of violence, characteristic of the followers of Francis, does not mean the renunciation of action.*** *However, the brothers and sisters should take care that their interventions are always inspired by Christian love.*

Constitutions - article 22.1, 22.2, 22.3

Wash yourselves; make yourselves clean; remove the evil of your doings from before my eyes; cease to do evil, learn to do good; seek justice, rescue the oppressed, defend the orphan, plead for the widow.

Isaiah 1:16-17

The Spirit of the Lord God is upon me; he has sent me to bring good news to the oppressed, to bind up the broken-hearted, to proclaim liberty to captives, and release to the prisoners; to proclaim the year of the Lord's favor, and the day of vengeance of our God; to comfort all who mourn; to provide for those who mourn in Zion - to give them a garland instead of ashes, the oil of gladness instead of mourning, the mantle of praise instead of a faint spirit.
Isaiah 61:1-3

Coming to topics which are practical and of some urgency, the council lays stress on respect for the human person; everybody should look upon his or her neighbor (without any exception) as another self, bearing in mind especially their neighbor's life and the means needed for a dignified way of life, lest they follow the example of the rich man who ignored Lazarus, who was poor (Lk 16:19-31).

Today, there is an inescapable duty to make ourselves the neighbor of every individual, without exception, *and to take positive steps to help a neighbor whom we encounter, whether that neighbor is an elderly person abandoned by everyone, a foreign worker who suffers the injustice of being despised, a refugee, an illegitimate child wrongly suffering for a sin of which the child is innocent, or a starving human being who awakens our conscience by calling to mind the words of Christ: "As you did it to one of the least of these, my brothers or sisters, you did it to me"* (Mt. 25:40).

The varieties of crime are numerous: all ***offenses against life itself****, such as murder, genocide, abortion, euthanasia, and willful suicide; all* ***violations of the integrity of the human person,*** *such as mutilation, physical and mental torture, undue psychological pressures; all* ***offenses against human dignity,*** *such as subhuman living conditions, arbitrary imprisonment, deportation, slavery, prostitution, the selling of women and children, degrading working conditions where people are treated as mere tools for profit rather than free and responsible persons; all these and the like are criminal; they poison civilization; and they debase the perpetrators more than the victims and militate* *against the honor of the creator.*

Pastoral Constitution on the Church in the Modern World
Gaudium et Spes - Vatican II - Paragraph 27

Justice is well understood when we consider it in the light of relationships. Trinitarian spirituality places relationships at the top of its values. When we speak of injustice we almost always speak of practices that fail to support relationships. Injustice creates animosity, frustration, fear, anger, hatred, even death. None of these qualities support a loving relationship. They fracture relationships and develop separation. People may than seek revenge and reprisals of one sort or another.

Even if the violence is the "silent treatment" it does nothing to strengthen a relationship. Even if it is only killing words that degrade and diminish people, it fractures relationships. When Franciscans desire to act justly, they are asking themselves to do the things that create and sustain relationships. It widens the awesome responsibility that is needed when we choose to love others - always.

It covers every relationship; + between friends + between men and women + between spouses + between rich and poor + between citizens and strangers + between killers and lovers + between parents and children + between relatives and enemies + between victim and criminal + between dictators and servant leaders + between people of different beliefs + between the arrogant and the gentle + between the refugee and the home-maker + between people of greed and people of need.

Justice is based on good relationships that seek the good of the other person. People too easily create chasms rather than sidewalks; walls rather than bridges; fences rather than openness; rationalizations rather than honesty. Though justice is not easily achieved, it is God's way to invite people to relate to one another.

Here is my servant, whom I uphold, my chosen, in whom

my soul delights; I have put my spirit upon him; he will bring forth justice to the nations. He will not cry or lift up his voice, or make it heard in the street; a bruised reed he will not break, and a dimly burning wick he will not quench; he will faithfully bring forth justice. He will not grow faint or be crushed until he has established justice on the earth; and the coastlands wait for his teaching.

Isaiah 42:1-4

The link between justice and relationship moves us to develop personal perspectives and actions that build relationships. Trinitarian spirituality moves us to grow in the ways of justice. Sensitivity to injustice makes us aware of the many ways that people are denied human dignity and how often there is separation instead of community.

We develop an ability to realize how destructive negative words and attitudes can be. We use positive words and attitudes in relationships. A positive Franciscan spirit grows within us. Our lives, in word and action, reflect this spirit. We develop a spirit of justice and act on it wherever justice is called for. We collaborate with others to challenge injustice wherever it is found. We deliberately choose not to become "one issue" people. We support action for justice wherever it is needed. To act otherwise would not fit our Franciscan identity.

What does the Rule ask of us? To *be in the forefront in promoting justice by the testimony of their human lives and their courageous initiatives.* We are not bystanders any more. Franciscans get involved. We involve ourselves in wise ways, observing, judging, and acting. We use common sense. We get help if that is needed. We seek trained help if that if needed. We seek training if that is needed. We support professional help if that is needed. But doing nothing is no longer a choice for us.

Justice also refers to our relationship with God. We do not neglect our God-relationship as we deal with members of the human family. We do whatever is needed to strengthen our relationship to God. We realize that we can do nothing without God's help. Our Franciscan spirit lives in a world created by a God who loves all people and the earth on which they live. We offer praise and thanksgiving to God because it is a matter of justice.

Among other attitudes, here are two attitudes that challenge our attempt to be people of justice.

The use of force to achieve goals. It often means violence of some sort that may end in physcial death or death of a person's reputation or livelihood. Both the innocent and the guilty suffer. Property is destroyed or lives are shattered. The impact on perpetrators and those who are harmed is generally not in accord with the Gospel. Yet, in our human struggles, force may seem the only recourse in some situations. Some people seem to respond to nothing else. We are obviously not living in the Kingdom of God in every corner of our world nor in the heart of every person on earth. But the inevitable consequence of the use of force is destruction of some sort. It causes separation among people that can take years to heal.

Who speaks up for other ways to deal with conflict? Will people in power, or people protecting possessions and wealth speak out? Some may. The voices of gospel people must address these issues. We must, at the very least, encourage people in power to use every means available before even thinking about using force. Franciscans must be among the people who speak up. To be silent is not an option for us. But we will never use violence as a way of dealing with injustice. Seeking justice is easy to talk about but hard to achieve.

The use of a variety of means to protect wealth, property and lifestyles. Any one of us can become used to a comfortable style of living. Some may have more luxury than others, but we are susceptible to protecting what we have. If it seems necessary to use force in order to maintain our comfortability we may be strongly tempted to do so. This may move us to actions that are unjust.

Manipulating financial accounting can occur. Paying less than a living wage can deprive others of basic needs. Using economic tools to keep others in their place will seem normal. Fear tactics can intimidate people and keep them from protesting unjust practices. People with little or no power are easily overlooked and overpowered. Immigrants can easily be branded, with or without an honest evaluation. Since they have no power they can be easily dismissed in order to protect what we have and have no intention of sharing. Employees and employers must be certain their actions lead to justice for everyone concerned.

In these situations dialogue is often avoided. Those in power use power to get what they desire. Laws are established that protect individual groups but are not in the interest of the common good. People loved by God and with inalienable human rights do not deserve unjust treatment. Franciscans work for justice without dividing people into good and evil. We face human obstacles in our efforts. But the Kingdom of God cannot tolerate injustice no matter who does it or how well it is portrayed!

Franciscans strive to bring people together in a society known for its dedication to justice. We will not act in ways that deepens the chasm between peoples. Our interaction with involved people will prayerfully search for a way that has positive results for all concerned. We cannot tolerate actions that deny basic human dignity for anyone involved.

Franciscans will get truthful information, approach the parties with care, concern, and respect - acting in ways that achieve the goals we seek. We want people to live together peacefully after serious dialogue.

This is the ideal. But relationships are not easily nor quickly healed. Opinions and attitudes do not change automatically because of our actions. People do not immediately feel comfortable with others who shortly before were the "enemy." Society does not immediately respond to another way of seeing things. We will need to persist in building a world where justice reigns.

Changing unjust systems is more effective than dealing with individual injustices. It is also more difficult. Franciscans are involved in a **both/and** situation. We will work to correct individual unjust actions. We will act to bring about justice for individuals who are the victims of injustice. But we will also work to create social systems that support justice rather than creating situations that are unjust. Both situations call us to work for justice, taking *courageous initiatives* to accomplish that goal.

An individual Franciscan can not do everything that pertains to justice. We seek to develop a common spirit and vision that recognizes injustice in life and works to change it. Individuals may take a leadership role or a supportive role. That will be determined by the people and the situation where injustice occurs. Being faithful to the Rule includes faithfulness, *individually and collectively,* to promote justice *by the testimony of their own lives and their courageous initiatives (SFO Rule #15).* The SFO Rule is clear!

Jesus' words at the last judgment scene in Matthew's gospel lists some things that need to be done for people in need. Sometimes those needs arise from injustice. Sometimes they happen because of the negative actions of an individual or society. In either case Jesus expects us to respond. Our response reveals another dimension of what the Kingdom will look like. In the following text Jesus requires us to respond as a normal way of living the Gospel.

Then the king will say to those at his right hand, "Come, you that are blessed by my Father, inherit the kingdom prepared for you from the foundation of the world; for I was hungry and you gave me food, I was thirsty and you gave me something to drink, I was a stranger and you welcomed me, I was naked and you gave me clothing, I was sick and you took care of me, I was in prison and you visited me." Then the righteous will answer him, "Lord, when was it that we saw you hungry and gave you food, or thirsty and gave you something to drink? And when was it that we saw you a stranger and welcomed you, or naked and gave you clothing? And when was it that we saw you sick or in prison and visited you?" And the king will answer them, ***"Truly, I tell you, just as you did it to one of the least of these who are members of my family, you did it to me."***

Matthew 25:34-40

A key element in this story is our relationship to these people. What happens in this story is precisely what we are called to do in cases of injustice and need. We know the result in the second part of this story in Matthew for those who ignore neighbor needs (Matthew 25:45).

Whatever the injustice may be we cannot ignore it. Our skills may give us an opening to do something. We have a fraternity of people pledged to help with their skills and talents. In addition, many other people are concerned for justice and will help. The issues of injustice are opportunities for learning. We hope to learn well and do better in our next contact with injustice - even within a fraternity!

Jerusalem, Jerusalem, the city that kills the prophets and stones those who are sent to it. How often I have desired to gather your children together as a hen gathers her brood under her wings, and you were not willing!

Luke 13:34

The United States has many organizations that address issues of peace and justice. Changing circumstances will require groups to change in order to meet new problems and issues. Franciscans have developed some organizations that promote peace and justice in our world. Our Franciscan groups strive to help us to be effective in matters relating to issues of peace and justice.

One group is called ***Justice, Peace and the Integrity of Creation*** **(JPIC)**. JPIC groups are widespread, both within the Franciscan family and in other church groups, both Catholic and non-catholic. JPIC within the SFO looks for ways to support secular Franciscans in living articles #14 to #19 of the Rule more effectively. It also collaborates with other JPIC groups on issues concerning human dignity and care for creation.

Team members (of JPIC) *will serve as resource persons to all the SFO's in the U.S., responding to questions/concerns and clarifying the Franciscan response to societal issues.*

Document on JPIC prepared for NAFRA - October, 2007

Embracing ways and means to implement the SFO Rule will never end. Changing circumstances will require us to change as well. Franciscans seek to be faithful to the signs of the times. We will pattern our actions and structures both to the needs of the present moment and to future needs.

Franciscan Action Network **(FAN)** is an organization seeking to help the entire Franciscan family and others to deal with a variety of issues that affect people, especially poor and marginalized people.

The Franciscan Action Network is a network of U.S.-based ministries, institutions and persons following the spiritual and social movement begun by St. Francis and St. Clare of Assisi more than 800 years ago. Together, we seek to amplify our public voice and use our collective power to humbly advocate and act for inclusive and transformed social policy and social structures arising out of the U.S. Federal Government and related Washington, D.C. based institutions. Through our work, we hope to help build a society rooted in social justice, peace and care for all of creation.

FAN Mission Statement - news@franciscanaction.org

FAN will *amplify our public voice* to be heard more effectively in the USA. We avoid demonizing people who disagree with us, trying to understand their point of view and offering our own. Our advocacy focuses on people-needs, showing care and concern (Love). Sharing information from differing, but fair and truthful viewpoints, enable Franciscans to make good choices about public issues.

Franciscans International **(FI)** widens our concerns to embrace the global needs of the poor and others without a voice. We speak for them to people in positions of power, many of whom consult FI about isssues debated at the UN.

Franciscans International is a non-governmental organization (NGO) *with general consultative status at the UN, uniting the voices of Franciscan brothers and sisters from around the world. We operate under the sponsorship of the Conference of the Franciscan Family (CFF) and serve all Franciscans and the global community by bringing spiritual, ethical, and Franciscan values to the United Nations and international organizations.*

We closely follow the tradition of Saint Francis and Saint Clare, striving to put Franciscan ideals into practice at the international level. We are guided by the Saint's loving concern for the poor, care of creation, and peacemaking. As the poorest people are being exploited in systemic ways, and global peace is increasingly threatened, Franciscan commitment is needed more urgently than ever.

www.franciscansinternational.org

These organizations serve the SFO at a number of different levels. They are servant-groups who can assist us to a just way of living our Franciscan life in the midst of society.

Building a just and civil order, wherein each person receives what is his or her due, is an essential task which every generation must take up anew. *... The Church cannot and must not take upon herself the political battle to bring about the most just society possible. She cannot and must not replace the State. Yet at the same time she cannot and must not remain on the sidelines in the fight for justice. She has to play her part through rational argument and she has to reawaken the spiritual energy without which* *justice, which always demands sacrifice, cannot prevail and prosper.*

God is Love *(Deus Caritas Est)* - Benedict XVI - Paragraph 28.a

The direct duty to work for a just ordering of society ... is proper to the lay faithful. *As citizens of the State, they are called to take part in public life in a personal capacity. ... it still remains true that* ***charity must animate*** *the entire lives of the lay faithful and therefore also their political activity, lived as "social charity."*

Ibid - Paragraph 29

+++

Readings/Questions for dialogue

Francis and Franciscan Spirituality
Poverty & Joy - Wm Short OFM - Page 30-32

The Anonymous of Perugia - Chapter IV
Francis of Assisi - The Founder - Vol II - Page 41-42

Love, Rules, And Grace
United States Catholic Catechism for Adults - USCCB
Page 318

1. How is the practice of justice related to the ways of relationship?

2. What are some areas of modern life that need exploration (and change?) in regard to the practice of justice?

3. When Franciscans work for justice what virtues will they practice? What things will they avoid?

4. How does the *testimony of* your human life promote justice? Explain.

5. How can you integrate love and compassion into the practice of justice? Why is this important?

6. What is the role of JPIC, FAN and FI (or other structures that may develop) in our Franciscan life ?

7. Why is it important to have solid facts when working for justice? How can Franciscans confront injustice without breaking relationships with those being confronted?

8. Scripture reflection: 1 Timothy 6:3-19. How do these words of Paul address our work for justice? In your own words, describe some of the qualities Paul is asking of Timothy and those he serves.

We have an alternative economic vision that is a more solid foundation for security and peace. Rather than the dominant picture of inevitable competition, ambition and greed, Alexander of Hales, for example, saw economics as the activity by which mutual needs were recognized and supplied. By the end of the 13th century, friars were promoting a just wage, a just profit, and a fair interest on loans. Franciscans also struggled with issues of need, necessity, indigence, abundance, prosperity and what to do about surplus. They knew firsthand society's need to recognize the "law of necessity" - the right of each person to be materially sustained in his or her basic human dignity by one's neighbors. In Franciscan terms, we do not exist as competitors under a stingy Lord but rather are bound in the communion of a good and generous God, so that the exchange of goods and services builds up the human family under God.

<u>*Building a More Evangelical World*</u> - North American OFM, Conventual, and Capuchin Animators of Justice, Peace and the Integrity of Creation - November 11, 2004

Chapter twenty four

The Gift of Work

16. Let them esteem work both as a gift and as a sharing in the creation, redemption, and service of the human community.

1. Rule 16 *For Francis, work is a gift and to work is a grace. Daily work is not only the means of livelihood, but the opportunity to serve God and neighbor as well as a way to develop one's own personality. In the conviction that work is a right and a duty and that every form of occupation deserves respect, the brothers and sisters should commit themselves to collaborate so that all persons may have the possibility to work and so that working conditions may always be more humane.*

2. Leisure and recreation have their own value and are necessary for personal development. Secular Franciscans should maintain a balance between work and rest and should strive to create meaningful forms of using leisure time.

Constitutions - article 21.1, 21.2

Human work, whether it is done independently or as an employee, proceeds from the human person, who as it were puts a personal seal on the things of nature and reduces them to her or his will. By their work people ordinarily provide for themselves and their family, associate with others as their brothers and sisters, and serve them; they can exercise genuine charity and be partners in the work of bringing God's creation to perfection. Moreover, we believe by faith that through the homage of work offered to God humanity is associated with the redemptive work of

Jesus Christ, whose labor with his hands at Nazareth greatly added to the dignity of work. This is the source of every person's duty to work loyally as well as of their right to work; moreover, it is the duty of society to see to it that, in the prevailing circumstances, all citizens have the opportunity of finding employment. Finally, remuneration for work should guarantee to individuals the capacity to provide a dignified livelihood for themselves and their family on the material, social and spiritual level corresponding to their roles and productivity, having regard to the relevant economic factors in their employment, and the common good.

The Church in the Modern World (Gaudium et Spes)
Vatican II - Paragraph 67

The Autumn, 2007 issue of TAU-USA (Page 17), had an article by Sally Haddad SFO. She asked a question at various fraternity gatherings: *What kind of work do you do?* Often she received answers about distributing communion, working in soup kitchens etc. What she didn't often hear was that someone was an accountant, an electrical engineer, a cook at a school cafeteria, supervisor at a manufacturing plant, or parents caring for their children. People quickly think of volunteer "work" when asked the question.

Of course these answers are perfectly legitimate if that's what you are doing. But article #16 also addresses the work that supports our lives. In the work-a-day world we have opportunities to share *in the creation, redemption and service of the human community.*

In these secular places we share the Gospel. It may be through "holy" conversations. But probably we are more effective through a life showing honesty and compassion. Words and discussions help, but the final criteria is how you live and work and act on the job, whatever it may be. It is difficult to say something can't be done when you are doing it! To influence people at work you will also need time for reflection. It will bring a redemptive touch to your presence at work.

Whether work is done at home as a parent, at school as a teacher, or in the marketplace in other jobs, the inner spirit is the same. In each case people are being served - family, patients, students, clients, customers, friends. The quality of our work and our spirit will identify us as Franciscans. Work requires qualities necessary in all relationships.

The crafting of things used by people is a work of *creation.* Whether it is a physical creation like furniture or jewelry or an artistic creation, we participate in the process of creation. We might develop creative designs. We might develop the structures that make it possible to create the finished product. We may have lesson plans for the classroom or a recipe concocted for supper. We may imagine new plans to further the work of a business. We may heal a broken body or fight infections. We share in the work of creation in many different ways.

When the Rule invites us to *share in redemption* we face a challenge. Jesus redeemed us by a loving self-giving in his life. This was crowned by his loving self-giving on the cross, an expression of total love for the sake of others. If this is part of what redemption means, then love and respect for others will be part of our work-spirit. In his book, Spirituality@work, Gregory Pierce gathers many stories about people and their work. One story stood out for me. It represents the redemptive power of work that is done with love and respect.

I worked for a CEO in a major billion-dollar state government organization several years ago who comes closer to living the spirituality of work than anyone I have known. She was direct and honest but never disparaging of others. She was strategic but not conniving. Her power came from her vision, not just from the authority she held by virtue of her position. She was gentle in her correction or direction of others - affirming but not mushy. She was passionate but not emotional, smart, tolerant of other views, but always clear about her own. She always listened *before deciding anything. She was able to change her mind, but she was also deeply convinced about her own values. She treated others like she wanted to be treated, and others who worked for her eventually began to behave that way too.* *

Spirituality@work - Gregory F. A. Pierce - Page 25

Franciscans should have little trouble accepting and imitating this example. Whether you are a man or a woman the qualities displayed in the story can be practiced by anyone. Respectful and firm actions can influence others to similar positive values. The presence of such a person gives people permission to do the same. If it has been done it can be done. Each of us will put our fingerprints on how we do it. But we know it is possible. It is our Franciscan way.

You are the light of the world. A city built on a hill cannot be hidden. No one after lighting a lamp puts it under a bushel basket, but on the lampstand, and it gives light to all in the house. In the same way, let your light shine before others, so that they may see your good works and give glory to your Father in heaven.

Matthew 5:14-16

Through our work we bring light to the workplace and to the people who work there. Whether our work is paid or not, we offer light through our good working spirit. We bring the love of God to each situation. Whether we are homemakers, employees or employers, self-employed, a volunteer or internet sevice representative, we give the same example. This spirit of work does two things. First, it keeps us aware of our commitment to sharing in the creation, redemption, and service of others. Secondly, it offers people an example of what a gospel life looks like. We do not hide our skills, commitment, respect, compassion or reverence under a bushel basket. We put them in plain sight so people can see what gospel people do. In everyday working situations we offer an example of Kingdom living.

---

* Story told by Timothy Schmalz - Social Worker, teacher, writer, husband, father and grandfather - Phoenix, Arizona

Such is the vision of Franciscans. But reality can be very demanding. How do police deal with criminals who resist? How does an employee deal with a supervisor who has no idea of respect? How do mothers or fathers deal with a recalcitrant teenager? How does a working teenager deal with addictive parents? How does a person in the military deal with learning about ways to win in war? How do owners and employees deal with bankruptcy and economic downturns? How do workers react to low-paying jobs that make great demands but offer little remuneration? How does one deal with dishonesty at work? Discrimination? Bias? People who curse and downgrade fellow workers?

Work can be a place that has little attraction other than a paycheck. How do Franciscans deal with situations that are far from models of healthy relationships? If we had one answer that would be wonderful. But life isn't that simple.

We do know a few important things about ourselves. We will not allow negative situations to influence us to act in like manner. It may seem like the only way to survive, but it can destroy personal integrity which we must not lose. Community/fraternity support becomes an important issue in these cases.

We must not become violent in these situations. The temptation may be great. But our personal integrity does not permit us to go against our vision of life. Whether in word or action, we persist in being faithful to our Franciscan calling. Finding ways to deal with the chaos at work may not be easy. An appeal to authority may or may not be feasible. Many situations do not submit to outside intervention.

Similar cases can make work a difficult place. We must maintain our Franciscan spirit when there is nothing at work to support it - besides our sense of faithfulness. Talking with other Franciscans can help us be faithful. It may not solve the problems at work but it does enable us to be true to our profession as secular Franciscans.

Even in the best of work situations we need to know when to say "no" to taking on more responsibility. We weigh the different factors involved. If we are family people we ask serious questions. Will this reward us with more income but keep us away from the family for longer periods? Is the increased salary worth the loss in family relationships? Will more income stabilize a rocky marriage or friendship? Are there other things more important than buying new things? In short, we may discover that saying "no" is an important part of the spirituality of work.

Is there a time to say that we have invested enough effort and time in dealing with work issues? We need to recognize when we have done enough rather than becoming so involved that we are too tired to live. We recognize that for now we have done enough. The same is true for volunteer activities. There will always be a need. But it need not be a matter of laziness or indifference to recognize that more volunteering is beyond what I can presently handle. Its opposite is to have so little involvement that we never take time for others - hardly a Franciscan trait.

That "other" person at work is loved by God. Like it or not that is true. Calling this to mind may help to change how we act toward them. Or - we may feel they are so far from an image of God that I can ignore the fact that God loves them. What a good way to become spiritually schizophrenic! I can now pick and choose who is loved by God. I also need to inform God about this new insight of mine. Don't be surprised if God is surprised.

With what shall I come before the Lord, and bow myself before God on high? Shall I come before him with burnt offerings, with calves a year old? Will the Lord be pleased with thousands of rams, with tens of thousands of rivers of oil? Shall I give my firstborn for my transgression, the fruit of my body for the sin of my soul?

He has told you, O mortal, what is good; and what does the Lord require of you but to do justice, and to love kindness, and to walk humbly with your God?

Micah 6:6-8

In the arena of work as well as elsewhere, Franciscans allow the Gospel and their Rule of life to guide their attitudes and actions. In a world where *getting ahead* can be a prime motivation, Franciscans are willing to forego *getting ahead* if people would be hurt or diminished by that action. The Rule reminds us how to act - *with a gentle and courteous spirit accept all people as a gift of the Lord and an image of Christ* (Rule #13).

Franciscans accept this desire of God as expressed in the SFO Rule. Wherever we work we will follow the Rule. Since we professed to do so, we will do so!

He (Francis) *also admonished the brothers not to judge anyone, nor to look down upon those who live with refinement and dress extravagantly or fashionably. For, he would say, their God is ours, the Lord who is capable of calling them to Himself and justifying those called. He also used to tell them he wanted the brothers to show reverence to these people as their brothers and lords. They are brothers, because we were all created by one Creator; they are lords, because they help the good to do penance by providing them with the necessities of life. He added: "The brothers' way of life among the people should be such that whoever hears or sees them glorifies and praises the heavenly Father with dedication."*

Let no one be provoked to anger or scandal through you, but may everyone be drawn to peace, kindness, and harmony through your gentleness. For we have been called to this: to heal the wounded, bind up the broken, and recall the erring. In fact, many who seem to us to be members of the devil will yet be disciples of Christ."

Legend of the Three Companions - Francis of Assisi - The Founder
Vol II - Page 101-102

In all our meanderings around the places of work, it becomes evident that we are imperfect and sometimes inadequate for tasks. Accepting this reality makes us aware of our need for God and community. We are not going to finish God's work on our own. We need the help of God. Learning this is a gift. It overflows into other areas of life if work is not the only thing we do (Hopefully!). If work totally dominates our lives we are unbalanced.

Leisure and recreation have their own value and are necessary for personal development. Secular Franciscans should maintain a balance between work and rest and should strive to create meaningful forms of using leisure time.

Constitutions - article 21,2

There are jobs that require a 24-hour response and availability or something similar. Work of this sort creates stress, boredom, or excitement, depending on the task. The involved individual may find a need for creativity in order to maintain healthy personal development.

The SFO Constitutions wisely remind us of the value of leisure and recreation. Having time alone can be helpful. Anyone raising a family and working at the same time can realize how naive this sounds. But it is worth the effort to create space for leisure in life. We are able to control only so much of our time. We look to the period we can control in order to create space for things that bring joy and relaxation. Such decision-making helps us keep a balance in our life. It helps us in refreshing our inner spirit.

People who are retired may have a greater amount of time within their control They involve themselves in volunteer work without making choices that create stress and develop unhealthy habits. The article about leisure also applies to them. Franciscans, in their particular circumstances, choose to create as balanced a life as possible. It is part of who we are as Franciscans. It helps us to be human in our relationship with one another.

In work, as in all other activities of life, relationship is important. Franciscans continue to uncover what is needed to nurture relationships. Reflection requires time. Being overextended hinders such time. Hence the need to provide space for relaxation and leisure time. Our ability to work is a gift. Through it we share in the creation, redemption and service of others as well as ourselves. But when it cripples our ability to have and sustain relationships it needs to be evaluated.

Meaningful work and relaxing leisure time are partners in keeping us healthy and "sane." Despite the difficulties often encountered in keeping this balance, the result is worth the effort. It is integrated into our profession of the Franciscan way of life. Be faithful!

+++

Readings/Questions for dialogue

Reflections ... on the Church's Social Teaching: Major themes
United State Catholic Catechism for Adults - USCCB
Page 421- 424 (Up to: *The Poor in our Midst*)

Franciscan Prayer - Ilia Delio OSF
From: Page 82 *"Francis wanted his followers ... "*
To: Page 84 (1st seven lines)

God is Love *(Deus Caritas Est)* - Benedict XVI
Paragraph 28.a

Recommended: *On the Way to Work* - Stories & Reflections on Living as Christians Today - Vinal Van Benthem SFO - Twenty-Third Publications.

1. The word "work" covers a multitude of actions. List the actions in your life you would list as "work."

2. How is work a sharing in creation? Redemption? Service?

3. What qualities are especially important for Franciscans in their work? Why?

4. Why is leisure needed for a healthy personal life? How do you blend leisure and work to achieve a good balance?

5. How does your manner of working reflect upon the relationships in your life?

6. How does the spirit of consumerism influence our need for work? Evaluate the impact this may have on your Franciscan life!

7. Scripture reflection: 1 Thessalonians 5:12-24. How does the message in this passage apply to your spirit at work? What particular insight does this text offer to you? How will you implement it in your work?

+++

Secular Franciscans function in the world
as Christ-like people doing their
normal jobs
in a Christ-like way.
We, as Secular Franciscans,
have the advantage
of employing the teachings of St. Francis
to use the Gospels to find our way
in a highly complex and ambiguous world.
We have the advantage of our life-long
commitment to learn,
through the example of St. Francis,
how to go from Gospel to life
and from life to Gospel.
We have the advantage of monthly
SFO gatherings, where ongoing formation
continually shows us new or different
ways of looking at the world
and our place in it. We have the luxury
of sharing with our sisters and brothers
the triumphs and frustrations of our daily lives
and listening to each of them
share their joys and sorrows.

George W. Irving SFO - TAU-USA
Winter 2008 - Issue 61- Page 29

Chapter tweny five

In Their Family ...

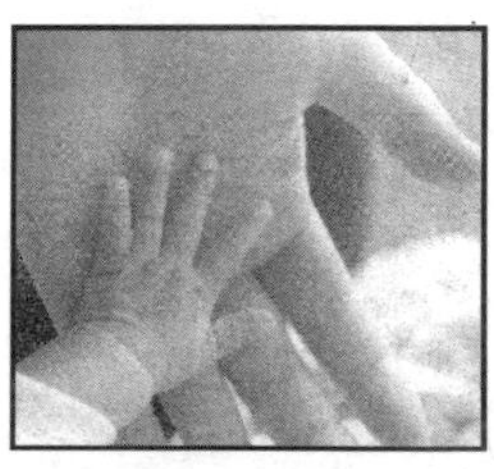

17. In their family they should cultivate the Franciscan spirit of peace, fidelity, and respect for life, striving to make of it a sign of a world already renewed in Christ.

By living the grace of matrimony, husbands and wives in particular should bear witness in the world to the love of Christ for his Church. They should joyfully accompany their children on their journey by providing a simple and open Christian education and being attentive to the vocation of each child.

1. Rule 17 ***Secular Franciscans should consider their own family to be the first place in which to live their Christian commitment and Franciscan vocation.*** *They should make space within it for prayer, for the Word of God, and for Christian catechesis. They should concern themselves with respect for life in every situation from conception until death. Married couples find in the Rule of the SFO an effective aid in their own journey of Christian life, aware that, in the sacrament of matrimony, their love shares in the love that Christ has for his Church. The way spouses love each other and affirm the value of fidelity is a profound witness for their own family, the Church, and the world.*

2. In the fraternity:

+ *the spirituality of the family and marriage and the Christian attitude towards family problems should be a theme for dialogue and for sharing of experiences;*

+ *they should share the important moments of the family life of their Franciscan brothers and sisters, and* ***they should give their fraternal attention to those - single, widows, single parents, separated, divorced - who are living difficult situations;***

+ Rule 19 *they should create conditions suitable for dialogue between generations;*

+ *the formation of groups of married couples and of family groups should be fostered.*

3. The brothers and sisters should collaborate with the efforts undertaken in the Church and in society to ***affirm both the value of fidelity and respect for life and provide answers to the social problems of the family.***

Constitutions - article 24.1, 24.2, 24.3

Out of the conviction of the need to educate children to take an interest in community, "bringing them the awareness of being living active members of the People of God" (*Apostolicam actuositatem* no 30) *and because of the facination which Francis can exercise on them, the formation of groups of children should be encouraged. With the help of a pedagogy and an organization suitable to their age, these children should be initiated into a knowledge and love of the Franciscan life. National statutes will give appropriate orientation for the organization of these groups and their relationship to the fraternity and to Franciscan youth groups.*

Constitutions - article 25

The Christian family forms an environment within which faith is professed and witnessed. When family members pray together, engage in lifelong learning, forgive one another, serve each other, welcome others, affirm and celebrate life, and bring justice and mercy to the community, they help each other live the faith and grow in faith. Some families may not understand themselves as a domestic church. Perhaps they consider their family too broken to be used for the Lord's purposes. They need to remember that a family is holy not because it is perfect, but because God's grace is at work in it.

United States Catholic Catechism for Adults - USCCB - Page 376

The family is the basic unit of society. A healthy family is the prerequisite of a healthy society. ***The authority,***

stability, and loving relationships that are found in families are essential for a society that wants to sustain freedom, security, and community responsibility.
United States Catholic Catechism for Adults - USCCB - Page 383

A good family in the neighborhood, parish, city and country contributes much to life in these structures. Though even the best parents cannot guarantee that their children will be the best, the odds are better than in dysfunctional families. If families are the "domestic church," then the human qualities that show up in families will likely show up in Church and society.

In addition, it seems sad that we have so few canonized saints among married people. What parents, children and extended family members contribute to church and society are without measure. The situations families address as a matter of course would stress out many people - and might even bring more than a little stress to Franciscan parents.

The adjustments that marriage brings require changes in the spouses. What initially seemed delightful can become boring. What looked so exciting during courtship may look like irresponsibility later on. The need for conversion and re-viewing relationships is normal stuff in marriage. The first pregnancy brings new discoveries about one's generosity. The possibilities of a miscarriage or other possibilities can bring worry and distress. When the wonder of having the first child is past and all-night feedings and crying babies create havoc in sleep habits, conversion is needed. Dialogue is needed. Lots of love is needed.

At the beginning of family life, parents face an unfamiliar parade of new demands. Within this parade are the wonderful moments of family life as well as difficult moments. First words, learning to walk, the child doing funny things, memories being stored, this unique new life brings joy even though new needs must be met. These are moments the parents savor.

Things change in small or large ways as children grow. A night out requires investment in a baby-sitter. Plans can never be just about husband and wife. Now a new person (or persons) must be taken into account. With financial costs increasing, it becomes labor intensive to have the financial resources needed for clothes and shoes and food and beds and technical tools and transportation. With increased school activities and homework and boy/girl friends and report cards - the need for patience and financial needs multiply. Love is challenged in many ways.

Teen-age discoveries about sex and reaching for independence while wanting security are important but taxing. Being responsible at home and sharing chores and many other things use up energy and patience within family life. Waiting for young people to get home at night or for them to participate in family affairs creates another dimension of controlled chaos. Wondering about drug and alcohol addictions and the influences that touch young people requires large doses of gentleness and understanding and firmness - and forgiveness and reconciliation.

Home is the place where the Franciscan vision and reality meet, we might even say "clash." Being Franciscan doesn't make everything fine. The same issues arise in Franciscan homes as elsewhere. The Rule especially focuses on *a spirit of peace, fidelity, and respect for life* - especially in family life. Achieving this spirit requires a faithfulness to one another (for both spouses and children), prayer, family communication (more than cell-phone talk), forgiveness and interaction within the family circle. If relationships are to be maintained, energy and reflection are needed to know *how* to show love in dozens of delightful or difficult situations.

The mixtures of joy and concern, laughter and tears, anger and gentleness, separation and unity, silent treatment and faithful dealing with issues require the skills of a mediator and referee and a communicator all wrapped up in one. At the same time, however, these situations sharpen our ability to create a spirit of *peace, fidelity and respect for life* within the family. To grow in these qualities is a natural response to the Franciscan call to conversion. Family life is fertile ground for such growth.

"Two men looked out through prison bars,
The one saw mud, the other, stars."

It can be a matter of where you look
and what you look for.
Whether it matters to you
that God is alive or
whether your only concern
is that you are alive!
Things start within our hearts
and our perspectives and
the way life looks to us.

We reflect on how people see us,
or how we see us,
or how Jesus sees us.
The Spirit operates in our hearts,
where it counts
and makes a difference.

The Spirit reaches people in different ways.
Sometimes through prayer, or through pain,
or through love, or through people,
or through hatred, even.
Through loneliness and loss.
Through pain and sorrow and joy

The Spirit always blows with a breath of kindness
forever waiting for us
to provide an opening in our heart
that lets the Spirit break out.
Like a mother bending over her child,
we wait, wait for the warmth
and power of Spirit-love to come forth!

Cultivate peace - We will address the global issues of peace in article #19 of the SFO Rule. In this chapter our focus is peace within the family.

Families are people. Where you have more than one "people" there is the possibility of conflict, large or small. Among family members the parents are usually the ones who set the tone of family life. They create the atmosphere of peace or chaos, of welcoming or exclusion or somewhere in between these bookends. Within this atmosphere are revealed the ways in which conflict is handled. The balancing act returns to center stage. How do families deal with conflict without also creating separation among family members? This applies not only to the period when children live at home but also when they have left home and somehow conflict rears its head.

A couple of things come to mind in managing conflict. We have already spoken of dialogue among participants. The nature of dialogue will differ according to the ages of the family members involved. But nurturing dialogue, at whatever age, is worthwhile not only for the present situation but also as a learning for the future. Despite the fact that we were all children at one time, we now have the possibility of creating a situation that may differ from our own background. One key element is the listening process. It gives people a sense of being respected. That allows for some mutuality in the conversation. It may also help in getting the facts straight.

When dialogue leads to a better understanding of the situation and the feelings involved, there may be need for: 1) Taking time to pray together in order to call on the Holy Spirit for assistance in the process. 2) For people to accept responsibility for their actions. 3) For people to be willing to change negative/frustrating actions which will require conversion. 4) For people to forgive others if they were hurt by their actions. 5) To develop tools to continue dealing with all the feelings and hurts that may occur.

Of course, using this process is good for positive situations as well. It can lead to better communication and a greater trust level among family members. It is not magic, but it can help. Families may have many reasons to celebrate and communicate with joy. Developing a listening and concerned attitude will allow for peaceful and joyful family gatherings as well as a willingness to tackle difficult issues.

If you learn other effective ways and means, use them! There are many ways to achieve peace within the family.

Cultivate fidelity - This sounds like a directive for the spouses. It certainly applies to them. Faithfulness between husband and wife give both of them a sense of security in their relationship. In our society there are plenty of temptations to test fidelity in marriage.

Fidelity, like so many qualities we talk about, does not stand alone like a scarecrow. It will require of the spouses a deep, loving commitment to one another. Relationships go through a series of situations that test the quality of spousal love. To be faithful will require honesty in revealing oneself. It requires a trustworthy person to receive spousal sharings. Spouses realize their humanness and are not surprised by the imperfections of a spouse. Forgiveness and reconciliation may be needed. Loving, honest interaction allows the relationship to become more secure.

Fidelity lives in the arms of a prayerful person. A growing relationship with God will normally enhance a growing relationship with a spouse. Once again trinitarian spirituality moves within the relationship.

In her teaching, the Church gives us a picture of family life that begins with the total gift of love between the spouses evidenced in their resolve to remain exclusively faithful until death. This promise, made before God in the midst of family and friends before an authorized priest or deacon, is supported by the continuing presence of Christ in the life of the spouses as he pours into their hearts the gift of love through the Holy Spirit. The couple does not walk alone and possesses the graced freedom to respond to natural and supernatural help.

United States Catholic Catechism for Adults - USCCB - Page 286.

It can seem difficult, or even impossible, to bind oneself for life to another human being. This makes it all the more important to proclaim the Good News that God loves us with a definitive and irrevocable love, that married couples share in this love, that it supports and sustains them, and that by their own faithfulness they can be witnesses to God's faithful love. Spouses who with God's grace give this witness, often in very difficult conditions, deserve the gratitude and support of the ecclesial community. (CCC, no. 1648)

Ibid - Page 287

Cultivate respect for life - In the context of family life respect for life covers the whole life of the family members. It begins with the belief in the sacredness of life. It builds on that fundamental faith-belief to cultivate a passionate respect for life throughout the lives of family members:

a) respect for life at conception, in the womb and protection and love at the beginning of life.
b) respect for the early years of life - showing love with touch and caress - all the ways that love finds expression in the early years of life.
c) respect during the growing years of life, concern for education - intellectual, faith-wise and emotional. Teaching youngsters ways to express love for one another.
d) respect for the teenage years of life and their struggles to discover their identity, sexuality and the development of skills to function independently - preparing for adulthood.
e) respect for the life of family members as they move from home and live independently but remain connected to their family. This part of respect for life continues as people grow older.

f) respect for life as family members grow older, respecting their lives and avoiding euthanasia or any actions that deliberately hastens the natural end of life.

These ideas about respect for life are focused on family life. It touches the moments of family relationships from the beginning of life to the coming of Sister Death.

There are many other issues about respect for life beyond the family. Guarding innocent lives in the womb; protecting the sick from unethical actions to limit life; recognizing that the death penalty does not respect life; realizing the care that must be taken with regard to power of attorney; or the written documents about the care people wish to receive when seriously ill; the desire to stop violence and conflicts that take innocent lives and wars that destroy the lives of people in the military as well as civilian victims.

We embrace the vision to respect all human life. We work to protect the lives of people no matter who they are or how bad they may be. It is the way of our Franciscan love. True christian love cannot be choosey. It is universal as we try to imitate the God who loves all people. For the same reason, we work *to create conditions of life worthy of people redeemed by Christ* (SFO Rule #13). All life is precious and we will live by that belief. We know how impossible this can be without the power of the Holy Spirit. Hence we are a prayerful people.

The Rule asks spouses to witness, by their love, to the love Christ has for the Church. Spouses make that love present as one image for expressing Christ's presence to and love for the People of God. Consider the direction of Rule #17:

They should joyfully accompany their children on their journey by providing a simple and open Christian education, and being attentive to the vocation of each child.

SFO Rule #17

Parents are reminded of the fact that their home is a domestic church. That church is a place where the members learn about their faith and their role/ministry in life. They may be called to a single life, to a married life, to life as a religious or a life in the priesthood or other forms of ministry in Church, at work, or in serving others.

As the children grow, parents help them discover where they might best serve Christ. Whatever the call, Franciscans are attentive to the presence of a call. They support it in every way they can. Their prayerfulness will assist in recognizing the call. The atmosphere of the home will be supportive in helping children find their way in life.

Many books on marriage are written by unmarried people (like myself) and address the vision about marriage without always considering day-to-day needs. Other books encourage values and ideas that may not fit our Catholic vision. Books and programs may consider only a few of the needs of marriage. Some needs may be met by developing a group within the fraternity to dialogue about marriage issues. There are groups within the church that deal with marriage issues from the couple's point of view. Make use of those that are helpful to you, your spouse and your family.

Competent Franciscans should find ways to assist youth programs in their parish or neighborhood. Participating in youth programs is an opportunity to bring the Franciscan spirit to young people. It is not necessary to make youth groups a recruiting resource for fraternity life. Primarily we participate in youth ministry as a way to bring Franciscan ideals and values to young people. The Holy Spirit may call them to be Secular Franciscans, but that is not our primary goal. Involving young people in mission trips and service ministries gives them a fresh way to experience God. A young person wrote this about a mission trip:

My experience in South Dakota was simply amazing. This trip opened my eyes to what the world around us is really like. I learned that you just can't think about yourself, but you have to respond to the needs of others. (Teenager from St Maria Goretti Parish - Madison, WI)

+++

Franciscans who are divorced or separated need support from fraternity members. The needs in these situations call for compassionate help. The needs of the children are of special importance. We do not limit our love. The way spouses express love to each other requires a prayerful attitude and a common sense way of showing love. It is another area of life where we model our Franciscan vision. No one and no place is outside the focus of our love.

He also said, "With what can we compare the kingdom of God, or what parable will we use for it? It is like a mustard seed, which, when sown upon the ground, is the smallest of all the seeds on earth; yet when it is sown it grows up and becomes the greatest of all shrubs, and puts forth large branches, so that the birds of the air can make nests in its shade."

Mark 4:30-32

+++

Readings/Questions for dialogue

The Little Flowers of St. Francis
Francis of Assisi - The Prophet - Vol III
Chapter 12 - Page 585-586

The Purposes of Marriage / Effects of the Sacrament
United States Catholic Catechism for Adults - USCCB
Page 283-285

The Spirit of Prayer & Holy Devotion
Poverty & Joy - Wm Short OFM - Page 81

1. Who are the most influential persons in family life? Does it always remain the same? Explain.

2. How does a family develop a (Franciscan) spirit of peace?

3. Why is fidelity such an important quality in family life?

4. Explain how the love between spouses is a witness to Christ's love for the Church.

5. What quality or qualities would you say are most important for parents in relating to their children at different points of their lives? .. in the early years? .. beginning school? .. as teenagers? .. when they leave home for jobs or further education? .. after they get married? .. as single people having a life of their own?

6. What contribution do Franciscans bring when they work with school, neighborhood or church youth groups?

7 Scripture reflection: Ephesians 3:14 21. How does this text give you hope to be able to express love to everyone in your life?

The mountaintop is where we traditionally think about finding God. If we conceive of heaven as being somewhere "up," then it is logical to think that the higher up we go the closer we get to God. Unfortunately, this line of thinking has made us susceptible to the belief that our day-to-day life here on earth is farther away from God. So we, like Peter and James and John, look for ways to remain on the mountaintop. (Mk 9:2-10).

... What would have happened if Peter, James, and John had built their tents and remained on the mountaintop? I probably wouldn't be sitting here writing about their experience. Nor would you be reading my words. What if Martin (Luther King Jr) *had chosen to stay on the mountaintop? What would our world look like today?*

Spiritual seekers have always sought the mountaintop encounter with God. But the true mystic knows that we are not meant to stay there. If the life, death and resurrection of Jesus Christ are to have any meaning in our world today it is up to us to bring its message back down from the mountaintop and into our homes and communities, back to places where we work and play. Are we builders of the kingdom? Or are we satisfied with being builders of tents?

<u>On the Way to Work</u> - Vinal Van Benthem SFO
Twenty-Third Publications - Pages 168-169

Chapter twenty six

Universal Kinship

18. Moreover they should respect all creatures, animate and inanimate, which "bear the imprint of the Most High," and they should strive to move from the temptation of exploiting creation to the Franciscan concept of universal kinship.

4. Following the example of Francis, patron of ecologists, they should actively put forward initiatives that care for creation and should work with others in efforts that both put a stop to polluting and degrading nature and also ***establish circumstances of living and environment which would not be a threat to the human person.***

Constitutions - article 18.4

We show respect for the Creator by our stewardship of creation. ***Care for the earth is a requirement of our faith.*** *We are called to protect people and the planet, living our faith in relationship with all of God's creation. This environmental challenge has fundamental moral and ethical dimensions that cannot be ignored.*

United States Catholic Catechism for Adults - USCCB - Page 424

In creating the universe, God entrusted the resources of the earth to the stewardship of all people. The Church, applying this truth, upholds the principle that the universal destination of the goods of the earth is meant for the common good of all people. At the same time, the Church stands by the right of private property.

Ibid - Page 426

Environmentalists are often not appreciated by many people. But their message is wider than just the stereotype that they are *tree-huggers*. Our ability to live in harmony with the natural world is important for all people. When we mis-use, ignore, or abuse nature there are usually consequences. To ignore these consequences is not very wise. It may be easy to ignore warnings and continue to exploit nature. But, sooner or later, we experience negative results because of what we have done or failed to do. Pollution, poisoned streams, ground water contamination, loss of oxygen-bearing forests, climate change and other issues touch our ability to live in harmony with nature. Like the exploitation of people, the exploitation of nature can bring unhealthy results.

Reverence and respect for nature is a Franciscan perspective that is part of our lives. As good stewards, we choose to find ways to protect nature's resources so they are available to all people - and to the children of future generations. Wherever we work and live we promote healthy responsibility and concern for earth's resources. To do otherwise would make us poor stewards. This perspective may not always be popular, but it is part of our identity as Franciscans. Once again we look to things that concern the common good and not exploitation for personal gain.

The earth is the Lord's! If we are stewards than we are also responsible for our stewardship. We have spoken a great deal about reverence and respect for people. This text of the Rule opens our minds to another area **to show respect and reverence - to all creatures, animate and inanimate**. As always, we act on sound information and not on hearsay evidence. The "truth" is our partner in our ability to care for the earth and its resources. We are challenged to show concern and responsibility by caring for Mother Nature.

It is more than recycling. It relies on a Franciscan spirit that is in tune with God's creative love at work in giving us a world to live in. Having been put in charge of this world we are responsible to care for it. Most of us will probably not be living in a space vehicle in the near future. Our earth is presently all we have. Taking care of it is in our best interests. Our use of the earth, its resources, its contributions to life, the oxygen we breathe as well as the water we drink and the fruit we eat and the seeds we plant need sensitive people to use them wisely.

It is God's earth and requires respect from those who love God and whom God loves. Followers of Francis should be known not just as bird lovers or people who work hard to protect nature. As stewards of God's earth we fulfill our role in every necessary way. We will tackle problems of wasting earth's resources. We will protest exploiting and abusing the earth merely for the sake of profit. We will dialogue with people and encourage respect for all of creation and for all creatures.

If exploitation is the "name of the game" we will ask to sit down with exploiters and try to convince them to respect God's creation. If big profits are involved, this will be a difficult task. But we do not evade the issue because money and power are allied against our ideas. Neither will we demonize the exploiters. Rather we will treat them with respect even when we disagree with their ideas or actions.

Respectful confrontation may not lead to immediate success. But we will be consistent in calling for an end to exploitation - of people or nature. We know that nature's resources are limited. As the population of our earth grows the demands made on nature's resources will grow. Good stewardship will move us to find better ways of growing food; to develop a delivery system that makes the food available to all; to find ways for people in the food chain to make a reasonable profit without denying food to people.

If overuse or misuse of earth's resources by a few begins to endanger life on planet earth, we will share that information. We want to help people make better decisions about their use of natural resources. Problems like global warming and forms of poisoning or pollution must be tackled both individually and through government action. Franciscans have a sense of *universal kinship* and share it with others. We will pursue whatever will accomplish the task of protecting earth's resources so our children's children do not live in a wasteland. Without forever crying "wolf," we will persist in doing whatever it takes to care for creation. A variety of programs surrounding ecology and the use of nature's gifts are available. We will join with others in adding our Franciscan spirit and voice to the need for good stewardship (JPIC).

The motivation is clear in the Rule. Creation bears *the imprint of the Most High* (SFO Rule //18). Beyond what we have already addressed, there is another gift that nature brings us - beauty. The flowering plants of earth bring exquisite color and form into our lives. The majestic sweep of mountains reveal a power beyond what we humans can do. There is the wonder of a beautiful stream or river that flows to the ocean and waters the earth. Rain and rainbows bring vivid colors to the sky. Lightning flashes and the roll of thunder create a symphony that is hard to equal. The quiet corners of the earth and its animals provide quiet space for an aching heart They are all gifts of creation.

In November of 1979 John Paul II named St. Francis the patron saint of ecology. The Pope said:

St Francis is justifiably ranked among those famous saints who have respected nature as a marvelous gift of God to humankind. He knew how to honor each one of the works of the Creator. Moved by the divine Spirit, he also sang the magnificent Canticle of the Sun, in which he first and foremost gave praise, glory, honor and thanksgiving to the Supreme, Almighty and Good God for Brother Sun, Sister Moon and the stars of heaven."

Quoted in: Build with Living Stones - SBU - Unit 13 - Page 5

Canticle of the Creatures (Sun) -1225

Most High, all-powerful, good Lord, Yours are
the praises, the glory, and the honor and all blessing.
To you alone, Most High, do they belong,

and no human is worthy to mention Your name.
Praised be You, my Lord, with all Your creatures,
especially Sir Brother Sun,
Who is the day and through whom You give us light.
And he is beautiful and radiant with great splendor,
and bears a likeness of You, Most High One.
Praised be You, my Lord, through Sister Moon and the stars,
in heaven You formed them clear and precious and beautiful.
Praised be You, my Lord, through Brother Wind,
and through the air, cloudy and serene
and every kind of weather,
through whom you give sustenance to your creatures.
Praised be You, my Lord, through Sister Water,
who is very useful and humble and precious and chaste.
Praised be You, my Lord, through Brother Fire,
through whom You light the night,
and he is beautiful and playful and robust and strong.
Praised be You, my Lord, through our Sister Mother Earth,
who sustains and governs us, and who
produces various fruit with colored flowers and herbs.

Praised be You, my Lord, through those
who give pardon for Your love,
and bear infirmity and tribulation.
Blessed are those who endure in peace
for by You, Most High, shall they be crowned.

Praised be You, my Lord, through our Sister Bodily Death,
from whom no one living can escape.
Woe to those who die in mortal sin.
Blessed are those whom death will find in Your most holy will,
for the second death shall do them no harm

Praise and bless my Lord and give Him thanks
and serve Him with great humility.

Canticle of the Creatures
Francis of Assisi - The Saint - Vol I - Page 113-114

From the time of his conversion, Francis grew in his relationship with God. As trinitarian spirituality was embraced by Francis, his concern not only for people but for all of creation continued to grow. It was a natural result of his intimacy with Jesus. As love took over his heart, nothing was left out of the reach of that love. His respect for all of creation blossomed and found numerous expressions. There are many stories about his relationship to and care for creatures who crossed his path.

As he was going along further in that same fervor he raised his eyes, and along the road he saw some trees in which there was an almost infinite multitude of birds. Saint Francis marvelled at this and said to his companions: "You wait for me here on the road, and I'll go and preach to my sisters the birds." He entered the field and he began to preach to the birds that were on the ground. And quickly the birds that were in the trees all came down to him and together remained still while Saint Francis finished preaching, and did not leave until he gave them his blessing. And according to what Brother Masseo later told Brother James of Massa, as Saint Francis went among them, touching them with his tunic, not one of them moved.

The Little Flowers of St Francis
Francis of Assisi - The Prophet - Vol III - Page 593

(You may want to read the rest of the story, read the last 2 lines of page 592, the whole of page 593 and the conclusion on page 594)

Beyond doubt, Francis not only praised God's gracious love bestowed on Francis, but showed concern for all of God's creatures as well. It sprang from a sense of gratitude for God's continuing gifts to Francis and all people. Francis probably didn't know the word "ecology." But he showed a consistent love for creation because it is God's creation. He knew that relationship to God included a universal relationship to all of God's creatures. They became his brother and sister. Re-read his *Canticle of the Creatures* to discover the warmth of his relationship with creation.

Francis' clarity in responding to creation with love developed because his penitential life brought him to intimacy with Jesus. In turn, his spirit was open to a simple relationship to all creatures whom God loves. It could hardly be otherwise. May we also embrace such a spirit!

Reflection questions/Readings

Little Flowers of St. Francis
Chapter 22 - *"How St Francis Tamed the Wild Doves"*
Francis of Assisi - The Prophet - Vol III - Page 604

64. What kind of bond exists between created things?
Compendium - Catechism of the Catholic Church
USCCB - #64 and #65 - Page 24

Earthly goods destined for all
Pastoral Constitution on the Church in the Modern World
Gaudium et Spes - Paragraph 69

1. Why are Franciscans concerned about all of creation? What motivates Franciscans to respect and reverence all of God's creatures and the resources of earth?

2. Explain the nature of our stewardship in regard to creation. How does stewardship show itself in daily life?

3. What does the *Canticle of the Creatures* teach you about the spirit of Francis? How does it influence your own spirit in regard to all creatures and all of creation?

4. Why is the exploitation of nature's resources a concern for us humans? How do we show respect for nature?

5. What spirit do we bring when we find it necessary to confront people who exploit creation or, even worse, exploit people? What does our Franciscan spirit expect of us in such situations?

6. What are some practices you could adopt that would show your concern for creation? What practice(s) are you going to adopt?

7. Scripture reflection: Psalm 19: 1-6 / Psalm 33:1-9. What truth do these psalms express about the earth? What response do they ask of the readers? How do these texts support the focus of this chapter?

Chapter twenty seven

Bearers of Peace

Fly, bird, fly over all borders, over barbed wire and minefields, fly and sing everywhere a song of peace.

19. Mindful that they are bearers of peace which must be built up unceasingly, they should seek out ways of unity and fraternal harmony through dialogue, trusting in the presence of the divine seed in everyone and in the transforming power of love and pardon.

Messengers of perfect joy in every circumstance, they should strive to bring joy and hope to others.

Since they are immersed in the resurrection of Christ, which gives true meaning to Sister Death, let them serenely tend toward the ultimate encounter with the Father.

1. Rule 19 ***Peace is the work of justice and the fruit of reconciliation and of fraternal love.*** *Secular Franciscans are called to be bearers of peace in their families and in society:*

+ *they should see to the proposal and spreading of peaceful ideas and attitudes;*
+ *they should develop their own initiatives and should collaborate, individually and as a fraternity, with initiatives of the Pope, the local Churches, and the Franciscan Family;*
+ *they should collaborate with those movements and institutions which promote peace while respecting its authentic foundations.*

2. While acknowledging both the personal and national right to legitimate defense, they should respect the choice of those who, because of conscientious objection, refuse to bear arms.

3. ***To preserve peace in the family,*** *the brothers and sisters should, in due time,* ***make a last will and testament for the disposition of their goods.***

Constitutions - article 23.1, 23.2, 23.3

1. Even in suffering, Francis experienced confidence and joy from:

- *the experience of the fatherhood of God;*
- *the invincible faith of rising with Christ to eternal life;*
- *the experience of being able to meet and praise the Creator in the universal fraternity of all creatures.*

Rule 19 *Following the Gospel, Secular Franciscans, therefore, affirm their hope and their joy in living. They make a contribution to counter the widespread distress and pessimism, preparing a better future.*

2. In the fraternity, the brothers and sisters should promote mutual understanding and they should see to it that the atmosphere of their meetings is welcoming and that it reflects joy. They should encourage one another for the good.

Constitutions - article 26.1, 26.2

1. Rule 19 *The brothers and sisters, progressing in age, should learn to accept illness and increasing difficulties and to give a deeper sense to their life. This should be undertaken with increasing detachment as they set out for the Promised Land. They should be firmly convinced that the community of those who believe in Christ and who loved one another in Him will go forward into eternal life as the "communion of saints."*

2. Secular Franciscans should commit themselves to create in their environment and, above all, in their fraternities, a climate of faith and hope so that "Sister Death" may be regarded as a passage to the Father, and all may prepare themselves with serenity.

Constitutions - article 27.1, 27.2

Come, let us go up to the mountain of the Lord, to the house of the God of Jacob; that he may teach us his ways and that we may walk in his paths. For out of Zion shall go forth instruction, and the word of the Lord from Jerusalem.

He shall judge between the nations, and shall arbitrate for many peoples; they shall beat their swords into plough-shares, and their spears into pruning hooks; nation shall not lift sword against nation, neither shall they learn war any more.

Isaiah 2:3-4

How beautiful upon the mountains are the feet of the messenger who announces peace, who brings good news, who announces salvation, who says to Zion, "Your God reigns."

Isaiah 52:7

For the kingdom of God is not about food and drink but righteousness and peace and joy in the Holy Spirit. The one who thus serves Christ is acceptable to God and has human approval. Let us then pursue what makes for peace and for mutual edification.

Romans 14:17-19

PEACE

Within our lifetime we have rarely been at peace in our world. If our country was not at war, there were wars among other nations. It seems as though the desire for peace is a futile search. True peace is not easy to achieve. That is true among individuals as well as groups and nations. The awesome consequences of war live all around us. The destruction of property, the spirit of soldiers returning home who struggle to live in the ordinary confines of everyday life. Families and individuals who struggle to return to something resembling normalcy. People who mourn the loss of loved ones because of war and bombs and bullets and suicide bombers.

Within cities and neighborhoods there may be a spirit of violence as a means of power that locks doors and escalates fear. Within families there is the violence of absence and abuse and non-caring attitudes. So many things in our world kill the spirit of hope and bring despair. So many people grow up ashamed of themselves, lacking any real identity because of their treatment in homes or in a society that is dysfunctional. Many social needs cry out for solutions.

The Church suffers from people in authority abusing youngsters and diminishing trust. People in public positions abuse trust and allow corruption that makes it difficult to trust public officials, teachers, police or whomever. These things together create an atmosphere that makes a peaceful society difficult to find.

It is not surprising then that the SFO Rule states that peace must be *built up unceasingly.* There is no vacation from the work of being *bearers of peace.* Peace is not our only responsibility, but it is a vital one. We bring our Franciscan spirit to tackle problems that diminish the possibilities for peace. True peace requires more than the cessation of violence.

Respect for and development of human life require peace. Peace is not merely the absence of war, and it is not limited to maintaining a balance of powers between adversaries. Peace cannot be attained on earth without safeguarding the goods of persons, free communication among men, respect for the dignity of persons and people, and the assiduous practice of fraternity. Peace is "the tranquility of order" (St. Augustine, De Civ. Dei, 19,13, 1:PL 41, 640). ***Peace is the work of justice and the effect of charity.*** (Cf. Isaiah 32:17; cf. GS 78 Paragraphs 1-2).

Catechism of the Catholic Church - no. 2304 - Page 554

Our work for peace will encompass a variety of approaches:

+ Creating an atmosphere where people are free is part of peacemaking. + Creating a society that respects the dignity of people is part of peacemaking. + Developing a process for enemies to reconcile and forgive is part of peacemaking. + Changing minds and hearts so that dialogue is used instead of violence is a way of peacemaking. + Developing jobs and wages that allow families to meet basic needs for human living is peacemaking. + Building bridges for relationships is a way of peacemaking. + Providing places and people to help change degrading and abusing situations is a part of peacemaking. + In short, creating a society where relationships are more important than wealth and power will help us live up to the name - *peacemakers.*

Not surprisingly our dedication to peacemaking is built on the foundation of relationships. Trinitarian spirituality walks into our lives, touching us with the spirit that helps us deal with the consequences of conflict, big or small.

The SFO Rule #19 puts it directly: we *should seek out ways of unity and harmony through dialogue.* Why is that a part of our spirit? The Rule is clear when it says that we *trust in the presence of the divine seed in everyone.* We have already written of becoming aware of the image of Jesus in other people. We know the work it takes for such trust to become part of our spirit. As that spirit deepens in us we will more naturally be peacemakers.

An important element of the Franciscan spirit of peace is our readiness to recognize *the transforming power of love and pardon.* When people/nations are in conflict they are often overwhelmed by feelings of animosity, anger, hatred and "getting even." It will take time to tame these feelings. But experience shows us that clinging to them keeps us controlled by negative feelings. We are NOT free! When we allow the transforming power of love and pardon to enter our lives we will be moving toward freedom. We will also create a place of peace for others.

Whenever you stand praying, forgive, if you have anything against anyone; so that your Father in heaven may also forgive you your trespasses.

Mark 11:25

Do not judge, and you will not be judged; do not condemn, and you will not be condemned. Forgive, and you will be forgiven; give, and it will be given to you. A good measure, pressed down, shaken together, running over, will be put into your lap; for the measure you give will be the measure you get back.

Luke 6:37-38

JOY & HOPE

This part of article #19 is an interesting one. Notice that there is an expectation that joy and hope are part of our lives. Of course, if we are perfect Franciscans that is true. However, reality tells us that perfection may not always be ours. The Rule is doing more than nudging us here. It shares a declarative statement: *Messengers of perfect joy in every circumstance ...* The question is, would we answer that statement with a "Yes, I am" or a "No, I'm not?" If "No,"what do we need to bring joy into our lives?

Joy goes far beyond the ability to laugh in life. Joy is connected with a peaceful spirit. It allows us to perceive God-at-work in our lives. There is a sense that we are cared for and loved. We are "somebody" to God and God loves us no matter how poorly we respond to God's love. There is an inner sense of peacefulness that is a partner with joy.

The things that diminish joy are like a list of things that diminish peace. Anger, resentment, hatred, frustration can keep joy from being part of life. Too much busyness and lots of chatter can diminish joy. Taking things for granted or dominated by desires for material things can push joy aside. Lack of quiet reflective time can put roadblocks in the way of joy. A negative sense about our own identity or any form of self-hatred leaves little room for joy. Worry contrasts with a sense of joy. Would-have, could-have, should-have concerns are not partners with joy.

Why? Joy grows when we are at ease with ourselves and our world. Joy grows when we can forgive people and discover a new freedom of spirit. Joy blossoms when we can rejoice at others' good fortune. Joy happens with each new realization of being loved by God. Joy is fruitful when we experience a gentle reaction to life's quirks and can smile at our own inconsistencies. In fact we don't so much seek joy as discover that it comes when gospel values and ideals take root in our lives. It walks into our lives when we are faithful to the secular Franciscan Rule. It is linked to the integrity of being what we profess to be. It finds support in a good sense of humor.

A Franciscan becomes aware that many of the things we do are small, sometimes insignificant. There is always the temptation to want to do big things, make an enormous difference among people, and design and build things that bring us fame. The temptation is understandable. For a Franciscan to give in to the temptation is where the "rubber hits the road." Profession invites us to give whether we get a lot of credit or not. Our love is offered freely and delights to see people find new life in what we offer.

Unless the Lord builds the house, those who build it labour in vain. Unless the Lord guards the city, the guards keep watch in vain. It is vain that you rise up early and go late to rest, eating the bread of anxious toil; for he gives sleep to his beloved.

Psalm 127: 1-2

Joy comes to us when we trust God. Joy comes to us when we are faithful to our profession. Joy comes to us when we forgive and reconcile and collaborate in doing good. Joy comes when our relationship with Jesus and the Trinity grows and blossoms. Joy comes when we seek positive solutions rather than negative judgments and words of condemnation. Joy comes in viewing the wonders of creation and the smile of a baby. Joy comes when good plans reach fulfillment.

... *to bring joy and* ***HOPE*** - Hope is another expression of the wonder of being in God's hands. Hope, like faith and charity, relies on the gracious love of God.

For in hope we were saved. Now hope that is seen is not hope. For who hopes for what is seen? But if we hope for what we do not see, we wait for it with patience.

Romans 8:24-25

Hope is based on God's faithfulness to his promises. Because of our belief in a loving God, we trust in God's care for us. God's promises are not made lightly. God is always faithful to the covenant. The covenant is not dependent on our faithfulness (Thank you, Jesus!). The love of God consistently relates to us. God always keeps his covenant with us.

Father, we acknowledge your greatness: all your actions show your wisdom and love. You formed man in your own likeness and set him over the whole world to serve you, his creator, and to rule over all creatures. Even when he disobeyed you and lost your friendship you did not abandon him to the power of death, but helped all men to seek and find you. Again and again you offered a covenant to man and through the prophets taught him to hope for salvation.

Eucharistic Prayer #4

God is faithful; by him you were called into the fellowship of his Son, Jesus Christ, our Lord.

1 Corinthians 1:9

God is faithful, and he will not let you be tested beyond your strength, but with the testing he will also provide the way out so that you may be able to endure it.

1 Corinthians 10:13

Scripture points out the source of our hope. Our hope can include our talents and gifts to deal with issues. But the *bottom line* for hope is God's faithfulness and love for us.

Hope is our readiness to do something because we recognize that it is a good thing to do. We hope for success, but it does not dictate to us. Whether or not we succeed, if it is worth doing we do it. Success depends on the power the Spirit of God brings to the situation and to us.

In the light of hope we patiently await the touch of God to enable us to do good even when we may not feel like it. Hope nourishes us when the odds seem to be against success. Hope gives us strength to continue when we are worn out. Hope reminds us that this is God's work and not our own. Hope may invite us to change our tactics or to give prayerfulness an opportunity in our ministry. Just when we believe we can do no more nor go no further on our Franciscan journey, hope says, in the name of God: *Fear not, for I am with you.*

Hope happens in little things. During my writing of this text I was looking for a book I wanted to use to stimulate some ideas for one of the chapters. I couldn't find it in my room or in our library. I was frustrated because the author was a good friend and I was certain she had given me a copy. I gave up on finding it and thought I might order a copy through *Amazon.com.* It was time for evening prayer. I entered chapel and sat next to a visiting friar. Guess what book he had brought along to read? The very book I wanted! Even without hope of getting the book quickly or praying about it, it was given to me. God must love those little surprises of hope which are unexpected!

Be attentive to God's surprises, big and little. No detail is too insignificant for God. It's no wonder gratitude is such a natural response for Franciscans!

SISTER DEATH / RESURRECTION

In an earlier chapter I mentioned that we would deal with the *resurrection* later on. This is the "later on." The resurrection fits here because we want to talk about Sister Death and her entry into the room of our lives. Sharing ideas about *resurrection* gives us reason for hope when Sister Death invites us to "pass over."

If there is no resurrection of the dead, then Christ has not been raised; and if Christ has not been raised, then our proclamation has been in vain and your faith has been in vain. ... For if the dead are not raised, then Christ has not been raised. If Christ has not been raised, your faith is futile and you are still in your sins.

But in fact Christ has been raised from the dead, the first fruits of those who have died. For since death came through a human being, the resurrection of the dead has also come through a human being; for as all died in Adam, so all will be made alive in Christ.

1 Corinthians 15:13-14, 16, 20-22

You that are Israelites, listen to what I have to say: Jesus of Nazareth, a man attested to you by God with deeds of power, wonder and signs that God did through him among you, as you yourselves know - this man, handed over to you according to a definite plan and foreknowledge of God, you crucified and killed by the hands of those outside the law. But God raised him up, having freed him from death, because it was impossible for him to be held in its power.

... This Jesus God raised up, and of that all of us are witnesses. Being therefore exalted at the right hand of God, and having received from the Father the promise of the Holy Spirit, he has poured out this that you both see and hear.

Acts 2: 22-24, 32-34

Belief in the resurrection is a matter of faith. Scripture does not have witnesses to the actual moment of resurrection. That part of it is a mystery. But scriptural authors write about the many consequences of the resurrection within the believing community.

Mary of Magdala gives witness to the empty tomb and the presence of Jesus (John 20:11-18). Peter and John run and see the empty tomb (John 20:3-10). The disciples in their locked room give witness to the risen Christ (John 20:19-23/Luke 24:36-49). Thomas gives witness that it is really Jesus (John 20:26-29). The couple on the way to Emmaus discover Jesus in the breaking of bread (Luke 24:13-35). The ascension scene reveals Christ's return to the Father and his exaltation (Luke 24:50-53/Mark 16:19-20). Peter is taught about love (John 21:15-19).

The resurrection of Jesus is a sign of the power of the Father at work to vindicate the life and loving self-oblation of Jesus. It shows that death is not an end of everything. The disciples and the adversaries of Jesus thought it was. Jesus' enemies were happy to have Jesus out of the way. They concocted a story to explain away the resurrection (the disciples stole the body!) and to avoid the implications of the resurrection. Jesus' passion, death, and resurrection not only guarantee the meaning of Jesus' life but touches the meaning of all human life and death. This is a matter of believers testifying to believers.*

The resurrection of the dead fulfills our trust in a loving God. Death is not the end for us. It is a doorway to a new life accompanied by Sister Death. What a tragedy the death of Christ must have been for those who had faithfully followed him in the hope that he was the savior.

The two people on the road to Emmaus even expressed their sorrow: *We had hoped he was the one to redeem Israel* (Luke 24:21). Death had seemingly trumped their hope. Jesus' answer was a bit frustrated: *Oh, how foolish you are, and slow of heart to believe all that the prophets declared. Was it not necessary that the Messiah should suffer these things and then enter into his glory?* (Luke 24:25-26). Distress was turned into joy. Unbelief changed to faith.

The resurrection is meant to do the same thing for us. Our weak faith is challenged by something only the Giver of life could do. It confirms our belief. It gives us hope in the face of the temptation to unbelief. It offers a gift of life in the presence of Sister Death. We know this by faith and not by scientific research or exploration of documents. The mystery of the resurrection gives us a spiritual value that confirms our belief in the Lord of life.

I pray that the God of our Lord Jesus Christ, the Father of glory, may give you a spirit of wisdom and revelation as you come to know him, so that, with the eyes of your heart

---

* Cf. Understanding Catholicism - Monica Hellwig - Page 102ff

enlightened, you may know what is the hope to which he has called you, what are the riches of his glorious inheritance among the saints, and what is the immeasurable greatness of his power for us who believe, according to the working of his great power. God put his power to work in Christ when he raised him from the dead and seated him at his right hand in the heavenly places, far above all rule and authority and power and dominion, and above every name that is named, not only in this age but also in the age to come. And he has put all things under his feet and has made him the head over all things for the church, which is his body, the fullness of him who fills all in all.

Ephesians 1:17-23

Together with the hope that Jesus' resurrection gives is also the assurance that God is with us in pain and suffering. We are not alone nor are we being punished for something when sickness and suffering strike our lives. Suffering and pain are not unusual companions on our human journey. How we deal with them makes a difference for Franciscans. We use medical help to alleviate pain and suffering.

Yet we humans cannot solve every form of suffering nor escape the entrance of Sister Death. Because of our trust in God, our relationship with God through Jesus Christ, and through the presence of the Holy Spirit, we learn to deal with suffering. Its relationship to Jesus' suffering draws us to him. Suffering, when it keeps us from ordinary activity, becomes our activity for the moment. It does not separate us from life but is, at present, a part of our life. If we offer our entire self to God, then this suffering is now united to Jesus and becomes our activity of the moment. Instead of controlling us, we bring suffering to the chalice that makes it redemptive in its union with Jesus.

On the Cross, Jesus bore the full weight of evil and removed its power over us. He provided a new meaning for suffering by giving it redemptive power. By his grace we are able to unite our pain to his redemptive passion. St. Paul witnessed this when he wrote, "I rejoice in my sufferings for your sake, and in my flesh I complete what is lacking in the afflictions of Christ on behalf of his body, that is, the church." (Colossians 1:24)

United States Catholic Catechism for Adults - USCCB - Page 252

We are given new insight and understanding of suffering through the words of Paul. Suffering comes to us human beings. We are not being punished by God for our sinfulness. God's love is too rich to do that. Neither will we neglect normal medical treatment that can control or eliminate suffering. We will unite ourselves with Christ and bring redemptive power to our suffering. It will not be a waste of time though it keeps us from our ordinary activities. Instead, engaging the suffering becomes our activity for the moment. Francis shows us the way.

As his illness grew worse, he lost all bodily strength, and deprived of all his powers, he could not even move. One of the brothers asked him what he would prefer to endure: this long-lasting illness or suffering a martyr's cruel death at the hands of an executioner. "My son," he replied, "whatever is more pleasing to the Lord my God to do with me and in me has always been and still is dearer, sweeter, and more agreeable to me. I desire to be found always and completely in harmony with and obedient to God's will alone in everything. But to suffer this illness, even for three days, would be harder for me than any martyrdom. I am not speaking about its reward but only of the pain and suffering it causes."

Life of St Francis - second book - Thomas of Celano
Francis of Assisi - The Saint - Vol I - Page 275

Franciscans deal with suffering with wisdom and faith. Jesus shows the way and Francis follows his example. May we be able to do the same. Faith reveals that death is a passageway to new life - far beyond our expectations. For death is not the end as Jesus' resurrection reminds us. Hence, we are able, in faith and love, to deal serenely with the coming of Sister Death.

Readings/Questions for dialogue

Chapter 8
How St. Francis explained those things that are perfect joy
Francis of Assisi - The Prophet - Vol III - Pages 579 to 581

Christ is Risen! Alleluia! / A Transcendent Event
United States Catholic Catechism for Adults - USCCB
Page 93-94 / 95

The Sacrament of Anointing of the Sick
Compendium - Catechism of the Catholic Church
no. 313-320 - Pages 90 to 92

1. Make a list of things you can do to be a bearer of peace. How many do you practice in daily life?

2. What quality of faith must be incorporated as we seek the ways of unity and harmony through dialogue?

3. How does the transforming power of love and pardon show itself in actual practice in your life?

4. Why are joy and hope important qualities in today's world? Describe how you practice them in your life.

5. How can you bring joy and hope to others?

6. How can suffering take on new meaning for us? Explain the process.

Sister Death
Michael Gaffney OFM Cap
Capuchin Cemetery
Mt Calvary, WI

7. Why do we welcome Sister Death? How can we prepare for a welcoming attitude to her?

8. Why is the resurrection important to the practice of our faith?

9. Scripture reflection: Psalm 139: 1-18, 23-24. How does this text bring you hope? What does it say about God's concern for us?

Chapter twenty eight

Fraternities: Gathering as one

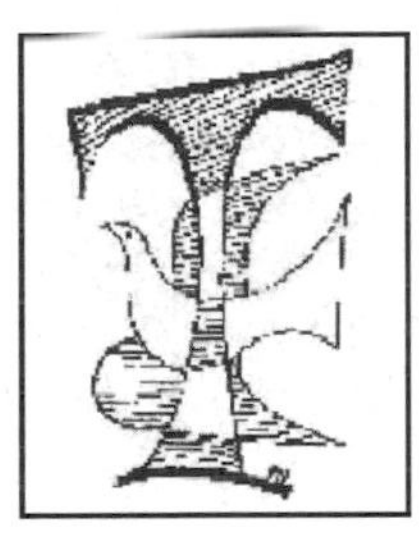

SFO RULE - Chapter three

20. The Secular Franciscan Order is divided into fraternities of various levels - local, regional, national and international. Each one has its own moral personality in the Church. These various fraternities are coordinated and united according to the norm of this rule and of the constitutions.

1. The fraternity of the SFO finds its origin in the inspiration of Saint Francis of Assisi to whom the Most High revealed the essential quality of life in fraternal communion.

2. Rule 20 *"The SFO is divided into fraternities of various levels," the purpose being to promote, in an orderly form, the union and mutual collaboration among the brothers and sisters and their active and communal presence in both the local and the universal Church. The SFO shall also support the commitment of the fraternities in their service to the world and specifically to the life of society.*

3. The brothers and sisters gather in local fraternities established in connection with a church or a religious house, or in personal fraternities, constituted for specific and valid reasons recognized in the decree of establishment.

<u>Constitutions</u> - article 28.1, 28.2, 28.3

1. Local fraternities are grouped into fraternities at various levels: regional, national and international according to criteria that are ecclesial, territorial, or of another nature. They are co-ordinated and connected according to the norm of the Rule and the Constitutions. This is a requirement of the communion among the fraternities, of the orderly collaboration among them, and of the unity of the SFO.

2. Rule 20 *These fraternities, that each have their own juridical personality in the Church, should acquire, if possible, a civil juridical personality for the better fulfillment of their mission. It pertains to the national councils to give guidelines concerning the motivations and the procedures to be followed.*

3. National statutes should indicate the criteria for the organization of the SFO in the nation. The application of these criteria is left to the prudent judgment of the leaders of the fraternities concerned and of the national council.

Constitutions - article 29.1, 29.2, 29.3

Associations whose members share in the spirit of some religious institute while in secular life, lead an apostolic life, and strive for Christian perfection under the higher direction (Altius Moderamen) *of the same institute are called third orders or some other appropriate name.*

The Code of Canon Law - Canon 303

Our appropriate name is the *Secular Franciscan Order.* This chapter deals with structures, laws and definitions. Our Franciscan vision needs structure to assist its implementation. This is true in the Church as well as in secular society. Structures are meant to support the vision and not hinder it. SFO structures serve the Franciscan vision.

As members of the SFO it is important to know our standing in the Church. The SFO is a *Public Association of the Christian Faithful.* The SFO is constituted of faithful lay members and clergy among the people of God and is approved by the Holy Father. It enjoys the privilege of being pastorally and spiritually *assisted* by the brothers of the First Order and Third Order Regular.

As indicated earlier in this book, **the SFO is autonomous** (having its own law) **and international**, having members throughout the world, who are united by their *profession* as secular Franciscans. The Secular Franciscan Order thus possesses three features: *autonomy, unity and secularity.*

5. The Secular Franciscan Order is a public association in the Church. It is divided into fraternities at various levels: local, regional, national, and international. Each one has its own jurdic personality within the Church

Constitutions - article 1.5

1. The vocation to the SFO is a specific vocation that gives form to the life and apostolic activity of its members. Therefore, those who are bound by perpetual commitment to another religious family or institute of consecrated life cannot belong to the SFO.

Constitutions - article 2.1

2. The SFO, as an international public association, is connected by a special bond to the Roman Pontiff from whom it has received the approval of its Rule and the confirmation of its mission in the Church and in the world.

Constitutions - article 99.2

Being a *privileged Public Association* gives us special responsibilities to the Church and the Franciscan Family. The Church assigns us the mission to be a model in our inner life in the Church and in our outreach to the world. This is no little responsibility. When a fraternity is canonically established it possesses a public juridic personality in the Church.*

Our Franciscan vision, understood and embraced, brings a particular spirit to the Church and the world. Our lives will show that spirit in all areas of human life both in our service in the Church and in our mission to the world. Our profession of the SFO Rule consecrates us. Though we are in the world we choose not to be influenced by its non-gospel values, attitudes, or policies. In that sense secular Franciscans "leave the world."

---

* In the Church the SFO is under the juridiction of two Roman congregations - the *Congregation for the Institute of Consecrated Life* and the *Society of Apostolic life.* Generally speaking, they do not intervene in SFO affairs unless there are specific issues to be addressed or important information to be shared.

Profession incorporates people into the SFO. Though profession is done at a particular fraternity site, the person making profession becomes a member of an international Order called the SFO. Profession establishes a permanent relationship with our Franciscan brothers and sisters throughout the world.

Much of Franciscan life takes place at the local level. But we must never forget that we are part of an international Order. The SFO has people of different cultures; different languages; living in various places; having different skin colors; influenced by different social systems; having various relationships within the Church. We express the Franciscan spirit throughout our planet and within the Church. We have unity, but we are not monolithic. The expression of the Franciscan vision wears many faces. E.g. Franciscan nurses model the gospel in a way different from a worker in an auto assembly factory or a clerk in a supermarket. All of them embrace the Franciscan vision. They express the Franciscan vision in the circumstances in which they live and work.

But though there may be a variety of ways to express the Franciscan spirit, all of us contribute to building the Kingdom of God and re-building the Church, the People of God. John Paul II addressed the international chapter of the SFO on November 22, 2002. His words focus on the reason for our existence.

1. ... The Church expects from the SFO, one and only, a great service in the cause of the Kingdom of God in the world of today. The Church desires that your Order should be a model of organic, structural and charismatic unity on all levels, so as to present itself to the world as "a community of love." The Church expects from you, Secular Franciscans, a courageous and consistent testimony of Christian and Franciscan life, leaning towards the construction of a more fraternal and gospel world for the realization of the Kingdom of God.

... 4. You Secular Franciscans, by vocation, live belonging to the Church and to society as inseparable realities. Therefore, you are asked, above all else, to bear personal witness before all in the environment in which you live: "in your family life; in your work; in your joys and sufferings; in your associations with all men and women, brothers and sisters of the same Father; in your presence and participation in the life of society; in your fraternal relationships with all creatures" (Constitutions - article 12:1). *... you are certainly asked for the testimony of consistency and firmness in fulfilling the promises made at Baptism and at Confirmation, renewed and confirmed in your Profession in the SFO.* ***In virtue of your profession, the Rule and General Constitutions must represent for each one of you the reference point for everyday experience, on the basis of a specific vocation.*** *If you are truly spurred on by the Spirit to achieve the perfection of charity in your secular state, "it would be a contradiction to settle for a life of mediocrity, marked by a minimalist ethic and a shallow religiosity"* (Novo Millennia Ineunte 31). *It is necessary to commit oneself with conviction to the "high measure of ordinary Christian life"* (Ibid) *to which I invited all the faithful at the end of the great Jubilee of 2000.*

5. I do not want to conclude this message without recommending you to consider your family as the primary environment in which to live the Christian commitment and the Franciscan vocation, giving within it space for prayer, to the Word of God and to Christian catechesis, and making every effort to respect all life, from conception and in all situations, until death. It is necessary to act in such a way that your families "who show convincingly that it is possible to live marriage fully in keeping with God's plan and with the true good of the human person; of the spouses and especially of the children who are more fragile." (Novo Millennio Ineunte 47)

Message of the Pope to the 10th General Chapter of the SFO
John Paul II - The Vatican - November 22, 2002

This text of John Paul II invites us to reflect on the nature of the call to be secular Franciscans. It sometimes happens that profession is accepted as the end of formation. Nothing could be further from the truth. It is the beginning of a life lived in fraternity that requires regular conversion and *ongoing formation*. Our Franciscan life is given preference in making personal decisions. Ordinarily nothing takes preference except for special circumstances. This is also true in regard to attendance at the regular gatherings of the local fraternity.

Profession makes it clear that we are part of the SFO and its identity within the Church. We are called to impact the secular world with our Franciscan spirit. In that world we live and work and play. The *rite of profession* gives a clear direction for us to follow:

*I, N.N., by the grace of God, **renew my baptismal promises** and **consecrate** myself to the service of his kingdom. Therefore, in my secular state, I **promise** to live all the days of my life the gospel of our Lord Jesus Christ in the Secular Franciscan Order **by observing its rule of life.** May the grace of the Holy Spirit, the intercession of the Blessed Virgin Mary and our holy father, St. Francis, and the fraternal bonds of community always be my help, so that I may **reach the goal of perfect Christian love.***

Ritual of the SFO - Page 23-24

When we make *profession* in the SFO, God's love accompanies us on the journey. God gives the call and gives us the ability to live our Franciscan life each day and in every place. God's love continues the transformation to which the Holy Spirit calls us. The Holy Spirit accompanies us on every step of our journey of *ongoing formation*. The Gospel challenges us to live a gospel life with dedication and love. The special relationship between us and the Trinity requires us to nurture all our relationships.

3. Insertion into a local fraternity and participation in fraternity life is essential for belonging to the SFO. Appropriate initiatives should be adopted according to the directives of the national statutes, to keep those brothers and sisters united to the fraternity who - for valid reasons of health, family, work or distance - cannot actively participate in community life.

Constitutions - article 53.3

A local fraternity is the basic structure of the SFO. It is important that all the members cooperate in building a vibrant community that models Franciscan life. When questions of canon law arise in a fraternity, it is wise to consult a canon lawyer to help with the issue. Guesswork often creates more problems than it solves. Recognizing our lack of knowledge in canonical matters is the way of wisdom. Seeking canonical help is a way of dealing with reality - which is where God is found.

The *Regional* fraternity and its executive council assures the link between the local fraternities, the region and the national fraternity (Constitutions - article 61.1). In a country the *National* fraternity and council unites all the local and regional fraternities with the International fraternity. The *International* fraternity unites the Catholic Franciscan fraternities throughout the world. Within the international fraternity the *Presidency* coordinates, animates, and guides the SFO at the international level and attends to the resolution of urgent problems (Cf. Constitutions - article 70.1 to .4).

Secular Franciscans at every level are joined to and supportive of the fraternities of each level. They recognize servant-leaders who strive to animate Franciscan life in the fraternities at all levels. The interchange of creative ideas; sharing ideas about issues that arise in life; collaboration in ministry and social action are normal tasks for secular Franciscans. In all we do; in our discussions and conversations; in our dialogue among ourselves and with others - we show respect and reverence. We do everything possible to maintain healthy relationships. We invite people on all sides of an argument to have the *common good* as their goal. We remind one another that the good of the SFO is important in our conversations.

Our goal is unity and understanding rather than winning arguments or whining. We explore better ways to be Franciscan and bring our spirit to the Church and the world.

Not least importantly, the spirituality of reconciliation, so evident in Francis' peaceful dialogue with Malek el-Kamil during the fifth crusade, reminds us of what has been called "The Spirit of Assisi," a spirit of respectful and attentive dialogue among members of differing religious traditions. War and threats of war among nations, invoking God as their justification, contradict that Franciscan understanding of "the Most High God who is good, all good, the highest good." In the figure of the Poverello those who continue to struggle for reconciliation among nations and individuals may find a sign of hope. Whenever he spoke to people, or birds, or wolves, he always began with these words, with which I end: "May the Lord give you peace."

Poverty & Joy - Wm Short OFM - Page 130

+++

Readings/Questions for dialogue

Charity as a responsibility of the Church
God is Love *(Deus Caritas Est)* - Benedict XVI
Paragraph 20

Read the paragraph beginning with:
Through the Spirit, we are to take ... etc
Franciscan Prayer - Ilia Delio OSF - Page 113

A Mirror of the Perfection - Chapter 24
A Brother who neither prayed nor worked but ate well.
Francis of Assisi - The Prophet - Vol III - Page 275

1. How do fraternities at the local, regional, national and international level support and promote the unity of the SFO?

2. Why is *ongoing formation* so important after profession?

What issues need *ongoing formation* and dialogue at the local fraternity level? Name some and give reasons for their importance.

3. What elements for SFO life does the quotation from John Paul II illustrate (Pages 304 to 305) - i.e. what does the Church expect of us?

4. In your Franciscan life, what are the ways in which you will support the fraternities at the various levels?

5. How does canon law serve us and the Church? What resource do we use to clarify matters of canon law that arise in the SFO?

6. How do local fraternities show their love and concern for Secular Franciscans who, for good reasons, can no longer attend fraternity gatherings ?

7. Scripture reflection. Romans 8:26-39. How do these words reflect the total commitment of the SFO way of life? What words of this text of Romans are especially impressive to you?

A young couple moved to a new neighborhood. At their first breakfast the young woman saw her neighbor hanging the wash outside. *That laundry isn't very clean,* she said. *She doesn't know how to wash corrrectly. Perhaps she needs better laundry soap.* Her husband looked on but remained silent. This same conversation continued for a few weeks.

About a month later the woman was surprised to see a nice clean wash on the line. *Look,* she said to her husband, *she has learned how to wash correctly. I wonder who taught her?* The husband said: *I got up early this morning and cleaned our windows!*

++

Be certain the windows of your heart are clean before judging!

Chapter twenty nine

Servant Leadership

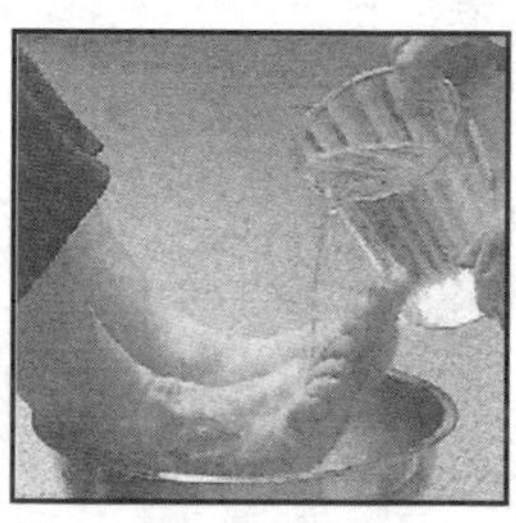

21. On various levels, each fraternity is animated and guided by a council and minister (or president) *who are elected by the professed according to the constitutions.*

Their service, which lasts for a definite period, is marked by a ready and willing spirit and is a duty of responsibility to each member and to the community.

Within themselves the fraternities are structured in different ways according to the norm of the constitutions, according to the various needs of their members and their regions, and under the guidance of their respective council.

1. Rule 21 *"On various levels, each fraternity is animated and guided by a council and minister* (or president)*." These offices are conferred through elections, in accordance with the Rule, the Constitutions, and their own Statutes. Only by way of exception or in the first phase of their establishment may fraternities exist without a regular council. The council of the higher level will make the arrangements necessary for this inadequate situation only for the specific amount of time it takes to get a fraternity back on sure footing or to establish a new fraternity; to give its leaders the proper formation and to carry out elections.*

2. The office of minister or councilor is a fraternal service, a commitment to hold oneself available and responsible in relation to each brother and sister and to the fraternity so that each one will realize his or her own vocation and each fraternity will be a true community, ecclesial and Franciscan, actively present in the Church and in society.

3. The leaders of the SFO at every level should be perpetually professed, convinced of the validity of the

Franciscan evangelical way of life, attentive to the life of the Church and of society with a broad and encompassing vision, open to dialogue, and ready to give and receive help and collaboration.

4. The leaders should see to the spiritual and technical preparation and animation of the meetings, both of the fraternities and of the councils. They should seek to inspire life and soul into the fraternities by their own witness, suggesting appropriate means for the development of the life of the fraternity and of apostolic activities in the light of the fundamental Franciscan options. They should see to it that the decisions made are carried out and they should promote collaboration among the brothers and sisters.

Constitutions - article 31.1, 31.2, 31.3, 31.4

1. The ministers and councilors should live and foster the spirit and reality of communion among the brothers and sisters, among the various fraternities, and between them and the Franciscan family. They should, above all, cherish peace and reconciliation in and around the fraternity.

2. Rule 21 *The ministers' and councilors' task to lead is temporary. The brothers and sisters, rejecting all ambition, should show love for the fraternity with a spirit of service,* ***prepared both to accept and to relinquish the office.***

Constitutions - article 32.1, 32.2

1. In the guidance and co-ordination of the fraternities and of the Order, the personality and capacity of the individual brothers and sisters and of the individual fraternities should be promoted. The plurality of expressions of the Franciscan ideal and cultural variety must be respected.

2. The councils of higher levels should not do what can be adequately carried out either by local fraternities or by a council of a lower level. They should respect and promote their vitality so that they fulfill their duties properly. The local fraternities and councils concerned should commit themselves to carry out the decisions of the international council and of the other councils of higher levels, and to implement their programs, ***adapting them when necessary to their own situation.***

Constitutions - article 33.1, 33.2

Where the situation and the needs of the members require it, sections or groups which gather members sharing particular needs, common interests, or the same choices, may be established within the fraternity under the guidance of one council.

Such groups can give themselves specific norms relative to their meetings and activities, ***firmly remaining faithful, however, to the requirements which arise from membership in the one fraternity.*** *National statutes may establish criteria suitable for the formation and functioning of these sections or groups.*

Constitutions - article 34

These articles of the Constitutions focus on qualities of Franciscan leaders and fraternity life. Specific details about the job descriptions of various offices can be found in the Constitutions (articles 49-52) and National Statutes (articles 1-15).

Issues of leadership, elections and dealing with issues are part of the Constitutions and National Statutes. Check these documents in order to act in accordance with them. *Read the job descriptions in the Constitutions* (articles 49-52) so you are aware of the duties when you run for an office or are appointed to a ministry in the fraternity. Competence is an important quality. It is difficult to offer servant-leadership if someone is incompetent to fulfill the office to which he/she is elected or appointed. Good leaders regularly use two basic phrases: "Thank you!" and "What do you think?" They are empowering words and need to be genuine when used by colleague-servant-leaders.

Leadership programs help. On the national level some programs have been developed. Training programs are important in order to develop good leaders for fraternity offices. This is an ongoing process and needs to be taken seriously. Creative ways of accomplishing this task is a gift for the SFO. Though workshops may not be absolutely essential, they are most helpful to fraternity life.

The spirit of anyone who is elected to office is one of being a servant after the model Christ used at the Last Supper i.e. washing the feet of his disciples. Jesus did not lose his authority nor his power to lead. Rather he gave a model of *how* to lead by being a servant. For Franciscans it means that the power or authority that officers possess is used for the common good and not for personal purposes or needs.

I did not come to be served, but to serve says the Lord. (Mt 20:28) *Let those who are placed over others boast about that position as much as they would if they were assigned the duty of washing the feet of their brothers. And if they are more upset at having their place over others taken away from them than at losing their position at their feet, the more they store up a money bag to the peril of their soul.* (Cf. John 12:4-6)

The Undated Writings
[IV Let no one make being over others his own]
Francis of Assisi - The Saint - Vol I - Page 130

As our Franciscan spirit grows, loving service is a natural consequence when we are called to serve. Our way of life implements the spirit Jesus shows at the last supper. The authority of office in the SFO is real. The power of a council is real. Power and authority are gifts from God. Franciscans use them to serve others in the fraternity as well as dealing with issues beyond the fraternity. When used in a spirit of service Franciscans with power and authority model the servant-leadership role.

In the SFO the council of a fraternity possesses the authority/power to serve the membership. Each fraternity has a council with its minister. The election to be a fraternity minister does not confer the power to do what he/she wants. The power given to the minister (together with the council) is to serve the brothers and sisters and to love them and put into practice the decisions of the fraternity and the council.

When we speak about authority and power in the Rule and Constitutions we find it expressed in the words - *animate and guide* and not *command and prescribe.* Servant-leaders always prefer to *animate and guide.*

You may have noticed that the **principle of subsidiarity** is part of the way in which Franciscan authority functions. (Constitutions - article 33.2). Issues that arise should be addressed at the level which is best suited to deal with them. Only if that level of authority is unable to handle the situation is it appealed to a higher level. Councils are expected to handle fraternity issues on their level. Whatever they can do they are expected to do! In situations when the Constitutions or National Statutes require the approval of a council of a higher level the affected council seeks that approval.

When dealing with issues of structure and law, servant-leaders should check the Constitutions and National Statutes to see what articles apply to the situation. The Constitutions and Statutes often offer direction for dealing with ordinary issues in fraternity life. If officers do not find guidance in the Constitutions or Statutes, they can appeal for direction from a council of the next higher level.

Leaders require clarity about the Franciscan *vision.* Only then can practical ways and means be developed to implement the *vision.* The *vision* helps us develop programs that are achievable. What we have done before is never quite enough. The *vision* always stretches us to do more.

Everyone needs to be affected by the *vision.* Though the total *vision* is never quite achieved, it can inspire, motivate, stretch and challenge, broaden and deepen the purpose and the meaning of a group's mission.* Leaders invite dialogue among the members to reflect on the *vision* and make it their own. The ongoing search for creative ways to live the *vision* brings together a symphony of ideas and attitudes

---

* Cf. *Elements of Spiritual Leadership* - Rev. Roger Statnick Ph.D - Human Development - Volume 25 #4 - Winter 2004 - Page 15.

that give flesh to the *vision* in this time and place.

Vision-clarity and recognizing how it fits into life, helps leaders make practical decisions about Franciscan life both individually and as a fraternity. The fraternity gradually becomes attuned to decisions that clearly give life to the *vision*.

Good decisions, made with the *vision* in mind, can move the group toward embracing and giving flesh to the *vision*! Since none of these decisions are infallible, leaders are flexible enough to adjust and refine decisions. The leadership of a fraternity constantly evaluates decisions to be certain they continue to support living the *vision*.

2. The fraternity, meeting in an assembly or chapter, discusses questions regarding its own life and organization. Every three years, in an elective assembly or chapter, the fraternity elects the minister and the council in the way established by the Constitutions and statutes.

Constitutions - article 49.2

The council leadership deals with many issues in fraternity life. Prioritizing the needs of the fraternity gives a sense of timing for working out solutions. Not everything is of equal importance. The council, in dialogue, will determine when, where, and how issues will be dealt with.

Leaders seek a **"both/and"** approach to issues. They seek ways where differing ideas are joined in a manner beneficial to the fraternity. The opposite attitude is an "either/or" approach which always has someone winning and someone losing. Separate groups then develop and some unity is lost.

As far as possible, councils, in important fraternity issues, seek the involvement of fraternity members with special skills. At times it invites the whole fraternity into a well-prepared dialogue about issues concerning the Franciscan vision, apostolic ministries or other needs that surface in fraternity life. This form of open dialogue gives ownership of the issues to the members of the fraternity.

E.g. *A possible issue for a **Regional** council:* Small local fraternities may find it difficult to develop a slate of nominees for their council. As this becomes more serious the fraternity can invite the Regional council's involvement. The regional Spiritual assistant and another member of the regional council can visit and dialogue with the fraternity. These officers can offer alternatives to the fraternity that fits their situation. They then encourage the fraternity to decide on the alternative that seems to fit their situation.

The regional council may approve the suggested alternative. Practical ways of communication with the members of the fraternity are devised. If the fraternity is deactivated or joins another fraternity, it is good to have a ritual to celebrate the change. The rite reminds everyone to continue to be faithful to their profession of the SFO way of life. The Regional council and the local council can develop reasonable ways for members to continue their communication with each other and offer support to one another. If they join another fraternity or become a cell of another fraternity, they continue their Franciscan life in the life of that fraternity.

Councils with their minister, at every level, will establish good relationships with Franciscans within their fraternity and region. Trinitarian spirituality requires this effort on the part of council members and the minister. Relationships within the fraternity as well as with people beyond fraternity borders are vital for maintaining healthy relationships.

Profession in the SFO can ultimately open the door that involves the individual in leadership roles. Accepting nomination to an office on the council should happen only after at least three years of experience in fraternity life. Each member contributes to fraternity life. The newly professed, using their skills in committee or other ministries, become experienced in fraternity life. When they are nominated for a council office they need to be competent for the role. A few years of living the Rule and gaining experience is encouraged and important before running for office.

Devote yourselves to prayer, keeping alert in it with thanksgiving. ... Conduct yourselves wisely towards outsiders, making the most of the time. Let your speech always be gracious, seasoned with salt, so that you may know how you ought to answer everyone.

Colossians 4:2, 5-6

When professed members transfer to another fraternity, that fraternity needs assurance that the formation of the transferee is solid and fits the spirit of the new fraternity. Dialogue with the council may lead to the decision to spend time in formation with the new fraternity. The transferee and council decide on the length of this formation process.

Readings/Questions for dialogue

Christianity and Social Progress *(Mater et Magistra)*
John XXIII - Paragraph 236 to 239

On the Way to Work
Vinal Van Benthem SFO - *See-Saw* - Page 67-68

Engaged Spirituality
Joseph Nangle OFM - *Contemplation* - Page 44 to 46

1. How do the councils at the various levels influence one another in the SFO?

2. Describe your understanding of being a servant-leader? What are some qualities needed by a servant-leader?

3. What are some responsibilities of a local fraternity council? Why would a know-it-all, domineering person be a poor selection for ministry on a council?

4. What gifts (competencies) do you bring to fraternity life? How can they best be used in the fraternity?

5. Profession is made in a local fraternity. Is that profession made only to the local fraternity or to something bigger? How would you describe the "something bigger?"

6. Explain how the Franciscan ***vision*** influences the daily life of a secular Franciscan. How does it influence your life?

7. How do the Constitutions and National Statutes assist the councils in their servant-leadership within the fraternity? Why is it important to be knowledgeable about the Constitutions and National Statutes?

8. Scripture reflection: Revelation 22:1-6. How do these words give hope to people in leadership? Where does the "light" to lead come from?

+++

Wisdom and Everyday decisions

... Several years ago I was attending a parish meeting. It was a Friday evening. One member of our committee arrived late and out of breath, having driven directly from the airport. Despite the fact that it was his wife's birthday and this would be their only chance to celebrate, he had chosen to come to the meeting rather than going home to his wife. Our pastor was delighted. The rest of us, however, asked him what in the world he was doing there and told him he should go home! Balance - and priorities.

... Society applauds the workaholic, that man or woman who makes lengthy "to-do" lists and then works diligently to check things off. This gospel (Luke 10:38-42) *reminds us that, while most of us are pretty good at the "work" part, it must be balanced by a genuine concern for human needs. ...*

On the Way to Work - Vinal Van Benthem SFO - Page 72

Chapter thirty

Fraternity Life

22. The local fraternity is to be established canonically. It becomes the basic unit of the whole Order and ***a visible sign of the Church, the community of love.*** *This should be the privileged place for developing a sense of Church and the Franciscan vocation and for enlivening the apostolic life of its members.*

1. Rule 22 *The canonical establishment of the local fraternity belongs to the competent religious major superior at the request of the brothers and sisters concerned and with the prior consultation and collaboration of the council of the higher level to which the new fraternity will be related according to the national statutes.*

The written consent of the local Ordinary is necessary for the canonical establishment of a fraternity outside the houses or churches of the Franciscan religious of the First Order or the TOR.

2. For the valid establishment of a local fraternity, at least five perpetually professed members are required. The admission and profession of these first brothers and sisters will be received by the council of another local fraternity or by the council of a higher level which will have provided for their formation in appropriate ways. The acts of admission and profession and the decree of establishment are preserved in the records of the fraternity. Copies are sent to the council of the higher level.

Constitutions - article 46.1, 46.2

1. Rule 22 *Each local fraternity, the primary cell of the one SFO, is entrusted to the pastoral care of the religious Franciscan Order that canonically established it.*

2. A local fraternity may pass to the care of another religious Franciscan Order in the ways determined by the national statutes.

Constitutions - article 47.1, 47.2

1. In the case of cessation of a fraternity, the patrimonial goods of the same, the library and the records are acquired by the fraternity of the immediately higher level.

2. In the case of revival according to the canonical laws, the fraternity will repossess any remaining goods, its own library, and records.

Constitutions - article 48.1, 48.2

3. The fraternities should bear in mind that they are subject to the vigilance of the local Ordinary (Bishop) *insofar as they perform their apostolic activities within the local churches. Secular Franciscans should, therefore, dialogue with their local Ordinaries and follow their directions, inasmuch as they are the moderators of the ministry of the Word and of the Liturgy and the coordinators of the various forms of apostolate in the local Diocesan church.* (Cf. SFO Rule - #6)

National Statutes (USA) - article 16.3

No one doubts the importance of the local fraternity. This is where the spirit of Francis finds its most basic experience. While the fraternities at other levels are important, the local fraternity is the foundation of all that is done regionally, nationally or internationally. Without the cooperation and support of the local fraternity the SFO would exist without a firm foundation.

It is also the reason why the formation process, both initial and ongoing, is so vital at the local fraternity level. To profess people who lack an understanding of our way of life would be ridiculous. The local fraternity establishes a healthy relationship to the rest of the SFO. The local fraternity does not function as an isolated unit. Regional councils, through the visitations, help to evaluate the local fraternity's Franciscan life. It is also guided to a unity of purpose and development of its Franciscan life through this relationship. E.g. The *regional* council and fraternity bring together ministers of the local fraternities in a given region. Together they assist one another in living the Franciscan life. The local fraternity ministers (and non-voting observors) gather at an annual *regional* chapter to dialogue about the life and development of the SFO in the region. While troubling issues can be addressed, the primary goal is to encourage one another and provide tools to live our Franciscan life with greater dedication. Every three years the local ministers and REC elect a Regional Executive Council to conduct the ordinary affairs of the region.

This same pattern is followed as *regional ministers* gather in a yearly *national* chapter to conduct the business of the SFO in the whole United States. The National executive council (NEC) implements the direction given by the annual chapter of NAFRA (National fraternity).

International chapters are held every three years (elections every 6 years), gathering representatives of SFO Catholic fraternities from around the world. The international chapter provides direction and guidance for leadership, formation, and other issues that create a sense of unity for the SFO. The International *Presidency* carries out the decisions of the general chapter. It collaborates with the Conference of General Spiritual Assistants who also assist with issues related to the Vatican or various Congregations. Being in relationship to the Church is part of our Franciscan vision.

The Franciscan vision benefits from the creative ideas that develop at all levels of fraternity life. The interaction between the fraternities at different levels is a gift to us. It keeps us in tune with one another as we create a symphony of Franciscan life around the world.

This interaction among the various levels of the SFO helps to fulfill the direction of the Rule relating to the local fraternity: *This should be the privileged place for developing a sense of Church and the Franciscan vocation and for enlivening the apostolic life of its members* (SFO Rule - #22).

Notice that the Church is described, in this article of the Rule, as *the community of love.* We recognize Francis' love and relationship with the Trinity and the whole of creation, human, animal and beyond. His love for the Church sprang from his awareness of Jesus and the mission of the Church to proclaim the Gospel.

He immediately went to visit the tomb of St. Peter, and after praying there he left the city. Setting out with his companions, he took the road to the Spoleto Valley. As they were going, they discussed among themselves the many gifts of different kinds the merciful God granted them. They had been graciously received by Christ's vicar, the lord and father of the whole Christian nation. How could they carry out his advice and commands? How could they sincerely keep the rule they had accepted and steadfastly safeguard it? How could they walk before the Most High in all holiness and religion? Finally, how could their life and conduct, by growth in the holy virtues, be an example to their neighbors?

Life of St. Francis - Thomas of Celano - The first book
Francis of Assisi - The Saint - Vol I - Page 213

This sounds a bit like what happens at regular fraternity gatherings. Through *ongoing formation* we find ways to live as the Church invites us through our approved Rule. How can *our life and conduct ... be an example to our neighbors? Ongoing formation* about daily life and the Franciscan vision helps achieve a clear Franciscan example.

The initial establishment of a fraternity is spelled out in the *Handbook for Spiritual Assistance in the SFO (2005).* The process takes time. It requires a complete progam of initial formation as well as the development of leadership in a newly forming fraternity. The sponsor for a new fraternity is either a neighboring fraternity or the regional council. The interaction is spelled out in the *Handbook for Spiritual Assistance to the SFO* (Segment B8-B12). Here are a few issues involved in founding a new fraternity.

1. A newly forming group is attached to a sponsoring fraternity by the regional executive council. A member of the new group is selected to be a non-voting liaison to the meetings of the sponsoring fraternity council.

2. Contact is made with the Provincial (or the Provincial Spiritual Assistant) of the 1st Order or TOR to which the new fraternity will be bonded. Once this takes place a spiritual assistant is appointed to *assist* the newly forming group.

3. The sponsoring fraternity's formation team conducts the orientation and initial formation for the new group. If there is a competent, perpetually professed member in the new group he/she can be invited to join the formation team.

4. The sponsoring fraternity deals with the new people in the same way as they do for their own people in *initial formation.* The council of the sponsoring fraternity admits people to *inquiry, candidacy* and *profession.* The minister of the sponsoring fraternity accepts the profession of the first group to make profession. The record of profession is kept in the register of the emerging fraternity.

5. During the final period of development, the sponsoring fraternity (or Regional Executive Council) selects a council from the new group. This council works with the council of the sponsoring fraternity as an internship for serving the emerging fraternity.

6. The canonical establishment of a fraternity ordinarily requires the permission of the local Ordinary. The minister Provincial (or PSA) of the province to which a fraternity is bonded, signs, and dates four copies of the *Document of Establishment.* He sends the copies to the local bishop. When he receives the bishop's approval and signature, he proceeds with the canonical establishment of the fraternity. A copy of the document of establishment goes to the

Bishop, the Regional council, the local emerging fraternity, and the Province to which the fraternity is bonded. Other elements of the process are spelled out in the *Handbook for Spiritual Assistance to the SFO* (Segment B8-B12).

We have spoken of our sense of Church in a number of pages of this text. Our sense of Church is for it to be a *community of love* shown through a gospel way of living.

In our culture, some have a resistance to institutions. Our history reminds us of the freedom of the frontier where the homestead was central and the fields endless - even though such traditions as wagon trains, communal barn-raising, and volunteer fire departments show us that even frontier freedom needed structure of some sort. But the sense of endless freedom is sometimes in tension with belonging to the Church as a community of believers.

When it comes to the Church, some claim that its institutional needs take a toll on the values of community and relationships. Institutions require time, money, and effort for their maintenance. Since the Second Vatican Council highlighted the Church as the People of God, does this not mean that our energies should be focused on people, not buildings, committees, laws, and rules? Should we not recapture the simplicity of Christ's relationship with his disciples and the intimacy of the early Church as described in the Acts of the Apostles?

In response, we would say this is not an "either/or" situation. There is no doubt that the Church is called to be a community of love in the Father, the Son, and the Holy Spirit. The risen Jesus himself presented a model of Church leadership based in love when he solicited three affirmations of love from Peter (Cf. Jn 21:15-17). *At the same time, though, the Church has many structures that are needed to build up the bond of love.*

The Church needs an institutional framework for its

stability, continuity, and mission for serving the cause of the Gospel and opening people to God's call to holiness. Problems with the institution are not arguments for its removal, but for its renewal. ...

Upon his Rock - A community of love
United States Catholic Catechism for Adults - USCCB -Pages 119 - 121

Our role in the Church is to support this *community of love*. Structures certainly can support the desire to show trinitarian love in our world. When structures support that goal, they serve well. When they hinder the goal of being a community of love, we dialogue about it and find ways for *its renewal*. **Our loyalty to the Church requires us to bring our Franciscan spirit to situations we confront within the Church.** Respectful dialogue seeks creative ways to help the Church to be a *community of love.*

Jesus certainly spoke often about the qualities of believers. In the Beatitudes he gave a list of things that identify his followers. He called for forgiveness and reconciliation as a normal part of life. He called for leaders who recognized their role as servants. He changed things, recognizing the need for fresh ideas. *You have heard it said, but I say ...* (Matthew 5:43-45).

For Franciscans, who are people of the Gospel, Jesus illustrates ways to give us a sense of Church. Jesus, in the Gospel, shows ways to establish and/or maintain relationships. He relates to the blind, lepers, Pharisees, tax-collectors, "Sons of thunder," as well as friendships with Lazarus, Martha and Mary. Mary Magdalen knew of his concern as did the ten lepers who were cured. Crowds were fed by Jesus both spiritually and physically. His disciples appreciated his acceptance of their slowness to understand. In short, our focus on relationships in the Franciscan Order fits the vision of gospel life as a *community of love.*

As Franciscans seek mutual relationships they reflect the goal of the Church as well. Hence, the development of our Franciscan vision coordinates with the Church's desire to be a *community of love.* This love is also the foundation for *enlivening the apostolic life* of the SFO.

Vision formation takes place initially in the local fraternity. Among the responsibilities of the local fraternity and its council is the formation of newcomers. The regional, national and international leaders share direction and content to assist the local council in their formation programs. The local fraternity is vital to the SFO and is not an isolated unit. The vitality of a local fraternity depends on their initial and ongoing formation programs.

The development of a good fraternity formation program is linked to implementing the direction from the higher councils. In the USA there are quality formation materials available from and recommended by the National formation commission and/or NAFRA.

Different levels of the SFO provide workshops and materials to help formation directors and their teams. Fraternities are encouraged to send their formation leaders to these programs. Since leadership changes as time passes, new people need similar training. Councils need to be aware of these programs and work to assist formation leaders to attend, especially with financial assistance.

Cardinal Stritch University in Milwaukee, WI has a Franciscan Center on its campus. They developed a list of Franciscan values that summarize some of what we have been saying (Paraphrased).

1. Franciscans create a caring community - Respect for individual dignity; hospitality; courtesy; kindness; friendship; openness; fostering loving relationships.

2. Sharing, compassion for others - Serving; caring for the poor and oppressed; concern for social justice issues; taking responsible social action; offering unselfish service; altruism.

3. Reverence of creation - Respect for all creatures; fostering a simple lifestyle; stewardship; human dignity and empowerment of people; concern for environmental issues.

4. Peacemaking - Healing and reconciliation; conflict resolution; forgiveness; care and understanding; eliminating fears; recognizing the need for prayerfulness.

Cf. STRITCH magazine - Summer, 1999 - Page 14

+++

Readings/Questions for dialogue

Saved in Hope *(Spe Salvi)* - Benedict XVI
Paragraphs 30-31

Doctrinal Statements
United States Catholic Catechism for Adults - USCCB
Page 122-123

The Undated writings
[V. Let no one be proud, but boast in the Cross of the Lord]
Francis of Assisi - The Saint - Vol I - Page 131

1. Why is the local fraternity considered so important in the SFO?

2. What qualities are required for the church to be a *community of love*? What do Franciscans do if there is a need for renewal in the Church?

3. Why is the local bishop's approval needed to establish a new fraternity of the SFO?

4. Please name at least two important ministries within a local fraternity? Why are they important to you?

5. Why is it important for local fraternities to maintain a close relationship with councils of higher levels? What are the advantages of such a relationship?

6. How has the Stritch University summary of *Franciscan Values* helped you put together the ideas we have shared about the Franciscan vision? How are your personal gifts supporting the Franciscan vision and apostolic ministries?

7. Scripture reflection. Luke 17:11-19. What quality does Jesus expect of people in the Kingdom of God? How do you express this quality in your life?

✚✚✚

St. Mary of the Angels
"The Portiuncula"

This church was originally the property of the Benedictines of Subasio. The Benedictines gave it to Francis and it became the center of Francis' community. In this little church Francis received Clare.

✚

It was built on a piece of land known as the "Portiuncula" (*The Little Portion),* a name which became attached to the little church. It was restored by St. Francis who made it the home of his Order because of his great love for the Mother of Christ to whom the church is dedicated.

✚

The warm atmosphere makes it seem like home to people who come here.

✚

The Portiuncula now stands within the basilica of St. Mary of the Angels.

Chapter thirty one

Membership in the SFO

23. Requests for admission to the Secular Franciscan Order must be presented to the local fraternity, whose council decides upon the acceptance of new brothers and sisters.

Admission into the Order is gradually attained through a time of initiation, a period of formation of at least one year, and profession of the rule. The entire community is engaged in this process of growth by its own manner of living. The age for profession and the distinctive Franciscan signs are regulated by the statutes.

Profession by its nature is a permanent commitment.

Members who find themselves in particular difficulties should discuss their problems with the council in fraternal dialogue

Withdrawal or permanent dismissal from the Order, if necessary, is an act of the fraternity council according to the norm of the constitutions.

✚

25. Regarding expenses necessary for the life of the fraternity and the needs of worship, of the apostolate, and of charity, all the brothers and sisters should offer a contribution according to their means. Local fraternities should contribute toward the expenses of the higher fraternity councils.

1. Rule 23 *Membership in the Order is attained through a time of initiation, a time of formation, and the profession of the Rule.*

2. The journey of formation, which should develop throughout life, begins with entrance into the fraternity. Mindful that ***the Holy Spirit is the principal agent of formation*** *and always attentive to collaboration with Him, those responsible for formation are:* ***the candidate, the entire fraternity, the council with the minister, the master*** *(director)* ***of formation, and the assistant.***

3. ***The brothers and sisters are responsible for their own formation,*** *developing in an ever more perfect way the vocation received from the Lord. The fraternity is called to help the brothers and sisters in this journey by means of a warm welcome, prayer, and example.*

4. ***The elaboration and adoption of means of formation*** *adapted to the local situations and offered as a help to those responsible for formation in the individual fraternities,* ***belong to the national and regional councils in common agreement.***

Constitutions - article 37.1, 37.2, 37.3, 37.4

1. Rule 23 *The time of initiation is a phase preparatory to the true and proper time of formation and is intended for the discernment of the vocation and for the reciprocal acquaintance between the fraternity and the aspiring member. It should guarantee the freedom and the seriousness of entrance into the SFO.*

2. The duration of the time of initiation and the forms employed in its development ***are established by the national statutes.****

3. It belongs to the fraternity council to decide possible exceptions to the time of initiation, keeping in mind the guidelines of the national council.

Constitutions - article 38.1, 38.2, 38.3

1. Rule 23 *The request for admission to the Order is presented by the aspirant to the minister of a local or personal fraternity by a formal act, in writing if possible.*

2. Conditions for admission are: to profess the Catholic faith, to live in communion with the Church, to be of good moral standing, and to show clear signs of a vocation.

3. The council of the fraternity decides collegially on the request, gives a formal answer to the aspirant, and communicates this to the fraternity.

---

* Refer to pages 1 to 4 in this book for an explanation of the periods of formation as well as article 40 of the Constitutions (Page 2-3). It would be well to re-read the first chapter in its entirety. The last sentence of article 40.1 of the constitutions is worth implementing: *These meetings* (of formation) *should be held, as far as possible and opportune, in common with the candidates of other fraternities.* This will require dialogue between fraternity councils. Re-read article 42.1, 42.2, on page 4 of this book.

4. The rite of admission is performed according to the Ritual. The act is to be registered and preserved in the records of the fraternity..

Constitutions - article 39.1, 39.2, 39.3, 39.4

1. Rule 23 *Having completed the time of initial formation, the candidate submits to the minister of the local fraternity a request to make his or her profession. Having heard the master of formation and the assistant, the fraternity council decides by secret ballot, on the admission to profession, gives its reply to the candidate, and informs the fraternity.*

2. The conditions for the (perpetual) *profession or promise of evangelical life are:*

+ *attainment of the age established by the national statutes (National statutes - 21 years);*
+ *active participation in the time of formation for at least one year;* (National Statues require longer period)
+ *the consent of the council of the local fraternity.*

3. Where it is held to be opportune to lengthen the time of formation, it must not be extended to more than a year beyond the time established by the ***national statutes.***

Constitutions - article 41.1, 41.2, 41.3

At this point in your initial formation you have a good idea of the goal and necessity of formation in the SFO. *Profession* is a permanent commitment. When you make profession your life is permanently connected to the SFO Rule and the guidance of the constitutions and national statutes. You make that choice with full knowledge of what it entails. For the rest of your life you need *ongoing formation* in order to face new situations and challenges in following the SFO Rule.

Realize your personal responsibility in responding to initial formation. Formation materials can guide your understanding but you put it into practice in everyday living. Your work and cooperation is required to achieve the goal of formation. Your continued understanding and implementation of the Franciscan vision is expected as you approach the permanent commitment of *profession.* This is done prayerfully and with understanding.

The time of *candidacy* includes living as a Franciscan to the best of your ability. Your presence at fraternity gatherings is expected. Your readiness to engage in fraternity ministries is part of your formation. Learning the ways of contemplative prayer is part of developing a prayerful perspective. *Participation in the meetings of the local fraternity is an indispensible presupposition for initiation into community prayer and into fraternity life* (Constitutions - article 40.3).

A style of teaching which is Franciscan in character and which fits the mentality of the persons concerned should be adopted (Constitutions - article 40.4). Formation sessions are not lectures but require interaction among the participants. We learn from one another as we explore the questions of each chapter as well as the readings. Formation sessions regularly share reflections on scripture. Local fraternity formation directors will schedule meetings that allows time to integrate the lessons, usually ***at least*** a full hour or more. Formation sessions offer pertinent **information**; allows for the **formation** of life in response to the information; and accepts the **transformation** of personal life that the Rule requires - developing a Franciscan manner of living and perspective on life.

PROFESSION

Profession in the SFO is a special action. The catholic person renews the call of baptism - to be one with Christ and fulfill the mission of the Church. At this point re-reading pages 49 to 56 in chapter five is important. The ideas shared there relate to understanding, faithfulness and integration of your life through the gift of profession.

Profession is a grace given by the Holy Spirit. It is the

Spirit who calls us to the SFO. It is the same Spirit who gifts us with *profession.* The Spirit enables us to live a Franciscan life - embracing permanently the choice to live the Gospel in the spirit of St. Francis of Assisi. **Profession incorporates us into fraternity life with all the consequences it brings with it.** Incorporated into the fraternity, which is a cell of the Church, the newly professed chooses to contribute to the Church through his/her commitment to the Franciscan way of life.

Profession places us within a fraternity-community where life will be lived. We live both our Franciscan and Church life connected to the fraternity-community. The two become one. It has some aspects of a sacramental action without being a sacrament. Renewing our commitment to the Church and the Gospel, *profession* reflects the choices of baptism. Profession requires that the candidate has received the sacrament of confirmation - the outpouring of the Spirit. *Profession* is total self-giving, imitating Jesus' self-giving on the cross. ***The minister of the candidate's local fraternity accepts the profession.***

Profession ordinarily takes place in the context of the Eucharist. If this is not possible, a liturgy of the Word should be the liturgical action for profession (Cf. *Ritual of the SFO* - page 5: 3.31) **The local spiritual assistant is the church-witness** to the profession. If the local SA is not able to be present he/she can delegate this role to another person who has at least some knowledge of the SFO and Franciscan spirituality. (Ritual of the SFO - Page 6 - 3.35).

As candidates prepare for profession, the formation team and candidates take time to reflect on the profession ceremony *(Ritual of the SFO* - pages 18 to 26) and review the essentials of Franciscan life. Conversations about Franciscan life is helpful for everyone. Notice how the Ritual refers to baptism and a renewed dedication to the Gospel and the Church. Profession, except for very serious reasons, is done in the presence of the whole fraternity.

The mission of secular Franciscans has more to do with "being" rather than with "doing." We are not defined by the tasks we perform but by the Franciscan spirit which prompts the tasks. The ministries themselves may be done by others but we bring the unique spirit of Francis to them.

1. The vocation to "rebuild" the Church ought to induce the brothers and sisters sincerely to love and to live in union with the local Church in which they develop their own vocation and realize their apostolic commitment, aware that in the diocese the Church of Christ is truly functioning.

2. The Secular Franciscans should fulfill with dedication the duties with which they are occupied in their relations to the local Church. They should lend their help to activities of the apostolate as well as to the social activities existing in the diocese. In the spirit of service, they should make themselves present, as the fraternity of the SFO, within the life of the diocese. They should be ready to collaborate with other ecclesial groups and to participate in pastoral councils.

3. Fidelity to their own charism, Franciscan and secular, and the witness of building fraternity, sincerely and openly, are their principal services to the Church, which is the community of love. They should be recognized in it by their "being" from which their mission springs.

Constitutions - article 100.2, 100.2, 100.3

Please read: Constitutions - articles 98, 99, 101, 102 and 103.

In an address on profession, Felice Cangelosi OFM Cap, put the idea of profession in this way: ... *Profession in the Secular Franciscan Order, as a promise to live the Gospel in the manner of St. Francis, aims to put before us the radical, light-filled and joyful style in which Francis listens to the gospel and commits himself to live it.*

If, after profession, secular Franciscans find difficulty in living the Franciscan way of life, they should dialogue with their minister and spiritual assistant (or the Council) to find ways of dealing with the difficulties (Cf. National Statutes 18.7).

1. Rule 23 *Members who find themselves in difficulty may ask, with a formal act, temporary withdrawal from the fraternity. The council will evaluate the request with love and prudence, after a fraternal dialogue between the minister and the assistant with the person concerned. If the reasons appear to be well founded, after the brother or sister in difficulty has been given time to reconsider, the council agrees to the request.*

2. The repeated and prolonged default in the obligations of the life of the fraternity and other conduct in serious opposition to the Rule have to be discussed by the council in dialogue with the person at fault. Only in the case of obstinacy or relapse may the council decide, with a secret vote, to suspend someone. It communicates its decision in writing to the person concerned.*

3. Voluntary withdrawal or the provision for suspension must be noted in the register of the fraternity. It involves exclusion from the meetings and activities of the fraternity, including the right of active and passive voice, but membership in the Order itself is not affected.

Constitutions - article 56.1, 56.2, 56.3

---

* Read articles 57, 58 and 59 (Constitutions) and article 18.7a, 18.7b (National Statutes) for guidance. All is done with a sense of respect, keeping a confidential record of the dialogue for reference purposes.

FINANCES

Franciscans are not angels who never have to worry about costs and money. That is an attractive idea but not practical. The *fair share* donation supports the SFO at all levels. Running a worldwide organization is no minor task and requires financial support At every level there are costs. E.g. Paying the "rent" when using space for gatherings or using a facility for profession etc. At a visitation the visited fraternity pays a stipend for travel connected to the visitation as well as for the ministry of the visitation by servant-leaders. Spiritual assistants deserve a stipend to support their service to the SFO. These are items that are included in the budget at all levels.

Formation materials cost money. Newsletters, stationary and postage are not paid by magic. Phone calls and travel for servant-leaders require funding. Computers and computer programs for officers may be part of expenses. Ministries require funding. Caring for the needy, especially in our own fraternities, need contributions. Liturgical functions require funds for ritual needs.

International, national, and regional councils may pay the cost of housing for attendees at their meetings. The *fair share* supports these costs. The personal contact of these meetings is important. Many Secular Franciscan servant-leaders could not afford to attend without financial help.

In Franciscan life we name our gift of money to the fraternity as a ***fair share.*** Stewardship calls us to support this way of life which is our way of life. The local fraternity receives money from its members. The local fraternity covers the costs of local administration and supports the councils of higher fraternities. *Regional fraternities* (The local ministers and regional executive council) establish, for the region, a ***fair share*** amount that is needed annually to meet the budget of the Region. This annual ***fair share*** donation from each fraternity enables the SFO to meet expenses.

The fraternity relies on generous ***fair share*** contributions from its members to support the higher councils. This is an obligation of the fraternity. It is achieved through the generous ***fair share*** given by the members. The financial needs of our Franciscan family require the support and generosity of the members. This contribution is part of our SFO responsibility and supports necessary structures and needs of the SFO at all levels.

Councils at all levels accept bequests and donations to support their work. You might remember the SFO in your will or with bequests. Such donations support the structures that serve us. Members contribute according to their means. This obviously differs for different members. It also changes as life situations change. Generosity is a key word when sharing a ***fair share*** with the fraternity.

The councils at every level give an annual financial report to the SFO members. In describing the regional council's responsibility to the membership, we read the following, which applies at all levels (also Cf. Constitutions - article 52.4, 52.5):

i. to make decisions regarding the use of available funds and, in general, to deliberate on matters regarding the financial management and the economic affairs of the regional fraternity.

j. to have, before its term of office is finished, the regional fraternity's financial and real estate situation audited by an expert who is not a member of the council or by the fraternity's board of examiners;

Constitutions - article 62.2i, 62.2j

We discourage fraternities from investing in real estate or other properties. Should it happen, the constitutions address the issue in article 54 which you can read at your leisure.

The duties of the local treasurer include the following:

a. to guard diligently the contributions received, recording each receipt in the appropriate register, with the date on which it was given, the name of the contributer, or the one from whom it was collected;

b. to record in the same register the items of expense, specifying the date and the purpose, in conformity with the directions of the fraternity council;

c. to render an account of his or her administration to the assembly and to the council of the fraternity according to the norms of the national statutes.

Constitutions - article 52.4

In financial matters the Rule/Constitutions expect accountability/transparency from servant-leaders. In like manner, fraternity members are accountable for living their Franciscan lives in accord with the Rule and Constitutions. This is a community responsibility. We help one another to be faithful to our profession. We seek ways to support each other in living the SFO Rule.

This sense of unity as an international fraternity was verbalized by American Secular Franciscans who attended the SFO General Chapter in Hungary in November, 2008:

We also were struck by a sense of belonging. To a real Order. Reaching all points of the globe. A belonging so intense it became overwhelming. A perspective so vast, yet so acute, that we could see our local fraternity, and our regional fraternity, and our national fraternity, as vital organs in a global body flush with oxygen-rich blood; and we could see a future of life-giving fraternities spreading out ... (Bob & Mary Stronach SFO)

We realize the importance of supporting the SFO with our lives and our finances. We are good stewards of our gifts. The SFO is a beneficiary of the faithfulness of our lives, the gift of our talents, and our generous financial support.

We thank God for the gift of life, but do we really live our lives? Rushing through my house this morning, preparing for work, I pass a window and my heart stops for one aching moment as I catch sight of the electric stain of sunrise spreading across the sky. Standing on the platform waiting for my train I close my eyes to more fully enjoy the wind washing my face with just an edge of spring in its touch.

Life, in all its wonder, surrounds us. We are immersed in it. In the warmth of spring, in the chill of autumn; when the morning sun rips open the fabric of the sky and at the end of day when the coverlet of darkness is drawn again and the earth surrenders to sleep. Life, "what God has prepared for those who love him" (1 Cor 2:9).

On the Way to Work - ... *For life*
Vinal Van Benthem SFO - Page 139-140

+++

Readings/Questions for dialogue

Statutes of the National Fraternity of the SFO in the USA.
Article 6.4 / Article 18.7, 18.9 / Article 19 / Article 25

Read the paragraph that begins:
Contemplation is the fruit of union ...
Franciscan Prayer - Ilia Delio OSF - Page 134

The Assisi Compilation
[He persuades the brothers to go joyfully begging for alms]
Francis of Assisi - The Founder - Vol II - Page 150-151

1. What has been the most important session of formation for you? Why?

2. What are your feelings about making a permanent commitment (Profession) to the SFO? Dialogue with formation personnel or other leaders about your doubts, fears, concerns or excitement as profession approches.

3. How do fraternity members contribute to your formation? What contribution has the local council made to your formation? What assistance during formation did the spiritual assistant offer? Please share your personal ideas about ways to improve the sessions.

4. Are you able to attend the regular fraternity gatherings on a consistent basis? What action will you take if you are unable to attend i.e. who would you inform? What do you contribute to fraternity gatherings other than the *fair share*?

5. How would you handle a situation where difficulties kept you from attending gatherings for a longer period? With whom would you dialogue about your situation?

Is it possible for you to help people get to the gatherings? What particular needs would you feel most able to meet?

6. *To preserve peace in the family, the brothers and sisters should, in due time, make a last will and testament for the disposition of their goods* (Constitutions - article 23.3). Have you made a last will and testament? Why is this important for everyone concerned? (You may wish to include the SFO in your will)

7. Scripture reflection: Luke 8:4-15. This parable is like an examination of our awareness of the Word. Become more aware of how you respond to Jesus and his words. Take time to reflect on how the Word (Jesus) and the words (of the Gospel) grow in your life? What steps would improve your "listening?" Share ideas as you feel comfortable doing.

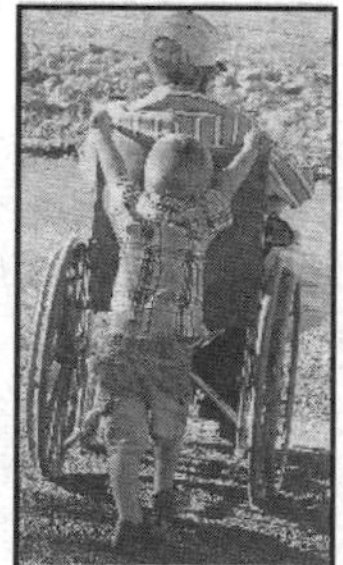

Charity is love received and given. It is "grace" (charis). Its source is the well-spring of the Father's love for the Son. It is creative love, through which we have our being; it is redemptive love, through which we are recreated. Love is revealed and made present by Christ (Jn 13:1) and "poured into our hearts through the Holy Spirit" (Rom 5:5). As the objects of God's love, men and women becomes subjects of charity, they are called to make themselves instruments of grace, so as to pour forth God's charity and to weave networks of charity.

Charity in Truth *(Caritas in Veritate)*
Benedict XVI - Paragraph 5

Chapter thirty two

+

Young & Old

Enriching the Franciscan spirit

24. To foster communion among members, the council should organize regular and frequent meetings (gatherings) *of the community as well as meeting with other Franciscan groups, especially with youth groups. It should adopt appropriate means for growth in Franciscan and ecclesial life and encourage everyone to a life of fraternity. This communion continues with deceased brothers and sisters through prayer for them.*

2. The fraternity has the duty to give special attention to the formation of the newly professed and of the temporarily professed, to help them become fully mature in their vocation and develop a true sense of belonging.

*3. **Ongoing formation** - accomplished by means of courses, gatherings, and the sharing of experience - aims to assist the brothers and sisters:*

+ Rule 4 *in listening to and meditating on the Word of God, "going from Gospel to life and from life to Gospel;"*
+ *in reflecting on events in the Church and in society in the light of faith, and with the help of the documents of the teaching Church, consequently taking consistent positions;*
+ *in discerning and deepening the Franciscan vocation by studying the writings of St. Francis, St. Clare and Franciscan authors.*

Constitutions - article 44.2, 44.3

1. Rule 24 *The fraternity must offer to its members **opportunities for coming together and collaborating** through meetings to be held with as great a frequency as allowed by the situation and with the involvement of all its members.*

2. Rule 6, 8 *The fraternity should come together periodically, also as an ecclesial community to celebrate the Eucharist in a climate which strengthens the fraternal bond and characterizes the identity of the Franciscan family. Where, for whatever reason, this particular celebration may not be possible, they should participate in the celebration of the larger ecclesial community.*

3. Insertion into a local fraternity and participation in fraternity life is **essential** *for belonging to the SFO. Appropriate initiatives should be adopted according to the directives of the national statutes, to keep these brothers and sisters united to the fraternity who - for valid reasons of health, family, work, or distance - cannot actively participate in community life.**

4. The fraternity remembers with gratitude its brothers and sisters who have passed away and continues its communion with them by prayer and in the Eucharist.

Constitutions - article 53.1, 53.2, 53.3, 53.4

*1. In the local fraternity, the perpetually professed of the same fraternity have active voice, that is can elect, and passive voice, that is can be elected. The temporarily professed have only active voice.***

Constitutions - article 77.1

The regular gathering of a local fraternity is vital for all the members. It is the place and time when secular Franciscans gather to share life experiences; ways of implementing the SFO Rule; discuss current church and society issues; pray together, take time to enjoy one another's company. The gathering may include reports and direction from the local council. Professed members have an opportunity to interact with people in the formation program and show them care and hospitality.

---

* Active, active-excused and lapsed membership is described in the *National Statutes* - article 18.7a, 18.7b. **Please read these texts!**

** More information on elections and connected items can be found in the Constitutions - articles 76, 77, 78, 79, 80, 81, 82.

Regular gatherings are often held monthly. While that may be somewhat of a tradition, having more frequent gatherings is certainly encouraged and can be helpful for enlivening our lives with a Franciscan culture.

Breaking the "once-a-month" habit may not always be possible but it is certainly worth some dialogue. Our dedication to one another in community may require more than a few hours a month. Even if a monthly gathering is four hours long, that is only 48 hours a year - about two days, in which to accomplish all the things the Rule, the constitutions and statutes expect us to achieve. Many fraternities have even shorter meetings. Frequent gatherings (even in smaller groups) are worthwhile so long as the groups maintain and fulfill their commitment to the main fraternity.

Creative imagination and recognition of both spiritual and interactive needs may call for more frequent gatherings. Of course, the planning invites the local council to engage the members in developing workable ways and means to have lively gatherings. Gatherings that continue formation in our Franciscan culture and spirit are vital. Within the lifetime of profession we are in need of the *ongoing formation* that assists *ongoing conversion*. Having more gatherings, by itself, is not the answer. What happens at the gatherings is what will attract people to attend.

+ Here is a list of some elements of a normal gathering +

Prayer - using the same prayer at each gathering does not widen the horizons of prayerfulness. A variety of prayer-forms at the gatherings helps members find a prayer form that is helpful for their daily prayer. Prayer forms can include the Liturgy of the Hours; Lectio divina; Franciscan Crown rosary; Stations of the Cross (Lent); inviting members to prepare a prayer for the gathering; using prayers that fit the liturgical season; having a prayerful remembrance of the deceased during November; have prayers of St. Francis/St. Clare at the gathering; focus the prayer on current needs in the Church and society; have special prayers for the feasts of St. Clare and St. Francis, as well as other special feasts; periodically celebrate the Eucharist together.

These ideas do not exhaust the possibilities. But they open the door to creative possibilities and keep us in touch with God and our ministry in the Church and the world. Prayerfulness is part of a gathering of Franciscans. Merely having a longer prayer is not always effective. Meaningful prayer filled with praise and gratitude reflects Francis' spirit.

Business - This may be long or short depending on the issues facing a fraternity. It gives the council and others time to share what is happening in the local fraternity as well as information from the higher level councils. It can offer ministry possibilities and a call for volunteers. The council can use this time to keep people informed about SFO news and views both within the fraternity and beyond.

Ongoing formation - This is ordinarily the longest period at the gathering (at least an hour or more). At its heart is the goal of helping the members master ways of expressing the Franciscan spirit in daily life. Whatever the issue, our goal is to touch it with a Franciscan flavor. Breaking into small groups may assist dialogue about issues.

Ongoing formation can deal with social issues; it can widen our ecumenical understanding, opening the door to relationship with other Christians, Muslims, Jews; it can focus on fresh insights into Franciscan spirituality including contemplation; it can dialogue about issues that divide us; it can dialogue about how to handle parish closings or misuse of authority in the Church or the world; it can build bridges between people labeled conservative or liberal; it can dialogue about ways to influence young people with the Franciscan spirit; it can share information about new formation materials; it can offer leadership training, especially before elections; it can focus on the needed competence of leaders and the willingness to be nominated for office; it can reflect on particular articles of the Rule or the Constitutions; it can report on regional, national and international chapters; it can share fresh insights into the way that Scripture is implemented or the ways of contemplation; it can share ways of dealing with conflictual situations; it can reflect on the words and stories of Francis and Clare; it may explore the insights of Franciscan authors. And the list goes on!

Ongoing formation is a natural consequence of profession, something that is never finished. The regular gathering offers important time for continuing our Franciscan growth.

Socializing - after all else is done, we definitely need time to enjoy one another's company. Food, of course, is a natural component for Franciscans. But this is time when you meet people you don't know well; you can take time to introduce yourself to newcomers; you can sit with someone you will be working with in ministry; you may want to catch up on what's happening in another's life; you may need time with someone going through a difficult period in life; special fun times includes inviting groups to share entertainment skills. This relaxing time keeps us balanced. It also deepens relationships which are so important to fraternity life. Some gatherings may simply be a time to have a good celebration together.

Gatherings are important! They should be well-prepared, perhaps assigned to different groups each time the fraternity gathers. The members are prayerful together; engage in dialogue; enjoy the fun; eat the food, and discover how their Franciscan love can find expression among themselves and in the secular world and within the Church. It is NOT a time to impose devotions or personal ideas on the fraternity or argue about how things should be done. If problems exist or issues need to be addressed, they are dealt with through dialogue and with respect.

Local fraternities in the same area may collaborate for some programs. Instead of having the same program in two, three, or four fraternities, it makes sense to have one program and invite the fraternities to the program. Fraternities in collaboration are able to pay a just stipend to speakers. The Constitutions/Statutes encourage collaboration for initial formation and ongoing formation (Constitutions 40.1 / National Statutes - article 19.c). In addition to supporting one another, Franciscans get to know one another. People are more comfortable working with Seculars they know.

With regard to *initial* and/or *ongoing formation*, when fraternities collaborate for formation they may select good people from each fraternity to serve on a formation team. Such collaboration has many advantages. Local councils are free to initiate such collaboration.

... *This formation* (initial formation) *should be carried out with frequent meetings for study and prayer and with concrete experiences of service and the apostolate.* ***These meetings should be held, as far as possible and opportune, in common with the candidates of other fraternities.***

Constitutions - article 40.1

Working together in this way also occurs on the regional and national level. Creating districts or clusters of fraternities within a region can bring people in the region closer together. District/cluster gatherings can reach many fraternities at one gathering. On the national level NAFRA has joined the regions in the country into geographic units. These smaller groupings meet at the NAFRA annual meeting and develop plans to enhance the SFO in their area.

Finally, all the members of a fraternity have the responsibility to promote the Order and invite people to join. Gaining new members is what keeps a fraternity alive. Otherwise it may disappear or find itself in a situation that calls for deactivation for lack of members or the inability to elect a council. Secular Franciscans give witness to their way of life and are in a position to attract new members. Each secular Franciscan takes this role seriously and prayerfully.

1. The promotion of vocations to the Order is a duty of all the brothers and sisters and is a sign of the vitality of the fraternities themselves. The brothers and sisters, convinced of the validity of the Franciscan way of life, should pray that God may give the grace of the Franciscan vocation to new members.

2. Although nothing can substitute for the witness of each member and of the fraternity, the councils must adopt appropriate means to promote the Secular Franciscan vocation.

Constitutions - article 45.1, 45.2

3. (For SFO members) *Fidelity to their own charism, Franciscan and secular, and the witness of building fraternity, sincerely and openly, are their principal services to the Church, which is the community of love. They should be recognized in it by their "being" from which their mission springs.*

Constitutions - article 100.3

Secular Franciscans are passionate about their vocation. They show a dedicated embrace of the entire Rule. They develop a passion for the Gospel, for the words of Jesus, and for the goal of proclaiming the teachings of Jesus, building the kingdom of God. What message does Francis communicate to us?

In a word, it was Jesus. To express it in such simple terms today may seem banal to us, or pious, or quaint. But for Francis, the discovery of Jesus, "Our Lord Jesus Christ," was the ongoing revelation of his whole life in the twenty years after his conversion. In his early years he discovered Jesus as the one who led him among the lepers, and made their presence "sweet" to him, rather than "bitter." He then discovered Jesus the preacher of conversion, announcing the reign of God. Over the years he began to see more clearly Jesus as the incarnate Son of God at Bethlehem, then as the Suffering Servant on Calvary; and finally, the Lord of all things, raised up in glory after his death. And in this Lord, the glorified Son, he also understood the trinitarian God.

It is through the "Lord Jesus Christ" that Francis understands Mary, the Church, the Scriptures, priesthood, the poor, his brothers and sisters, and all creatures. It is ultimately through and in Jesus that Francis understands himself.

Poverty & Joy - Wm Short OFM - Page 31-32

YOUTH, YOUNG ADULTS & THE SFO

Article #24 of the Rule speaks of meeting *especially with youth groups.* There are different ways of doing this (A-B-C).

A) One way is to be involved with youth groups sponsored by parishes or other groups. Our purpose is to expose them to the Franciscan spirit through our lives. The Franciscan spirit is attractive to many young people. Youth ministry opens the door to touching young people with our Franciscan spirit. As we gain their confidence we can share Franciscan ideas and ideals with them. We present them with the Franciscan spirit to add to their knapsack.

This may plant the seeds of an SFO vocation, but that is not our primary purpose. A secular Franciscan, faithful to his/her vocation, can influence young people and develop a relationship with them. A healthy relationship will allow us to touch their lives with the Franciscan spirit.

1. The SFO, by virtue of its very vocation, ought to be ready to share its experience of evangelical life with the youth who feel attracted to St. Francis of Assisi and to seek the means of adequately presenting it to them.

Constitutions - article 96.1

B) The Constitutions, articles #96 and #97 spell out another way of working with youth. This ministry more directly engages them in a fraternal development. In this situation the SFO provides *fraternal animation* and the 1st Order/TOR provides *spiritual assistance.* They assist young people in understanding the Franciscan spirit as it applies to young people. Again, it is for the sake of the young people and a way to share our Franciscan spirit.

1. The SFO fraternities promote the vocation to the Franciscan youth by means of appropriate and dynamic initiatives. They should see to the vitality and the expansion of the Franciscan Youth fraternities and will accompany youth in their journey of human and spiritual growth with proposals for specific activites and contents.

Constitutions - article 97.1

2. The Franciscan youth (YOUFRA)*, as understood by these constitutions and in so far as the SFO considers itself to be particularly responsible for it, is formed by those young people who feel called by the Holy Spirit to share the experience of the Christian life in fraternity, in the light of the message of Saint Francis of Assisi, deepening their own vocation within the context of the SFO.*

3. The members of the Franciscan Youth consider the Rule of the SFO as an inspirational document for the growth of their own Christian and Franciscan vocation either individually or in a group. After a suitable period of formation, of at least one year, they confirm this option with a ***personal pledge*** *before God and in the presence of the brothers and sisters.*

5. The Franciscan Youth has a specific organization, methods of formation, and teaching methods adequate for the needs of the world of youth, according to the existing realities in the various countries. The national statutes of the Franciscan Youth should be approved by the respective national council of the SFO, or in its absence, by the Presidency of the International Council of the SFO.

Constitutions - article 96.2, 96.3, 96.5

Franciscan Youth in the USA have statutes that guide their growth. For more information we recommend that you contact the *Youth and Young Adult councilor* of the National

Executive Council.

6. The Franciscan Youth as a component of the Franciscan Family requests from the competent secular leaders and religious superiors, respectively, fraternal ***animation*** *and spiritual* ***assistance****.*

Constitutions - article 96.6

Youth groups, with guidance as needed, develop programs and documents to stimulate their growth in the Franciscan spirit. Many young people are attracted to St. Francis and his spirit. SFO members are encouraged to share the Franciscan spirit with them.

Youfra is a temporary stage. It begins with adolescence and ends when a person reaches maturity. It is a call by the Holy Spirit. Young people respond with the desire to share experiences of the christian life in a community of young Franciscan believers, attracted by the vision of St. Francis of Assisi. In 2005 CIOFS published a document concerning Youfra. Among other things they wrote:

... one of the most important means will always be the close contact with the SFO fraternity. For this reason, the local fraternities should create spaces for the young, either by allowing them to participate in their meetings, or by entrusting them specific tasks in the fraternity. It is equally important that the SFO fraternities be flexible in their organization and that they seek creative ways of forming special groups in the fraternity under the guidance of the council of the fraternity.

CIOFS Document - *Youfra, A Way of Franciscan Vocation* - Article 26

Youth groups seek *fraternal animation* from the SFO and *spiritual assistance* from Franciscan religious superiors.

The Fraternal animator's presence in the group, together with that of the Spiritual assistant, will give Youfra the assurance that they are linked to the Franciscan family and will provide a unique opportunity to enrich their lives. Both individuals, in addition to their specific responsibilities of accompaniment and guidance, must also be engaged in the formation of the group

Koinonia - 2009-2 - Year 16 - No 62 - Page 3

Youfra is organized according to their own criteria, spelled out in their statutes. A method of formation suitable for young people (according the culture of each country) is used. Their formation program focuses on the needs of young people. Fraternal animators and SA's need sensitivity to the needs of young people. National statutes for Youth and Young adults (Approved by NAFRA/NEC) assist the process.

The formation program for youth and young adults is developed with the needs of young people in mind. That includes the length of time for formation as well as the age for admission etc. Formation is a time to recognize and love the Gospel according to the example of St. Francis. Youfra accompanies young people on their journey of formation and/or their discovery of the Franciscan vision.

Important: Those who serve young people need experience in working with youth. Any tendencies to physical or sexual abuse would block individuals from working with youth. A criminal background check may be required for people working with young people. This and other requirements of the Church and society cannot be ignored.

C) Members of Youfra who wish to become members of the SFO observe all the provisions of the SFO Rule, Constitutions and National statutes. They follow the path of *orientation* and *initial formation*. Young adults need the formative process to understand the responsibilities that come with membership in the SFO.

4. The members of Franciscan Youth who wish to belong to the SFO should satisfy the requirements of the Rule, the Constitutions, and the Ritual of the SFO. (They should also satisfy the directions of the National Statutes)

Constitutions - article 96.4

Readings/Questions for dialogue

Spirituality and eucharistic culture - Paragraph 77
Sacrament of Charity *(Sacramentum Caritatis)* - Benedict XVI

A Generation of Seekers - Page 6-7
United States Catholic Catechism for Adults - USCCB

God is Love *(Deus Caritas Est)* - Benedict XVI
Paragraphs 33, 35

1. What is the purpose of the regular gatherings of a fraternity? How is this purpose achieved?

2. How does collaboration among fraternities (E.g. for initial formation/ongoing formation) enhance our ability to live a Franciscan life?

3. What are the elements that are part of a local fraternity gathering? Which of them requires the most time? Why?

4. How do district/cluster gatherings of fraternities enhance a members' ability to be faithful to life in the SFO? How do personal relationships among Secular Franciscans assist in collaboration among fraternities?

5. What is the relationship between the SFO and Youfra or Youth and Young Adult groups? Explain.

6. Scripture reflection: John 17:20-26. How does this text give hope to all of us? What is the source of hope?

Every gun that is made, every warship launched,
and every rocket fired, signifies, in the final sense, a theft
from those who hunger and are not fed,
those who are cold and are not clothed.
The world in arms is not spending money alone.
It is spending the sweat of its laborers,
the genius of its scientists and the hopes of its children.

President Eisenhower - 1953 speech
to American Society of Newspaper Editors.

Chapter thirty three

Franciscan Family Connections

26. As a concrete sign of communion and co-responsibility, the councils on various levels, in keeping with the constitutions, shall ask for ***suitable and well-prepared*** *religious for spiritual assistance. They should make this request to the superiors of the four religious Franciscan families, to whom the Secular fraternity has been united for centuries.*

To promote fidelity to the charism as well as observance of the rule and to receive greater support in the life of the fraternity, the minister or president, with the consent of the council, should take care to ask for a regular ***pastoral*** *visit by the competent religious superiors as well as for a* ***fraternal*** *visit from those of the higher fraternities, according to the norm of the constitutions.*

2. The spiritual and pastoral care of the SFO, entrusted by the Church to the Franciscan First Order and the TOR, is the responsibility, above all, of their general and provincial ministers (major superiors). *The altius moderamen, of which canon 303 speaks, belongs to them. The purpose of the altius moderamen is* ***to guarantee the fidelity of the SFO to the Franciscan charism, communion with the Church, and union with the Franciscan family,*** *values which represent a vital commitment for the Secular Franciscans.*

Constitutions - article 85.2

2. This service of the religious ministers completes but does not substitute for the secular councils and ministers to whom belong the guidance, co-ordination, and animation of the fraternities at the various levels.

Constitutions - article 86.2

2. It belongs to the Conference of General ministers of the First Order and TOR:

a. to take care of relations with the Holy See concerning the approval of legislative or liturgical documents, which need to be approved by the Holy See;

b. to visit the Presidency of the International Council of the SFO;

c. to confirm the election of the Presidency of the International council of the SFO

Constitutions - article 87.2

1. The provincial ministers and the other major superiors, in the area of their own jurisdiction, guarantee the spiritual assistance to the local fraternities entrusted to their jurisdiction. They see to it that their own religious are interested in the SFO and that ***capable and well prepared persons*** *are appointed for the service of spiritual assistance.*

2. It is the specific competence of the major superiors, in the name of their jurisdiction:

a. to establish, canonically, new local fraternities and guarantee them spiritual assistance;

b. to animate spiritually and visit the local fraternities assisted by their own jurisdiction;

c. to keep themselves informed on the spiritual assistance given to the SFO.

3. The major superiors are responsible for the spiritual assistance to the local fraternities which they have established.

Constitutions - article 88.1, 88.2, 88.3

3. To be a witness of Franciscan spirituality and of the fraternal affection of the religious towards the Secular Franciscans, and to be a bond of communion between his Order and the SFO, the spiritual assistant should be a Franciscan religious, member of the First Order or the TOR.

4. When it is not possible to give such a spiritual assistant to the fraternity, the competent major superior can entrust the service of spiritual assistance to:

a. religious brothers or sisters of other Franciscan

institutes;

b. *diocesan clerics or other persons,* ***specially prepared*** *for such service, who are members of the Secular Franciscan Order;*

c. *other diocesan clerics or non-Franciscan religious.*

Constitutions - article 89.3, 89.4

1. The council of the fraternity at each level requests ***suitable and well prepared*** *assistants from the competent superiors of the First Order and the TOR.*

3. The competent major superior, having heard the council of the fraternity concerned, appoints the assistant according to the norms of these Constitutions and of the Statutes for Spiritual and Pastoral Assistance to the SFO.

Constitutions - article 91.1, 91.3

A few definitions are in order at this point.

Provinces - The First Order and TOR are divided into provinces. These are territorial areas in which the friars function. They do not have the same territorial boundaries as SFO regions. Provinces have individual names, e.g. Province of St Joseph of the Capuchin Order.

Provincial minister / General minister - The head of a province is called a Provincial minister (a major superior). The head of all the provinces in the world is called a General minister (a major superior).

Friar - name given to members of the First Order or TOR. The name simply means "Brother." The title "brother or friar" is often used whether the friar is ordained or not.

Provincial or General spiritual assistant - is a friar who is appointed by a provincial or the general to deal with SFO issues in their province or worldwide. Provincial SAs appoint local spiritual assistants to fraternities bonded to their province. They may also appoint a regional SA if they have fraternities in the region. The provincial minister determines the extent of the authority of a PSA.

Local spiritual assistant - a **qualified and well-prepared** person appointed by the Provincial or PSA of the Province to which a fraternity is bonded, i.e. either established by the province or the province has accepted the fraternity's transfer from another province. (Cf. Constitutions - article 89.4)

Conference of National Spiritual Assistants (CNSA) - four friars, each one representing a branch of the First Order and the TOR in the USA. They assist the National executive council and National fraternity of the SFO. Each friar is appointed by their conference of provincials (or their individual provincial) to represent their branch of the Order for a three year period (with a limit of twelve years).

One of the members of CNSA serves as president of CNSA for a two-year term. The CNSA members alternate in being president-in-turn. The president-in-turn is *ex officio* a member of the National executive council. The four CNSA members are *ex officio* members of NAFRA and attend NAFRA's annual meetings. CNSA members (and other spiritual assistants) do NOT vote on financial matters nor in elections.

Among other responsibilities the CNSA develops training programs for spiritual assistants (Provincial, regional and local SA's) and conducts workshops for them. The Conference deals with issues on the national level or issues that need to be communicated to the General spiritual assistants.

Jurisdiction - a term that indicates the area in which major superiors or others exercise power. E.g. He has *jurisdiction* in the state of New Jersey; or in the region of Franciscans of the Prairie; or in St. Barbara Province.

As you may realize, when we speak of a spiritual assistant, the accent is on "assistance." Spiritual assistants are part of the council at the different levels. They share ideas and reflections and invest their energy at council meetings. The council should listen to and respect the SA's ideas and opinions as they do for the other council members.

1. The principle task of the assistant is to foster a deeper insight into Franciscan spirituality and to co-operate in the initial and ongoing formation of the secular Franciscans.

3. The assistant participates actively and votes in the discussions and decisions taken by the Council or by the Chapter. He or she is specifically responsible for the animation of liturgical celebrations and spiritual reflections during the meetings of the Council or the Chapter.
Statutes for Spiritual & Pastoral Assistance to the SFO - Article 13.1, 13.3

2. The local assistant fosters communion within the fraternity and between the fraternity and the First Order or the TOR. In harmony with the local guardian or superior, the assistant sees to it that between the religious and the secular fraternities a real ***life-giving union*** *with each other exists. He or she fosters the active presence of the fraternity in the Church and in society.*
Ibid - article 23.2

1. The local Assistant, together with the Council of the fraternity, is responsible for the formation of the candidates and expresses his or her assessment of each of the candidates before profession.

2. Together with the Minister, the assistant discusses with the brothers or sisters in difficulty, who want to retire from the fraternity or who act in serious opposition to the Rule.
Ibid - article 24.1, 24.2

These articles clarify the responsibilities of a spiritual assistant. **SA's avoid dominating** the council or fraternity. They collaborate with the council and fraternity in nurturing the Franciscan life of all the members. They need understanding of Franciscan spirituality and familiarity with the functioning of a fraternity in the SFO. Whoever is recommended to be a local SA is expected to take the training program* provided by CNSA. Anyone who is ignorant of Franciscan spirituality, how the SFO functions, or the role of a spiritual assistant should not be appointed until he/she has completed the training course for SA's.

The local council informs their particular provincial (or PSA) of the need for a SA. They make the request in writing. They recommend people they judge to be *suitable and well-prepared.* (This process is also followed when the regional council requests the appointment of a regional SA) In the case of SFO members, the SFO General Chapter of 2008 approved the following requirements: *b) The Secular Franciscan SA must have been professed for a minimum of five years. c) The secular Franciscan SA must not belong to the same fraternity to which he/she is providing assistance.*

NB. In particular cases and for serious pastoral reasons the nominee may be a member of the same fraternity. Nominees are expected to take the training course provided by CNSA.*

A ritual for the installation of a spiritual assistant is found in the *Handbook for Spiritual Assistance to the SFO* (2005 - Segment B3-B5). The local council may edit the text.

1. By virtue of the ***vital reciprocity*** *between the religious and the secular members of the Franciscan Family and in regard to the responsibilities of major superiors, spiritual assistance to the fraternities of the SFO at all levels must be assured as a fundamental element of communion.*

Constitutions - article 89.1

Spiritual assistants bring together the *altius moderamen* required by the Church and the *vital reciprocity* required by the SFO Constitutions. People who are recommended to be spiritual assistants (regional or local) should ordinarily take the course prepared by CNSA. It will guide the nominee's relationships so that both the fraternity and the

---

* *Presently:* *Franciscan Family Connections* - 2007 - Smokey Valley Printing - Box 189 - Lindsborg, KS 67456 - 785-227-2364

nominee are enriched by his/her presence. Spiritual assistants are servant-leaders. Avoiding domination, they share their gifts with the SFO as true servant-assistants.

VISITATIONS

SA's conduct visitation of the fraternities. *Regional SA's* visit local fraternities in their region. *National Assistants* (CNSA) visit the regional fraternities in the USA. *International SA's* visit the national fraternities around the world. Thus the *vital reciprocity* with the SFO is maintained. Visitations offer an opportunity for respectful and loving inter-action between the First Order/TOR and fraternities at different levels. These visitations are called ***pastoral*** visitations.

The minister (or a delegated member of the council) at the regional, national and international levels visit fraternities within their scope of responsibility. These are called fraternal visitations.

Pastoral and fraternal visitations are generally done together. But the time constraints at many visitations may move national or regional executive councils to consider separate visitations in order to have more time to effectively achieve the goal of the visitation.

1. Rule 26 *The purpose both of the pastoral and fraternal visits is to revive (enhance) the evangelical Franciscan spirit, to assure fidelity to the charism and to the Rule, to offer help to fraternity life, to reinforce the bond of unity of the Order, and to promote its most effective insertion into the Franciscan family and the Church.*

Constitutions - article 92.1

2. Among the various initiatives to achieve the purpose of the **(fraternal)** *visit, the visitor will give special attention:*

- *to the validity of formation, both initial and permanent;*
- *to the relations entertained with other fraternities at the different levels, with Franciscan youth, and with the entire Franciscan family;*

+ *to the observance of the directives and of the guidelines of the international council of the SFO and of the other councils.*
+ *to the presence in the local Church.*

Constitutions - article 94.2

1. The ***pastoral*** *visit is a privileged moment of communion of the First Order and the TOR with the SFO. It is carried out also in the name of the Church and serves to revive the evangelical Franciscan spirit, to assure fidelity to the charism and the Rule, to offer help to fraternity life, to reinforce the bond of unity of the SFO and to promote its most effective insertion into the Franciscan family and the Church.*

2. The visitor strengthens the fraternity in its presence and mission in the Church and in society; verifies the relation between the secular and religious fraternities; gives special attention to programs, methods, and experiences of formation; gives attention to the collaboration and sense of co-responsibiilty among the secular leaders and the spiritual assistants; examines the quality of the spiritual assistance given to the visited fraternity; encourages the spiritual assistants in their service and promotes their continuing spiritual and pastoral formation.

3. ... For urgent and serious reasons or in case of failure on the part of the minister or the council to request it, the ***pastoral*** *visit may be carried out upon the initiative of the conference of spiritual assistants, having consulted the Council of the SFO at the same level.*

4. It is recommended that the pastoral and fraternal visits be carried out together, with agreement beforehand on the program. The visitor or visitors will in good time communicate the object and the program of the visit to the council concerned. ... They will draw up a report of the visit they have conducted, appending it to the records in the appropriate register of the fraternity visited, and will inform the council of the level which has conducted the visit.

5. In the visit to the local fraternity, the visitor or visitors will meet with the entire fraternity and with the groups and sections into which it is divided. They will give special attention to the brothers and sisters in formation and to those brothers and sisters who may request a personal meeting. Where required, they will proceed to the fraternal correction of the shortcomings possibly encountered.

Statutes for Spiritual & Pastoral Assistance to the SFO
Article 14.1, 14.2, 14.3, 14.4, 14.5

It is important to conduct the visitation in a respectful way. Both the visitors and the visited show respect and concern for one another. The visitation is a time for growth in the Franciscan spirit and not a time to create an atmosphere of fear or one that stifles dialogue. Even difficult problems are discussed in a reasonable and reverent manner. Trinitarian spirituality applies here as well as to our ministry outside the fraternity. Our relationship as brothers and sisters requires us to engage each other with a Franciscan spirit.

If emotions begin to dominate a conversation it is good to take a break for prayer. At times the dialogue can be limited to the people involved in a conflictual issue rather than involving the whole fraternity. These determinations are made by the visitors who recognize the need for such specific decisions. The visitors look to achieve the common good.

A post-visitation report is sent to the visited council by the visitors. They also keep a copy and share it with others who need to be informed. A common report or individual reports can be sent to those who need to be informed by the visitors.

The following article of the *Statutes for Spiritual and Pastoral Assistance to the SFO* also applies to local councils. Local fraternities can check to determine if the regional treasurer pays the visitors or if the local fraternity is expected to do so. If the local fraternity needs to offer a stipend, the local council determines a just amount.

2. The regional fraternity will present the National minister or his or her delegate and the representative of the Conference of National Spiritual Assistants, a stipend appropriate to the journey made and the length of the stay required at the time of fraternal and pastoral visits and also on the occasion of their presiding over and witnessing elections.

Statutes for Spiritual & Pastoral Assistance to the SFO - article 26.2

When national SFO personnel visit a *Regional fraternity* the above article #26.2 applies. Costs include the travel costs of the visitors as well as their room and board and a stipend for their ministry to the region. The stipend is given directly to each visitor at the visitation or shortly thereafter.

The triennial visitation of the *Regional fraternity* and *Regional executive council* is usually done on a weekend from Friday evening to Sunday morning. The time for the visitation should allow for plenty of opportunity for interaction with the regional fraternity, the regional executive council, SA's, formation personnel, people in formation and for ongoing formation/open-forum time.

The ***pastoral visitor*** at a *regional* visitation may take time to visit with a gatherings of the local SAs at some point in the visitation. The *Regional council* invites local spiritual assistants and informs them of the time for this meeting. An hour or more is a reasonable amount of time for this meeting. A visit to the regional fraternity and council should provide plenty of time for interaction during the visitation.

For triennial visitations of *local* fraternities the local council will provide time for the visitors to meet separately with the local fraternity council, with the entire fraternity, with anyone who wishes to see the visitors privately, with the formation personnel and the people in formation, and some time for the **pastoral** visitor to meet with the local spiritual assistant. Councils provide reasonable time for all these elements. It is courteous to offer possible dates and to make arrangements with the visitors (minister/SA) at least six months before the visitation to confirm a specific date.

The words that St. Francis addressed to his brothers apply to all facets of Franciscan life, including visitations.

Wherever the brothers may be and meet one another, let them show that they are members of the same family. Let each one confidently make known his need to the other, for if a mother loves and cares for her son according to the flesh, how much more diligently must someone love and care for his brother according to the Spirit! When any brother falls sick, the other brothers must serve him as they would wish to be served themselves.

The Later Rule - Chapter VI
Francis of Assisi - The Saint - Vol 1 - Page 103

Readings/Questions for dialogue

God is Love *(Deus Caritas Est)* - Benedict XVI
Paragraph 1 - *Introduction*

Start reading at the paragraph that begins:
The problem today is that we love many things ...
Franciscan Prayer - Ilia Delio OSf - Page 183 to 185

Poverty & Joy - Wm Short OFM
Page 74-75 - *Following the footsteps of Jesus*

1. What is the role of a spiritual assistant at the local level? List some qualities that a spiritual assistant should possess? How are spiritual assistants prepared for their service?

2. Who has the authority to appoint a spiritual assistant on the local or regional level? What process is followed?

3. What is the purpose of a fraternal and pastoral visitation (answer separately for each)? How often are visitations to the local and regional fraternity conducted? Describe the process that will initiate a visitation?

4. How long a period of time would you allow for the visitation of a *local* fraternity? Of a *regional* fraternity? What are some of the issues the visitors want to explore?

5. What spirit should be evident at the time of visitation? Describe why this spirit is so important to Franciscans?

6. Scripture reflection. Acts 4:13-22 - Explain how Peter and John became so bold when brought before the Jewish religious authorities. How does this text address you as you move to profession? How do we discern what is from God from what are merely personal opinions or desire?

+++

Thoughts on the time before Profession:

Initial formation is ending and *Ongoing formation* begins. Please be certain to read the material on profession on pages 366-367 in this book. *Here are other helps and hints:*

A. As you move to *profession*, make your request for profession to the fraternity council in writing. Acknowledge your desire to make profession and share your reasons for wanting to do this.

B. Dialogue with the formation team or formation director to become familiar with the profession ceremony as found in the *Ritual of the SFO.*

C. The formation personnel will determine a time for some form of retreat before your profession. If possible, this can be done in collaboration with other local fraternities who have candidates for profession.

D. The profession ceremony is done at a Eucharist, even at a parish Eucharist, if possible. (This obviously depends on the approval of the pastor and/or parish staff) If no priest is available, the profession takes place at a liturgy of the Word.

The Franciscan mission within the church does not consist in defending the faith against outside forces; there are other groups with that charism within the Church. The

Franciscan challenge is to accept Francis' call to heal and to mend and to call according to the Gospel. As loyal and committed Catholics, as Francis insisted we must be (cf.Later Rule 1 and 2), *we have the duty to do our part to challenge the Church to be imbued with these Gospel values, even to the point of prophetically speaking out when the Church is seen to act against such values. This demands the courtesy and courage of which we have already spoken.*

The Continuing Franciscan Task in the Church
Build With Living Stones - SBU - Unit 14 - Page 7

While he was still speaking to the crowds; his mother and his brothers were standing outside, wanting to speak to him. Someone told him, "Look, your mother and your brothers are standing outside, wanting to speak to you." But to the one who had told him this, Jesus replied, "Who is my mother, and who are my brothers?" And pointing to his disciples, he said, "Here are my mother and my brothers! ***For whoever does the will of my Father in heaven is my brother and sister and mother."***

Matthew 12:46-50

+++

Most High, glorious God,
enlighten the darkness
of my heart
and give me true faith,
certain hope,
and perfect charity,
sense and knowledge,
Lord,
that I may carry out
Your holy and true command.

Prayer before the Crucifix
Francis of Assisi - The Saint
Vol I - Page 40

Reflections on Profession

+ The vocation to become a Secular Franciscan is a gift of the Holy Spirit. *Profession* comes as a grace from the Holy Spirit. The celebration of *profession* acknowledges that vocational call in a liturgical action. It is our response to the Holy Spirit.

+ The grace of the Holy Spirit gives us the life-project of living a gospel-life. We are enabled to accomplish what we profess by the power and grace given by the Holy Spirit. The Spirit calls us to live the SFO Rule and enables us to do so.

+ Profession incorporates us into the international Order known as the Secular Franciscan Order. The newly professed enriches the fraternity and is enriched by the fraternity.

+ The Church accepts our profession in the presence of the fraternity and in the midst of the People of God (Church). We commit ourselves to follow the SFO Rule as our way of building the Kingdom of God.

+ Profession is the full and fruitful implementation of baptism. Sealed by the action of the Holy Spirit, the newly professed is called to fulfill this fresh commitment to baptism through his/her Franciscan vocation.

+ Profession has qualities of a priestly action. Since it is primarily done at the Eucharist,* those making profession give their entire life to the Church by living the life outlined in the SFO Rule. Like Christ in the Eucharist, the newly professed offers his/her entire self to God in love. Nothing is held back. Our whole life is given to Jesus through his Church and in the Secular Franciscan Order (Consecration).

+ Profession and the Eucharist are linked since both Christ and the newly professed offer their lives to the Father. This is a common act of self-giving love. Our life is a commitment *of* life and *for* life. What Christ manifests in his life, we manifest in ours - a total self-giving (Consecration) through faithful living as a Secular Franciscan.

---

* If no priest is available to celebrate Eucharist, a liturgical celebration of the Word is used.

+ The minister of the local fraternity, to which the candidate belongs, accepts the profession. The priest who presides at Eucharist (duly delegated by the local or regional SA, if necessary), represents the Church, gives witness to the fact that this is an ecclesial act; reassures the Church of the suitability of the candidates; and ratifies the profession in the name of the Church. The local SA is the primary Church witness and may delegate another to serve in that capacity if necessary.

+ Profession brings a permanent commitment to God and to Franciscan life through incorporation in the SFO. Franciscans build the Kingdom of God. We evangelize. We re-build the People of God where that is needed. We learn to love and relate in all circumstances. We forgive. We seek peace. We encourage people. We seek reconciliation. We pray. We celebrate. Living the Franciscan spirit and life is our task and our gift to the Trinity, the Church, and the world through our commitment to the SFO.

Jesus opens the door for our relationship with the Father and the Holy Spirit. He guides us in the way of truth. These words of St. Paul guide our spirit to imitate Jesus in our lives within the Church and the world - and with each other.

As God's chosen ones, holy and beloved, clothe yourselves with compassion, kindness, humility, meekness, and patience. Bear with one another and, if anyone has a complaint against another, forgive each other; just as the Lord has forgiven you, so you also must forgive. Above all, clothe yourselves with love, which binds everything together in perfect harmony. And let the peace of Christ rule in your hearts, to which indeed you were called in the one body. And be thankful. Let the word of Christ dwell in you richly; teach and admonish one another in all wisdom; and with gratitude in your hearts, sing psalms, hymns, and spiritual songs to God. And whatever you do, in word or deed, do everything in the name of the Lord Jesus, giving thanks to God the Father through him.

Colossians 3:12-17

Now to him who by the power at work within us is

able to accomplish abundantly far more than all we can ask or imagine, to him be glory in the Church and in Christ Jesus to all generations, forever and ever. Amen

Ephesians 3:20-21

✚✚✚

POSTSCRIPT

Initial formation opens the door for living a dedicated Franciscan life. It is only a beginning. Books, articles and other resources on the spirit and life of St Francis are innumerable. They continue to offer fresh insights into the image of Christ who is called Francis.

Your formation should continue without pause. New questions will arise as you live this life. New circumstances will call for prayer and dialogue to bring a Franciscan spirit to fresh circumstances. Your brothers and sisters in the Franciscan Family will walk with you. They will be people of all cultures, of all shapes and sizes, people with a plethora of ideas on how to live this way of life.

You are among them, sharing your insights and listening to theirs. The Holy Spirit will be in your midst with answers that develop from your conversations. You may love most Franciscans and there may be some whom you find difficult to love. What they do and how they live their Franciscan life may call for patience and understanding on your part. All of us struggle to treat each other with love and respect. But that is what we do as Franciscans!

At the heart of our motivation to live this life is Jesus, God's son, of whom the Father said: *This is my Son, the Beloved; with him I am well pleased;* ***listen to him!*** (Matthew 17:5)

The Scriptures consistently motivated Francis to do whatever pleases Jesus and the Father. From the poverty of the crib to the vulnerability of the Cross, Francis marveled at the humility and poverty of Jesus - and the length and breadth of Jesus' love which saves us. May our lives bring praise and gratitude to this gracious God who loves us with an everlasting love.

God saw everything that he had made, and indeed, it was very good.

Genesis 1:31

Continued ...

Applying all the care of his heart, to fulfill the words
of the new grace he had heard,
he became, by divine inspiration,
the proclaimer of evangelical perfection
and began publicly to preach penance with simplicity.
Moreover his statements were
neither hollow nor ridiculous,
but filled with the power of the Holy Spirit.
They penetrated the marrow of the heart
and provoked stunned amazement
in those who heard them.
But as he himself later testified,
he also learned by the Lord's revelation,
a greeting of this sort, that he should say:
"May the Lord give you peace."
Thus, in all his preaching,
he greeted people at the
beginning of his talk with the proclamation of peace.
Filled with the spirit of the prophets,
he proclaimed peace and preached salvation,
as the prophet said (Isaiah 52:7).
And it happened that by counsels about salvation,
he brought to true peace
many who had previously lived
at odds with Christ and far from salvation.

The Life of St Francis - by Julian of Speyer
Francis of Assisi - The Saint - Vol I - Page 379-380